▶ **Fifth Edition**

HUMAN
RELATIONS
DEVELOPMENT
A MANUAL FOR EDUCATORS

▶ **Fifth Edition**

HUMAN RELATIONS DEVELOPMENT
A MANUAL FOR EDUCATORS

GEORGE M. GAZDA
The University of Georgia and Medical College of Georgia

FRANK R. ASBURY
Valdosta State College

FRED J. BALZER
Forensic Psychologist
South Florida Evaluation and Treatment Center, Miami

WILLIAM C. CHILDERS
Care Medical, Athens, Georgia

ROSEMARY E. PHELPS
The University of Georgia

RICHARD P. WALTERS
Belhaven College, Jackson, Mississippi

Allyn and Bacon
Boston • London • Toronto • Sydney • Tokyo • Singapore

Vice President, Education: Nancy Forsyth
Series Editor: Ray Short
Editorial Assistant: Christine Shaw
Marketing Manager: Ellen Mann
Cover Administrator: Linda Knowles
Manufacturing Buyer: Louise Richardson
Editorial-Production Service: Walsh Associates
Cover Designer: Suzanne Harbison

Copyright © 1995, 1991, 1984, 1977, 1973 by Allyn and Bacon
A Simon & Schuster Company
Needham Heights, MA 02194

Library of Congress Cataloging-in-Publication Data

Human relations development : a manual for educators / George M. Gazda
    . . . [et al.]. — 5th ed.
        p.   cm.
    Includes bibliographical references and index.
    ISBN 0-205-16088-3
    1. Student counselors—Training of.   2. Educational counseling.
    3. Interpersonal relations.   I. Gazda, George Michael, 1931–   .
    LB1731.75.H86   1994
371.4'6—dc20
                                                                94-21193
                                                                CIP

Printed in the United States of America
10 9 8 7 6 5 4 3 2 1   00 99 98 97 96 95

In Memory
of
Dr. Nancy A. Haynie

Contents

Preface

We have prepared this manual and the accompanying *Instructor's Guide* to help train educators and prospective educators in the development of human relations skills.

We use the term *human relations development/training* broadly to include skill development in intrapersonal and interpersonal relationships. By *skill development* we mean developing expertise in listening and communicating in order to make problem solving easier for those who seek help. Expertise in listening/perceiving and communicating/responding is a potent way to prevent misunderstanding and is therefore essential both in preventing problems and in developing effective strategies or procedures for problem resolution. Throughout the manual we use *helping* and *facilitating* interchangeably. We also use *helpee* very broadly to mean at times someone who is actually seeking help and at other times someone with whom we are simply interacting.

By *educators* we are referring primarily to teachers, administrators, teacher aides, special education personnel, and student personnel services specialists such as counselors, school psychologists, school social workers, and the like. The target population is elementary and secondary educators, but, by slightly modifying certain exercises, college and university educators and others engaged in educational endeavors can use the manual as well. The manual was developed for use in both preservice and inservice education.

Procedures presented in the manual have been developed over several years with preservice and inservice teachers, administrators, and educational specialists. The manual has been modified and refined in its present form after having been used with several thousand undergraduate students enrolled in teacher education at the University of Georgia. In addition, input has been received from training several hundred inservice teachers, administrators, and other educational specialists.

The rationale for the model we use in this manual for human relations training is presented in Chapter 1; the model is developed and its effectiveness is demonstrated throughout the remaining chapters. The basic rationale for the model was developed by Robert R. Carkhuff and his colleagues. Their research on the development and effectiveness of this model is unequaled by any other human relations procedures used today. As a result, we feel confident that our adaptations of what has become internationally known as the "Carkhuff Model" are theoretically and empirically sound.

It has become increasingly obvious that interpersonal communication skills are a part of a larger family of related skills referred to in this manual as *generic life skills*. The other generic life skills are detailed, along with current research in this area, in Chapter 1, and interpersonal communication skills are placed in context with them. Chapter 1 continues with an overview of the interpersonal communication skills model dealt with in detail throughout the manual, along with original and current research support.

This fifth edition of *Human Relations Development: A Manual for Educators* has more changes than any previous edition. The adaptation of the Carkhuff Model that is featured in all previous editions remains essentially unchanged. In order to ensure ease in interpretation and implementation of the scales for each of the core dimensions, we have modified the four-point scale to a three-point scale. Illustrations for each of the three levels are given for each of the core dimension scales. We consider these three-point scales to be our "application" scales; however, for those who were accustomed to the four-point scales, we have retained them in the appendix. We now refer to these scales as our "research" scales.

Other major changes include the addition of two entirely new chapters. Chapter 2 includes two major features: the changing roles of teachers resulting from the restructuring schools movement and the special skills needed to teach those students with various learning and behavior disorders who are mainstreamed.

The second new chapter, Chapter 3, presents the rationale for multiculturalism in education along with the unique challenges that teachers face in communicating with multiethnic, multiracial, and multilingual issues. The entire text has also been revised to include numerous practice exercises that will enhance the trainees' communication with multicultural learners.

The *Instructor's Guide* that accompanies this manual has been revised in two significant areas: issues that relate to multicultural education, and the inclusion of several small group training exercises found to be effective by the text authors.

The model itself can only implement human relations skills development. Inevitably, it is the personnel who function as trainers who hold the key to the success or failure of this or any other training model. We wish, therefore, to underscore the importance of selecting healthy, high-functioning persons as trainers or educators. We recommend, further, that all potential trainers be trained in the model in this manual before they attempt to train others.

We do not pretend that all of the learning or skill development in human relations is contained in the exercises found in this manual and its accompanying guide. The manual and guide are *aids* for trainers who can develop audiovisual material of their own to supplement the exercises.

We wish to acknowledge the many individuals who have contributed to the development of this manual and its accompanying guide. Without the pioneering efforts of Robert Carkhuff the basic model could not have been developed. We thank Dr. Carkhuff for permitting us to adapt his model and scales to the educational setting. We are grateful to Tim Evans for his contribution of Chapter 25; to Nancy A. Haynie for her work on *The Instructor's Guide* and on portions of chapters; to Michael Baltimore for his contribution to Chapter 2 and his numerous helpful suggestions for improving the text; to my graduate assistant, Elizabeth Stewart, for her library research and editorial assistance; and to my secretary, Gaye Durand, for her typing and manuscript coordination.

▶ 1

Rationale

Effectiveness in teaching depends on a number of factors. Knowledge of subject matter, use of appropriate techniques and media, awareness of principles of applied learning, and skill in classroom management are among the elements frequently cited as contributing to effective teaching. (For discussion of effective *schools*, see Glickman 1990 and Goodlad 1985.) More important than these, however, are the skills you yourself possess—your life skills. Research by Brooks (1984) led to the identification of four *generic* life skills. These generic life skills have been named as follows: Interpersonal Communication/ Human Relations, Problem Solving/Decision Making, Physical Fitness/ Health Maintenance, and Identity Development/Purpose in Life (Gazda, Childers, and Brooks 1987).

Life skills are defined as all those skills necessary for effective living apart from the academic or "3R" skills. The term "generic life skills" refers to families of related skills. For example, Interpersonal Communication/Human Relations Skills include attending, listening, perceiving, verbal responding, and nonverbal responding, among others.

There is a remarkable similarity between the generic life skills and the goals of education in a democratic society. The National Assessment of Educational Progress (NAEP 1975), a division of the Education Commission of the States, cited the following seven areas, recommended by a planning committee, as *basic skills*: (a) consumer, (b) health maintenance, (c) interpersonal, (d) citizenship, (e) family relationships, (f) community resource utilization, and (g) career and occupational development. These skills bear a striking resemblance to the "Seven Cardinal Principles," defined by the Commission on the Reorganization of Secondary Education (*Cardinal Principles* 1918) over a half-century earlier. These principles are (a) health, (b) command of fundamental processes, (c) worthy home membership, (d) a vocation, (e) good citizenship, (f) worthy use of leisure time, and (g) ethical character. While the

1

language sounds somewhat quaint today, Shane (1976) contends that the principles "have retained their usefulness and their importance even after the passage of 60 years" (p. 59).

Similarly, Flanagan (1978) and the American Institutes for Research defined the quality of life for Americans and produced fifteen categories grouped under five headings as follows:

Physical and Material Well Being

Material well being and financial security
Health and personal safety

Relations with Other People

Relations with spouse (or girlfriend or boyfriend)
Having and rearing children
Relations with parents, siblings, and other relatives
Relations with friends

Social, Community, and Civic Activities

Activities related to helping or encouraging other people
Activities relating to local and national governments

Personal Development and Fulfillment

Intellectual development
Personal understanding and planning
Occupational role (job)
Creativity and personal expressions

Recreation

Socializing
Passive and observational recreational activities
Active and participatory recreational activities

It is obvious from comparing the NAEP basic skills, the Seven Cardinal Principles, and Flanagan's quality of life categories that there is a great deal of similarity among them. It also appears that the generic life skills proposed earlier encompass all of the skill areas described in these three lists. One skill area that repeats itself is interpersonal communication/human relations. (Hereafter abbreviated interpersonal communication skills.) This area is cited specifically by NAEP, is implied within several areas of the cardinal principles, especially "command of fundamental processes," and comprises one of Flanagan's categories by itself, while impinging on the other four.

The position we take in this text is that interpersonal communication skills are of primary importance in effective teaching, as well as in effective

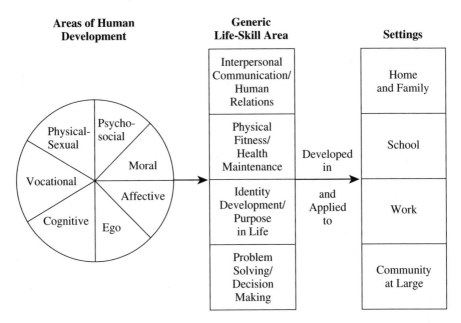

Areas of Human Development

Generic Life-Skill Area

Settings

FIGURE 1-1 **A Model for the Development and Application of Generic Life Skills.**

living. The development of such skills must be given attention at least equal to that currently devoted to materials, methods, and media in programs of preservice teacher education. Inservice education must also focus on further enhancing teachers' interpersonal communication skills. The remaining chapters deal with developing the rationale for communication skills training and with procedures for mastering these skills.

Interpersonal communication skills must be understood within the context of the totality of human development. Figure 1-1 illustrates the seven areas of human development from which the four generic life skills were identified. The figure also shows that one of the four areas where interpersonal communication is taught and applied is the school.

USE OF MODELS

The position we take in the text is that in order to master any life skill the most effective approach is to develop a model for the skill. When separate skills are taught willy-nilly and there is no complete rationale for showing relationship among the skills, nor any ordering for teaching the skills, the skills are soon lost or atrophied. However, when a sound model that provides a logical and scientific defense for its use is presented, the learner sees the whole picture and is motivated to master the component parts, because they fit together like a carefully machined group of gears. If one cog is imperfect, the gears will not mesh and the machine will not function, or it will function imperfectly.

Essentially we are speaking of what Egan and Cowan (1979) refer to as working models. According to them, working models (as opposed to models devised primarily to understand social phenomena) do the following:

they provide vehicles for translating theory and research into visualizations of how things work;

they constitute framework for action or intervention (delivery) by practitioners;

they suggest programs and the technologies needed to implement these programs;

they suggest areas of action-based research with "delivery" potential; and

they remain open to modification and development as they are influenced by new theory, research, and ongoing practice (p. 15).

RESEARCH SUPPORT

The model for human relations training described in this chapter and operationalized throughout the remainder of this manual has evolved from hundreds of studies based on the research of numerous counselors and psychotherapists. From the many studies of divergent theories and therapies, a common thread was discovered. Truax and Carkhuff (1967) carefully traced this thread, and they describe it as consisting of certain particular characteristics of the therapist. The characteristics first described were termed *accurate empathy, nonpossessive warmth,* and *genuineness.* The work of Carl Rogers (1957) served as the impetus to focus renewed interest on these and similar characteristics.

Working with Rogers at the University of Wisconsin, Truax, Carkhuff, and a host of others began to investigate the effect of the presence of the "common thread" in the therapist-client relationship. They did indeed discover that certain conditions or dimensions offered by the therapist, when present at high levels, led to growth on the part of the client and, when absent or present only at low levels, led to deterioration of the client. The accumulated evidence of the validity of the "core" conditions, or dimensions, as they were to be called, can be found in several volumes, especially in Rogers, Gendlin, Kiesler, and Truax (1967), Truax and Carkhuff (1967), Carkhuff and Berenson (1967), Berenson and Carkhuff (1967), Carkhuff (1969a, 1969b, 1971a, 1971b), and Berenson and Mitchell (1974).

As the research progressed, several new dimensions were discovered, and scales for rating these dimensions were developed (Carkhuff 1969a, 1969b; Carkhuff and Berenson 1967; Truax and Carkhuff 1967). Eventually Carkhuff (1969a, 1969b) refined, renamed, and standardized the scales of the core dimensions and added a rationale that seemed to complete the model for a helping relationship. Although further refinement of existing dimensions and scales and the search for new dimensions continues, there is now available a substantial body of research and knowledge to support a preferred mode of helping.

Studies on the effectiveness of this model for training undergraduates in teacher education have consistently shown significant increases in facilitative communication. Bixler (1972), Balzer (1973), Hornsby (1973), and Haynie (1981) studied the effects of interpersonal communication training, as outlined in this text, on preservice education majors. Based on approximately twenty class hours of training, students showed statistically significant gains at completion of training. Casey and Roark (1980) demonstrated statistically significant changes in facilitative responding and perception when the model was taught to junior high school students.

Childers (1973) found that student teachers who were trained in the model described in this text showed significantly less criticism, stimulated more student talk, and gave more indirect responses as measured by the Flanders system of interaction analysis during student teaching than a comparable untrained control group. Using the same model, Robinson (1976) demonstrated that elementary school students achieved statistically significant gains in language arts when taught by teachers trained in the model versus a comparable control group of students taught by untrained teachers.

Davis and Gazda (1975) demonstrated that the model could be used to increase significantly levels of facilitative responding and increase perceptual skills of a group of teacher educators who were members of the Association of Teacher Education.

We know of no other model for human relations training/interpersonal communication that has been so thoroughly researched and so carefully developed, and we therefore offer it to the trainer and trainee with considerable confidence in its validity. The credit for the model in its present form, however, goes to Robert Carkhuff, and we shall present the outline of his rationale as we interpret it from personal contacts, from his research and writings, and from our own application of the constructs to preservice and inservice training of teachers and other educators.

PERSONAL CHARACTERISTICS OF EFFECTIVE TEACHERS

One of the most comprehensive studies of teacher characteristics was made by Ryans (1960). The project involved over one hundred separate research investigations of some 6,000 teachers from 1,700 schools. For the purposes of this chapter, only selected findings from the total project are presented.

The Teacher Characteristics Schedule (TCS) is a 300-item, self-report inventory that was developed and used extensively in Ryans's project. Through factor analyzing numerous assessments of elementary and secondary teachers, three major patterns of teacher classroom behavior were identified (Ryans 1964, p. 76). These were as follows:

> *TCS pattern X:* warm, understanding, friendly versus aloof, egocentric, restricted behavior.
>
> *TCS pattern Y:* responsible, businesslike, systematic versus evading, unplanned, slipshod behavior.
>
> *TCS pattern Z:* stimulating, imaginative versus dull, routine behavior.

In one study in Ryans's project, school principals were asked to nominate outstandingly good and poor teachers. These teachers then completed the TCS. The good group attained significantly higher mean scores with respect to friendly and understanding behavior, organized and businesslike behavior, and stimulating behavior. The good teachers expressed a liking for personal contacts and were generous in their appraisal of others. The characteristics that distinguished the poor teachers suggested self-centeredness, anxiety, and restriction.

Several things were observed about the relationship between teacher behavior and student behavior in the classroom. Productive pupil behavior was related to the following teacher behaviors and characteristics: (1) understanding, friendly teacher behavior, (2) systematic, businesslike teacher behavior, (3) stimulating, imaginative teacher behavior, (4) child-centered educational viewpoint, (5) emotional adjustment, and (6) favorable attitudes toward pupils and democratic classroom procedures (Ryans 1964).

PERSONAL CHARACTERISTICS OF EFFECTIVE HELPERS

Characteristics of effective helpers are viewed as additive to those of effective teachers. A slight shift of focus is necessary, however, because not all desirable teacher behaviors are required to be an effective helper. For example, effective helpers do not necessarily *have* to be systematic and businesslike, but they *do* have to be understanding and friendly and they must be well adjusted emotionally. The remainder of this text is devoted to operationalizing a model for *helping relationships*, defined as facilitating personal growth and problem solving through effective interpersonal communications. Before turning to that task, however, a brief discussion of the characteristics of a helpful person appears warranted.

Fortunately, there is no *single* personality type that has been identified as the "helper type." There is, however, general agreement that there are *prerequisites* on which those who would be effective helpers can build. Without these prerequisites it is doubtful that any amount of training will enable one to be truly effective in a helping relationship. The prerequisites cluster around the concept of the "fully functioning" person, as elaborated in the writings of such contemporary social scientists as Rogers, Allport, Mead, Maslow, Fromm, and Otto. Yet who among us is "fully functioning"? It has been hypothesized (Otto 1970) that average "healthy" human beings function at only about 10 percent of their potential. If this is true, then the circle of those with the capability to help is exclusive indeed.

A closer look at the personal characteristics that may be prerequisites of effective helpers provides us with guidelines for training. By being cognizant of their own *values, motives, strengths, weaknesses, feelings, purpose in life,* and *current level of functioning,* aspiring helpers are better able to use the specific skills outlined in this text in effective helping relationships. We believe that by attending to these prerequisite characteristics while developing interpersonal communication skills, the prospective helper can approach more closely the ideal of the "fully functioning" person.

Awareness of *personal values* is directly related to how unconditional or nonjudgmental the helper can be when trying to help someone who has different values. The extent to which the helper is able to suspend judgments will determine the depth of the investment the helper has in the helpee[1]—an investment that is necessary if a helping relationship based on respect, understanding, and trust is to develop. The helper's ability to value and appreciate the helpee who has different values lies at the heart of this issue.

The helper's *motives and goals* are the product of his or her values. If a

---

[1]Helpee(s) is used throughout this manual to designate the person(s) seeking some kind of assistance at a given moment of time. The authors do not wish to imply that the helpee is the kind of person who is continuously in a state of emotional turmoil or some other difficulty. They have simply chosen this term as a succinct means of referring to a person on the help-seeking or help-receiving end of a continuum at a given moment. In other words, the helpee, by actively seeking assistance and understanding, may be showing a very positive behavior that in every respect is prevention oriented; whereas another helpee may be merely the passive recipient of the helper's action. Whether the helpee is seeker or passive recipient of help, the goal of the model is the same—to provide the conditions that enable the helpee to be actively involved in the solution of the problem and thereby to be willing to accept responsibility for action taken.

helper's goal is to transform the helpee into a behavioral "clone" of the helper, then the helpee's opportunities for growth and change may be limited to simply pleasing the helper. If the helper's goal is power, the helpee may be so manipulated as to become dependent on the authority of the helper. As a helper, your goals for the helpee must be constantly assessed against your own motives.

The emotional awareness of the helper is inextricably bound to his or her values and motives. Recognized *feelings* of disgust, revulsion, or horror may be early warning signals that the helper is unable to work with a particular helpee. Similarly, strong feelings of physical attraction or sympathy may also interfere with one's ability to help.

A keen awareness of one's *strengths and weaknesses* is also critical to the helper's ability to help. All helpers cannot be effective with all helpees. Unless personal areas of weakness have been resolved, it is unlikely that the helper will be able to assist a helpee whose problems center in those particular areas. Referring the helpee to someone else is the preferred course of action when helpee problems arise that coincide with the helper's own weaknesses. Helpers functioning at a high level can provide help to a broad range of helpees. Would-be helpers who have numerous personal deficits will probably not be able to help anyone.

Finally, having a clear vision of one's *purpose in life*, one's reason for being, enables the helper to communicate a vitality and enjoyment for living. This vitality, when shared with the helpee, can provide the helpee with a feeling of hope needed to undergird and sustain the relationship throughout the helping process. Such vitality also sustains the helper by permitting the helper to exert the energy and commitment that are essential to continuing to be helpful to someone else.

These prerequisite personal characteristics describe the kind of model that the helper is for the helpee. Additional treatment of the personal characteristics of a helping/helpee personality can be found in the following texts: Brammer (1993), Egan (1990), and Ivey (1988). We now look at the impact of modeling in promoting helpee growth and change.

MODELING AS A KEY COMPONENT OF THE HELPING RELATIONSHIP

Many reasons can be given to support skill training in interpersonal communication. One primary factor is that, when we are around others, they can observe things about us through several sensory modalities. We are thus *all models for others*. Even when we are not aware that we are being observed, our behavior may significantly influence the behavior of others. Modeling—defined as the imitation of others in the environment through observation, listening, and experimenting—is therefore a form of learning that must be taken seriously if we are interested in becoming more effective in our interpersonal relationships.

Every day we see the impact of modeling. We model the behavior, both appropriate and inappropriate, of those visible through media or "hype." All of us, to some extent, can be influential in the lives of others through our own behavior, which others observe and later incorporate into their own behaviors and response patterns. In school settings, the number of those affected is less than in mass media exposure, but the impact is usually greater, because of the level and intensity of the personal interaction between us as educators and the pupils who are modeling aspects of our behavior.

What are the behaviors pupils model? The possibilities are almost limitless, but we can discuss some of the more obvious elements. One way to understand the range of behaviors that might be modeled is to ask persons about the *qualities* they look for in a friend, or the *characteristics* they seek in individuals in whom they would confide if they needed to discuss something important. The following qualities and characteristics are more frequently listed:

someone who will listen to me;
someone with a sense of humor;
someone who communicates to me that they care;
someone who won't tell me what to do;
someone who won't judge me or try to impose his or her values on me;
someone who will have patience with me;
someone who will not tell everyone else what we talked about; and
someone who is confident and self-assured, who has his or her act together.

The list could go on, but these qualities would appear with overwhelming frequency any time a group of people is asked to describe a helpful person. What does this mean? The most obvious thing is that we can influence others in a positive way simply by the *interpersonal* skills we exhibit in our daily lives. If these are the qualities that others like in friends and confidants, it follows that they are also the qualities that helpees would like to possess in themselves.

We know that others, especially those who are at transitional points in their lives as a result of development stages or of changes resulting from other factors, will model the behavior of those around them. Knowing this, it makes sense to be concerned about the interpersonal skills that we are passing along, consciously or unconsciously, to students and others with whom we come in contact. The skills that enhance others' perceptions of us as helpful persons are discussed throughout this text. As skills, they are dimensions of our being with people that can be assessed, that permit identification of strengths and deficits, and that with practice we can enhance, building on our strengths and gradually eliminating our deficits. The process of learning to be an effective helper requires, more than anything else, a willingness to examine oneself interpersonally without threat, to accept feedback, and to be motivated to persevere in training. With practice the conscious processes of being aware of the types of communication requests helpees make, of responding appropriately, and of attending to their nonverbal behaviors become more unconscious and spontaneous. With practice and patience the teacher/helper thus becomes a positive model for effective interpersonal skills. The effect of such modeling on others is well worth one's investment in training.

THE GOALS OF HELPING

Generally speaking, the universally accepted goal of helping is to generate more appropriate behavior. The specific goals for a given helpee are determined by the helper and helpee collaboratively as they interact in the helping relationship. The nature of the interaction must be controlled by the helper, who is the expert on the conditions necessary for change to occur. When the helper's own behavior is controlled, it creates an atmosphere of security and trust that is a prerequisite for the first step or goal in helping. The conditions necessary for healthy, productive, interpersonal communication can be taught, systematically practiced, and incorporated into one's lifestyle.

Carkhuff (1971a) has outlined (and the authors have adapted) the three goals of helping as follows:

Helpee Self-Exploration

The first goal of helping is to facilitate helpee self-exploration. Before a helper can be of any assistance to a helpee, he or she must understand the helpee's problem in depth. Likewise, the helpee must know his or her own problem in all its ramifications to be fully involved in its solution.

The untrained lay "helper" frequently misses his or her first opportunity to help by being too willing to accept the helpee's initial statement of the problem of primary concern. The helper then often gives advice spontaneously on how the helpee should handle the problem. This is what we call "cheap and dirty" advice because it is "off the top of the head" of the helper and based on too little information. It is typically the kind of advice that the helpee has already considered and probably even tried but was still unsuccessful in solving the problem.

Helpee Understanding and Commitment

When the helpee is permitted to explore or is helped to explore his or her problems in depth, he or she is likely to understand them and him- or herself better. The role of the helper is to assist the helpee in making some kind of sense out of the many pieces of the puzzle. Typically, the helpee has thought about his or her problems a great deal, but because he or she did not have the necessary skills or responses, or because he or she could not put them together in the proper combination, the helpee was unable to change his or her behavior and so remained problem ridden.

Although self-understanding is generally considered to be a prerequisite condition for most types of problem solving, it is a well accepted fact among professional helpers that understanding alone is frequently insufficient in changing behavior. Witness, for example, the many people who know cognitively that smoking is harmful to their physical health, yet they persist in smoking. What is missing from the persons who know what is best for them and do not act to change in that direction is commitment. Therefore, during the second phase of helping, the helpee must not only understand his or her problems in depth, but he or she must also make a cognitive and visceral decision to follow through with a plan or program designed to correct the deficits.

Helpee Action

Often the most difficult step in problem solving is taking the necessary action to correct the identified problem. The helper and helpee must devise a plan of action which the helpee must follow to resolve the problem. It must be a plan that is possible to complete. That is, the helpee must be capable of taking the first of a series of steps or actions that will ensure the success of the next, and ultimately the successful resolution of the problem itself. In the process of arriving at a given course of action, helper and helpee consider alternate plans and the possible consequences of different plans before selecting one. (See Chapter 21 for a more complete description of implementation approaches.)

It is important to understand that not all teachers and educators will always be able to develop a sequence of actions that will lead to a desired outcome. Often the helper will be just one link in the chain. The helper may simply be the person who assists in developing a few key responses in the helpee's total repertoire of responses, ones that can be used in the future to help solve problems or enrich the life of the helpee.

THE CYCLE OF HELPING

If helpees will *self-explore*, this usually leads to a better understanding of their concerns and a commitment to change which, in turn, makes possible a more successful course of action. The action itself provides the ultimate feedback to helpees. Often they will need to refine or to alter their responses to arrive at the preferred behavioral outcome. Helpees repeat the cycle as often as necessary to lead them toward their goals.

The three-phase cycle that Carkhuff has outlined (and that we have adapted) for problem solving—*self exploration → better self-understanding and a commitment to change → more appropriate action or direction*—works for most people; however, there are exceptions. With individuals who are not in good contact with reality, it is usually necessary to reverse the cycle and first do something to get them back in contact with reality before understanding can occur. We are, at this point, generally describing the emotionally and mentally disturbed, and since most educators are not expected to deal extensively with this population, this type of helping will not be considered in this manual.

THE PROCESS OF HELPING

Table 1-1 contains the key concepts in the helping model developed by Carkhuff (1969a, 1969b, 1971b, 1972). Figure 1-2 represents the current version of Carkhuff's basic helping skills model. Aspy (1986) presents Figure 1-2 to illustrate how the helper employs helping skills to facilitate the helpee's movement through the learning process. Aspy (1986) describes the helping process as follows:

> The helpers, therefore, attend to the helpees in order to facilitate their involvement in helping; respond to the helpees in order to facilitate their exploration of their experience; personalize the helpees' experience in order to facilitate their understanding of their goals; and initiate to stimulate the helpees' action to achieve their goals. These helping skills apply as core conditions to all helping and human relationships, i.e., they represent a core of conditions that are shared by all helping orientations. (p. 252)

We begin our adaptation of the Carkhuff model with the procedural goals for basically normal individuals of all age levels. Of course, when dealing with a very young child, the adult communicates through direct action. For example, the adult communicates to the young child directly by cuddling, squeezing, feeding, cleansing, hugging, rocking, slapping, spanking, and so on. Often the adult adds words to describe the action even when the child cannot understand the words, and also responds with verbal and nonverbal expressions that express the way the adult feels about the child at the moment.

The first phase of helping is directed toward establishing a base, or building a good relationship, with the helpee. It might entail verbal expression, nonverbal expression, direct physical action, or a combination of all of these modes depending upon the age, intelligence, and degree of contact with reality of the helpee.

Preparing for a space shot and firing the rocket are analogous to the two

TABLE 1-1   Outline of the Key Concepts of a Helping Relationship

Facilitation phase	Transition phase	Action phase
Helpee describes symptoms. Helper suspends acting on evaluations. Helper's tenderness emphasized; helper "earns the right" to be judgmental later in the helping process.	Helpee defines problem and accepts responsibility for its change. Helper gently presses the helpee toward recognizing helpee's role. Helper cautiously and tentatively becomes more evaluative.	Helpee takes appropriate actions to solve problem. Helper may be judgmental. Helper's self-confidence and knowledge are emphasized.
Procedural goals: Self-exploration	Better self-understanding and commitment to change	More appropriate action or direction
Facilitation dimensions*	**Transition dimensions***	**Action dimensions***
Empathy (depth understanding)	Concreteness (ability to be specific)	Confrontation (pointing out discrepancies)
Respect (belief in)	Genuineness (honesty, realness)	Immediacy (helper and helpee telling it like it is in the "here and now")
Warmth (caring, love) (nonverbal)	Self-disclosure (ability to convey appropriately "I've been there too.")	

*Each of the eight dimensions involves the act of perceiving (becoming aware of) and the act of responding (acting on awareness).

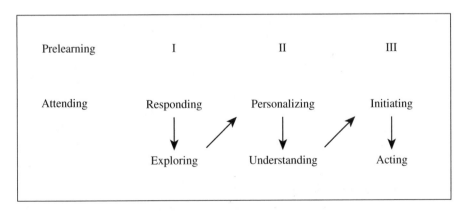

FIGURE 1-2   The Basic Helping Skills

basic phases of helping: facilitation and action. Before a rocket can be fired, many preparations must be made. First, a very strong base must be built under the rocket to hold it and to sustain the backward thrust when it is fired. Similarly, in a helping relationship, the helper must first use the less threatening (facilitative) dimensions to prepare and sustain the helpee for the more threatening but often necessary action of initiative dimensions. If helpers will carefully build their bases with helpees, they will help ensure their success when they use problem-solving approaches with helpees at a later action period. Carkhuff (1971a) succinctly stated the importance of the facilitation phase of helping when he said, "Even if you have just fifteen minutes to help, you must use five minutes or so responding [facilitating] to the helpee in order to find out for sure where the helpee is before starting to put the picture together [initiating] and acting upon that picture."

FACILITATION DIMENSIONS

Helpers begin to build their base with helpees by first responding with *empathy*, *respect*, and *warmth*. Table 1-1 shows how this leads to increased helpee self-exploration (the first goal of helping).

To achieve success in the first goal of helping, helpers must be able to refrain from acting on their judgments about helpees. Virtually no one can refrain from making evaluations or judgments about others, but we have found that helpers can refrain from *acting* on their judgments. This is especially important if their early evaluations or judgments are negative. For example, a helper may initially be repulsed by a helpee for a number of good reasons; nevertheless, if the helper can suspend acting on these feelings, something good or likable about the helpee usually shows up; at that point the helper can begin to invest in the helpee and build a base from which to work.

"Putting oneself in the shoes of another" and "seeing through the eyes of another" are ways of describing empathy. Empathy appears to be the most important dimension in the helping process (Carkhuff 1969a, p. 202). If we cannot understand—empathize with—a helpee, we cannot help this person.

Another facilitative dimension is respect. We cannot help people if we have no faith in their ability to solve their own problems. Respect develops as we learn about the uniqueness and the capabilities of helpees. It grows as we observe their efforts in many aspects of their lives. Helpers can usually demonstrate respect by good attending behavior and a belief in the capacity of helpees to help themselves, supporting them in their efforts, and not doing for them what they can do.

Warmth or caring is closely related to empathy and respect. We tend to love or have concern for those we know (understand) and believe in (respect). It is difficult to conceive of helping someone we don't care about. ("Help" here means to "make a significant investment in.") In this model, warmth is communicated primarily through nonverbal means, such as a smile, caress, touch, hug, and so on.

TRANSITION DIMENSIONS—HELPER ORIENTED

As the helper begins to develop a base with the helpee through empathy, respect, and warmth, the helpee self-explores in greater and greater depth. In fact, the clue to whether or not the helper is being successful in the early phase of helping is based on the degree to which the helpee uses helper responses to make deeper and more thorough self-explorations.

With repeated, interchangeable helper responses—responses that give back to the helpee essentially that which he or she has given to the helper—the helpee often begins to repeat him- or herself and "spin the wheels" or reach a plateau in self-exploration and understanding. It is at this point when the helper needs to encourage the helpee to risk more self-exploration, that the dimensions of *concreteness, genuineness,* and *self-disclosure* are carefully implemented. When the helper presses for greater concreteness or specificity on the part of the helpee, a certain degree of threat is introduced. The same thing occurs when the helper becomes more genuine and sets the stage—model—for the helpee to become more genuine. The helper's self-disclosure encourages greater intimacy in the relationship. which can lead to increased threat to the helpee. In other words, these three dimensions increase the threat level for the helpee, and they are thus *action-oriented* as well as facilitative. In addition to the relationship between level of threat and the action phase, these three dimensions are also involved in the problem-solving or planning stages of the action phase.

Specifically, *concreteness* refers to the helpee's pinpointing or accurately labeling feelings and experiences. The helper facilitates this by being specific, or at least as specific as the helpee has been. When the helper is more specific than the helpee, he or she is going beyond where the helpee is—the actions are *additive.* If the helper's *timing* of the use of additive concreteness is correct, the helpee can achieve greater understanding because his or her concerns were made more explicit.

Genuineness refers to the ability of the helper to be real or honest with the helpee. Helper verbalizations are congruent with inner feelings. Whether or not the helper's genuineness is useful to the helpee will often depend on the helper's ability to time his or her level of honesty to lead to greater trust and understanding. As Carkhuff (1971a, p. 21) has said, "Helping is for the helpee." And if the helpee cannot use the helper genuineness, it may be useless or even hurtful. The saying, "Honesty is the best policy," is not always correct, especially if brutal honesty is used with someone who is not capable of dealing with it for self-improvement. To illustrate, encounter groups are often harmful to certain persons, especially when, as is sometimes the case, frankness precedes the establishment of a solid base or relationship.

Self-disclosure by the helper, *if it is appropriate* or relevant to the helpee's problem, can lead to greater closeness between helper and helpee. If the helper has had a concern similar to that of the helpee and has found a solution to the problem, this can be reassuring to the helpee. Furthermore, the helpee's solution may even be similar to the one which was used by the helper. The success of Alcoholics Anonymous and other self-help groups is related to this dimension. Drinking alcoholics, for example, look to the "dry alcoholics" of AA for the solutions to their own problems. The "speaker" phase of AA thus uses the self-disclosure dimension.

When helper self-disclosure is premature or irrelevant to the helpee's problem, it tends to confuse the helpee or put the focus on the helper. The helper steals the spotlight.

TRANSITION DIMENSIONS—HELPEE ORIENTED

The facilitation-action dimensions of concreteness, genuineness, and self-disclosure can be used to predict the degree of success of the *helpee's help seeking*. The degree to which the helpee can be concrete about his or her problem (can label it accurately, for instance), can be honest and open with helpers, and can self-disclose at high levels with determine whether or not the helpee will, in fact, receive help. Of course, the other important factor in the help-seeking equation is the helper. If the helpee chooses to be concrete, genuine, and to self-disclose to a person who is incapable of helping, the helpee may become disillusioned or, worse still, hurt. Helping can be for better or for worse (Truax and Carkhuff 1967, p. 143).

Prospective helpers (educators) can predict the relative success they might achieve with a given student helpee. For example, helpers can rate student helpees on the scale for help seeking, that is their ability to be concrete about their needs and problems, their ability to be genuine with the helper, and their ability to disclose personally relevant material. These dimensions and others for rating helpees' potential for receiving help can be found in Appendix D. Also, in predicting whether or not helpees are amenable to receiving help, helpers may observe the degree to which helpees employ the basic defense mechanisms described in Chapter 4.

If prospective helpees talk about their concerns in vague and general terms (not concrete), are observed to be playing a role or relate in a superficial or phony manner (not genuine), and do not make personally relevant disclosures, helpers are relatively safe in predicting that these helpees will be difficult to help. Also, the process might require a relatively long period of time to develop the base—the first phase of helping—before any positive action can occur.

ACTION DIMENSIONS

The action of initiative phase of helping may be considered the most important phase. It is in this phase that tough decisions are made and the hard work must be done. It is the ultimate test of whether or not you, the helper, are in fact the "more knowing" individual, tough and confident enough to believe in both your own and the helpee's ability to devise a plan of action (strategy) and to follow through when the work gets difficult. The helper must be capable of helping develop a plan or strategy for the helpee that will lead to the successful resolution of the helpee's current problem and provide the helpee at the same time with a method for attacking future problems. Since teachers usually do not have the time or, perhaps, the special training in behavior problem solving, they should not expect to carry the primary burden of developing strategies for behavioral problem solving, but they should be partners in efforts developed by specialists.

If a helper has not resolved the particular problem or concern in question, it is highly unlikely he or she can assist a helpee with the problem. You cannot help someone else solve a problem you have not resolved yourself. This is a maxim that must guide all helping attempts. If helpers know themselves, they will be unlikely to enter into a helping relationship in a problem area that remains unresolved for them.

There is another cardinal rule in helping: One does not emphasize the action dimension until one has built the base. In other words, the helper does not confront the helpee without having earned the right to do so. Brutal honesty can be punitive and even harmful. *Confrontation* then, a key action dimension, can only be helpful when the helpee has learned, from earlier experience, that the helper is concerned about the welfare of the helpee and cares enough to risk the relationship by "leveling."

Frequently confrontation means dealing with discrepancies between what helpees have been saying about themselves and what they have, in fact, been doing. A common confrontation is one that assists a helpee to face the reality of a situation. The most threatening type of confrontation is one that does not allow a helpee to "save face." This is the type of confrontation that deals with the here and now. When you catch helpees behaving contrary to the way they claim to behave, and you confront them directly with it, it is difficult for them to deny it. They have few good means of defense and may use denial and other inappropriate short-term mechanisms that have long-term disadvantages. For example, if a mother catches her son in the cookie jar and accuses him of stealing cookies, the child may actually deny reality when the external threat is great enough. And so, by their use of threats, parents and teachers unknowingly are teaching children to lie and to deny reality.

Berenson and Mitchell's (1974) extensive research on the effects of the use of confrontation is quite sobering. They contend that confrontation is never necessary, but that it can be effective and efficient when used by highly functioning persons. Jacobs (1975) reported that, in a series of eleven studies on verbal feedback in groups, no evidence was found where negative feedback (one might consider this a form of confrontation of deficits) was advantageous to the group or recipient. Positive feedback (confrontation of one's potential) was rated as more believable, desirable, and impactful by recipients and donors with various populations of participants, types of leaders' manners and styles of delivery, and types and amounts of information exchanged. Jacobs furthermore contends that believability of information seems likely to be a necessary, although perhaps not always a sufficient, condition for attitudinal and behavioral change. In other words, the evidence is beginning to suggest that confrontation of one's deficits (negative feedback) must only be used by highly functioning sensitive helpers. Even then, the evidence suggests that the risk may be too great for potential benefits derived.

The other action dimension, *immediacy*, is often related to confrontation. It refers to what is really going on between helper and helpee. When helpees are unaware of their reactions towards helpers, helpers may need to describe or explain them. It includes "telling it like it is" between helper and helpee in the here and now. Helpees can gain a better understanding of themselves, especially how they affect others (in this case the helper), when helpers appropriately use the immediacy dimension. Once again, the helper must time the use of immediacy so that the helpee can use it productively.

The productivity of confrontation and immediacy can be guaranteed if the helper takes the position that "the customer (the helpee) is always right." By this we simply mean that, regardless of how brilliant and creative a helper's response may appear to be, if it cannot be used in solving the problem it is worthless—if not harmful—to the helpee.

Implementing a Course of Action

The courses of action that may be developed for helpees to achieve their goals or to give them direction may be many and varied. They may involve all four of the generic life skills.

The principles involved in implementing a course of action recommended by Carkhuff (1969a, p. 243) are summarized as follows: (1) the helper must check with the helpee at all stages of development and implementation to be sure that what is planned or performed is relevant to the helpee's functioning. (2) The focus of change should usually be on the helpee first and only secondarily on the helpee's relationships with others. (3) Only those measures or procedures that ensure the highest probability of constructive change are employed. (4) The emphasis is on outcomes and the achievement of attainable goals. The helper and helpee must be shaped by the feedback they receive.

Often the real test of helpers, as stated earlier in this chapter, will be whether or not they can develop appropriate plans of action for their helpees. Frequently helpees will be unable to develop their own courses of action and will require help in structuring their program. When helpees cannot participate fully in the program planning, Carkhuff (1969a) cautions helpers to develop programs that will "enable the helpee to carry some of the burden of responsibility for his own life" (p. 243).

If teachers and other educators can master the basic dimensions of the helping relationship that we have outlined in this chapter, they will prevent the development of many potential problem children and problem adults. Even with higher level functioning teachers in the classroom, other external factors such as the home, school, and community environment will produce child casualties. The teacher will need the assistance of educational specialists such as school counselors and school psychologists, reading experts, and special education experts working as a team in problem prevention and resolution.

Helping Involves Teaching and Learning

As helpers show empathy, respect, and warmth, helpees explore themselves and their problems. As helpers continue to show empathy, respect, and warmth, and display appropriate levels of concreteness, genuineness, and self-disclosure, helpees begin to understand themselves and their problems. After the base is built, helpers use positive confrontation and immediacy to help the helpees take action or find direction.

This description (as shown in Table 1-1) is oversimplified, but this is generally the pattern of helping. An important understanding is that during this process, helpers are really reinforcing certain behaviors and extinguishing others. Showing empathy, respect, and warmth generally reinforces whatever helpees say or do, which increases the probability of self-exploration and problem exploration.

Responding with appropriate levels of concreteness, genuineness, and self-disclosure results in more selective reinforcement. Helpers are no longer speaking strictly from the helpees' point of view. They begin to focus on aspects of helpee behavior that they think will be more productive, they begin to relate more of their own feelings which reinforce in a certain direction, and they point out discrepancies in helpee behavior. These helper behaviors increase the probability that helpees will understand themselves and their problems.

If an adequate relationship has been established, high levels of positive confrontation clearly reinforce certain kinds of behavior and extinguish others. These helper responses increase the probability that helpees will act on their problems and try to find some direction to follow which may solve their problems, such as additional life skills training.

The art of helping includes first knowing *how* to respond helpfully and then knowing *when* to seek higher levels on various dimensions or when to use interchangeable responses. Many beginning helpers learn to show interchangeable empathy, respect, and warmth but never become capable of displaying other, more action-oriented dimensions. They often say, "I don't want to be responsible if she makes the wrong decision so I always make sure it's her decision," or "I don't want her to become dependent on others to make her decisions." These are legitimate concerns, but they must be kept in perspective.

Helpers who display only interchangeable levels of empathy, respect, and warmth are not very selective in what they reinforce. This often results in helpees accepting their problems as permanent parts of themselves instead of solving them. If helpees are rewarded for discussing their problems over and over without moving toward some goal, they become desensitized to the problem and begin to think it's normal to have that problem.

It is extremely important for helpers to be aware of what behaviors they are reinforcing. The art of helping, therefore, includes knowing what behaviors to reinforce at a given time and how to do it. Beginning with the next chapter and continuing throughout the remainder of the book we develop a theoretical rationale to assist the helper to attend to and focus on helpee behavior and to respond appropriately to it.

REFERENCES

Aspy, C.B. 1986. "The Carkhuff models in human resource development." *Education,* 3, 252.

Balzer, F.J. 1973. "Interpersonal communication levels as a function of academic achievement." Unpublished manuscript.

Berenson, B.G., and R.R. Carkhuff. 1967. *Sources of Gain in Counseling and Psychotherapy: Readings and Commentary.* New York: Holt, Rinehart and Winston.

Berenson, B.G., and K.M. Mitchell. 1974. *Confrontation: For Better or Worse!* Amherst, MA: Human Resources Development Press.

Bixler, J.E. 1972. "Influence of trainer-trainee cognitive similarity on the outcome of Systematic Human Relations Training." Unpublished doctoral dissertation; University of Georgia.

Brammer, L.M. 1993. *The Helping Relationship: Process and Skills* (5th ed.). Boston: Allyn and Bacon.

Brooks, David F., Jr. 1984. *A life-skills taxonomy: Defining elements of effective functioning through the use of the Delphi Technique.* Unpublished doctoral dissertation; University of Georgia.

Cardinal Principles of Secondary Education. 1918. (Bulletin No. 35) Washington, DC: Department of the Interior, Bureau of Education.

Carkhuff, R.R. 1969a. *Helping and Human Relations: A Primer for Lay and Professional Helpers.* Vol. 1: Selection and Training. New York: Holt, Rinehart and Winston.

Carkhuff R.R. 1969b. *Helping and Human Relations: A Primer for Lay and Professional Helpers.* Vol. 2: Practice and Research. New York: Holt, Rinehart and Winston.

Carkhuff, R.R. 1971a. "Helping and human relations: A brief guide for training lay helpers." *Journal of Research and Development in Education* 4(2), 17–27.

Carkhuff, R.R. 1971b. *The Development of Human Resources: Education, Psychology, and Social Change.* New York: Holt, Rinehart and Winston.

Carkhuff, R.R. 1972. *The Art of Helping.* Amherst, MA: Human Resources Development Press.

Carkhuff, R.R., and B.G. Berenson. 1967. *Beyond Counseling and Therapy.* New York: Holt, Rinehart and Winston.

Casey, C., and A.E. Roark. 1980. "Outcomes of systematic human relations training with junior high school students." *Education* 101(1), 68–74.

Childers, W.C. 1973. "An evaluation of the effectiveness of a human relations training model using in-class student teacher observation and interaction analysis." Unpublished doctoral dissertation; University of Georgia.

Davis, K.L., and G.M. Gazda. 1975. "Results of the 1973 Association of Teacher Education human relations training summer workshop." *Education* 96, 184-189.

Egan, G. 1990. *The Skilled Helper* (4th ed.). Pacific Grove, CA: Brooks/Cole.

Egan, G., and M. Cowan. 1979. *People in Systems: A Model for Development in the Human-Service Professions and Education.* Monterey, CA: Brooks/Cole.

Flanagan, J.C. 1978. "A research approach to improving our quality of life. "*American Psychologists* 33, 138–147.

Gazda, G.M., W.C. Childers, and D.F. Brooks, Jr. 1987. *Foundations of Counseling and Human Services.* New York: McGraw-Hill.

Goodlad, J.I. 1984. *A Place Called Schools: Prospects for the Future.* New York: McGraw-Hill.

Glickman, C.D. 1990. *Supervision of Instruction: A Developmental Approach* (2nd Ed.). Boston: Allyn and Bacon.

Haynie, N.A. 1981. "Systematic Human Relations Training with neuro-linguistic programming." Unpublished doctoral dissertation; University of Georgia.

Hornsby, J.L. 1973. "The effects of group composition on systematic human relations training." Unpublished masters thesis; University of Georgia.

Ivey, A. 1988. *Interviewing and Counseling.* Pacific Grove, CA: Brooks/Cole.

Jacobs, A. 1975. "Research on methods of social intervention: The study of the exchange of personal information in brief personal growth groups." Paper presented at the Invited Conference on Small Group Research, Indiana University, Bloomington, April, 1975.

National Assessment of Education Progress. 1975. "Draft of basic skills objectives." Denver: National Assessment of Educational Progress, A Division of the Education Commission of the States.

Otto, H.A. 1970. *Group Methods to Actualize Human Potential: A Handbook.* Beverly Hills, CA: Holistic Press.

Robinson, E.H., III. 1976. "Students' perceptions of teachers' abilities to provide certain facilitative conditions and their relationship to language arts achievement gains." Unpublished doctoral dissertation, Duke University.

Rogers, C.R. 1957. "The necessary and sufficient conditions of therapeutic personality change." *Journal of Consulting Psychology* 21, 95–103.

Rogers, C.R., E.T. Gendlin, D.J. Kiesler, and C.B. Truax. 1967. *The Therapeutic Relationship and Its Impact: A Study of Psychotherapy with Schizophrenics.* Madison: University of Wisconsin Press.

Ryans, D.G. 1960. *Characteristics of Teachers.* Washington, DC: American Council on Education.

Ryans, D.G. 1964. "Research on teacher behavior in the context of the Teacher Characteristics Study." In B.J. Biddle and W.J. Ellena (Eds.), *Contemporary Research on Teacher Effectiveness.* New York: Holt, Rinehart and Winston.

Shane, H.G. 1976. "The seven cardinal principles revisited." *Today's Education* 65(3), 57–72.

Truax, C.B., and R.R. Carkhuff. 1967. *Toward Effective Counseling and Psychotherapy: Training and Practice.* Chicago: Aldine.

▶ 2

Teacher Roles: Their Changing Character

ROLE CHANGES EMANATING FROM RESTRUCTURED SCHOOLS

Public opinion polls show that a vast majority of teachers are dissatisfied with their jobs. Approximately 50% of those entering the teaching profession leave within five years and new teachers tend to come from the lower end of the academic pool. (Koppich, Brown, and Amsler 1990, p. 2)

The dissatisfaction and dropouts among teachers are of epidemic proportions. Equally disturbing is the high dropout rate of students from public elementary and secondary schools of this country, coupled with unsatisfactory learning achievement of graduates.

What are the factors behind the decline in public education? No comprehensive treatment of this question is intended here, but a few related factors will be cited. Many authorities point to the breakdown of the traditional family unit as a major contributor to problems in the schools. Working mothers, single parent families with less family supervision of children combined with extensive poverty in many areas of the country are indices of educational shortfalls. Related to these conditions is the increased violence in society.

Muggings, beatings, knifings and shootings characterize the environment that many children live in today. By the time they reach 8 years of age, these children have become hardened, insensitive and distant. They look and behave as though they have witnessed more pain and suffering than people three or four times their age. (Hranitz and Eddowes 1990, p. 4)

Stephens (1988) states: "Violence has become so pervasive that the Center for Disease Control in Atlanta is studying the problem of violence as an epidemic" (p. 2). According to Greenbaum and Turner (1989), approximately 5,200 of the nation's one million secondary school teachers are physically attacked at school per month. Webster (1986) contends: "Aggressive behavior is becoming a widespread and alarming problem in American society" (p. 56). Hranitz and Eddowes (1990) believe that reducing violence will be one of the most difficult tasks facing educators as the country enters the twenty-first century. This task will become very difficult because of the rising incidence of child abuse which has been shown to lead to a cycle of abuse as abused children become abusing parents and sometimes violent adults.

Obviously when the safety needs of students and teachers are not being met, learning suffers. Likewise, a system that is based on rewards and punishment for one's ability to learn or not learn rapidly generates a significant number of academic failures leading to low self-esteem and frequently aggressive, acting out behavior or withdrawal from the learning task. For many reasons, many endemic to the system, the traditional "factory" model of education is failing and reforms are being attempted. Passow (1989) points out that the reforms of the late 1970s and early 1980s began with "top-down" regulatory efforts to change the academic environment. By the middle of the 1980s, attention had shifted to the reverse or "bottom-up" efforts to restructure teaching and learning by "site-based" management efforts which gave the teacher a much greater role in planning the kinds of changes that were to take place in his or her local school site.

Bredeson (1992) views restructuring and teacher empowerment as antecedent conditions of role conflict, role overload, and role strain. Bredeson believes that teachers and principals could view restructuring as threats to their professional effectiveness or as opportunities for growth and enhanced professionalism.

Meier (1992) concludes: "Today it is clear that since we need a new kind of school to do a new kind of job, we need a new kind of teacher, too" (p. 594). Meier laments the fact that everyone wants improved results from the educational system, but she believes that there is not a lot of evidence of a serious will to change. Of the many things to be changed,

> At the heart of it is the question of how teachers can be changed— even what it means to "retrain" the educational work force. The change that must take place among the work force involves three tough tasks: changing how teachers view teaching and learning, developing new habits to go with that new cognitive understanding, and simultaneously developing new habits of work—habits that are collegial and public in nature, not so private as has been the custom in teaching. . . . (Meier 1992, p. 598)

Meier cites three major areas in which teachers' philosophy and roles must change, but she gives only one specific role change—collegial work habits. Others, such as Sarason (1971) several decades ago, cited the need for teachers to work collegially.

Peeler (1992) indicates that there seems to be a consensus among leading educators, psychologists, and philosophers that "tomorrow's adults must be prepared for a lifetime of inquiry, analysis, collaborative learning, problem-solving, and decision making" . . . and "that these abilities will be the 'basic skills' of the future" (p. 7). According to Peeler, this new definition of learning will require the teacher's role to shift to that more like a coach, facilitator, listener, model, guide, and mediator. Peeler also believes that the teacher will need to become computer literate and employ a highly interactive computer system to provide guidance and instruction to students.

Koppich, Brown, and Amsler (1990) point out that career ladder programs have added new roles for experienced teachers, including curriculum development, program development or staff development, supervision, evaluation, and training such as the California Mentor Teacher Program, shared decision making resulting from site-based management that includes making educational decisions about budgets, staffing, curriculum, and even how schools are organized. Teachers in restructured schools, state Koppich and colleagues, have served as "case managers" for groups of some twenty students, providing "personal attention and the sympathetic ear of a caring adult" (p. 5). In the Dade County, Florida system leaders are given "nine-week sabbaticals during which they conduct research, serve as mentors, develop new instructional methods, and design curriculum materials" (p. 5).

Collins and Hanson (1991) found teachers in the Dade County, Florida public schools participating in duties such as discipline, hiring, and team leadership not traditionally associated with teacher roles. In the middle schools of Dade County, teachers were involved as student advisors and worked with student services as well as in public relations.

Firestone and Bader (1991) have observed "Schools are not only expected to solve a great variety of social problems from the drug problem to the AIDS crisis but must also act as sources of day care, entertainment, and community cohesion" (p. 121). Obviously, these expanded services assumed by schools also add new roles for teachers that are frequently shared with specialists in the school setting such as counselors, social workers, nurses, and psychologists.

Inasmuch as the new roles of the teacher will significantly alter his or her traditional role as sole dispenser of information to a classroom of students to multi-faceted roles such as facilitator, coach, mentor, advisor, purveyor of good community relations, team teacher, and developer of educational models, expertise in the generic life skill of interpersonal communications/human relations could spell success or failure for the teacher in this era of restructured schools. Becoming an excellent communicator and human relations specialist are prerequisite to being a successful teacher.

ROLE CHANGES EMANATING FROM MAINSTREAMING

Statistics compiled by the U.S. Department of Education (1989) show that most elementary school students placed in special education classes are diagnosed as mildly mentally retarded, learning disabled, or behavior disordered. "Although children with mild handicaps have been physically mainstreamed into regular educational environments for quite some time, their social integration in these settings has often been unsatisfactory" (Cullinan, Sabornie, and Crossland 1992, p. 340).

Cannon, Idol, and West (1992) used an interdisciplinary panel of 105 experts from thirty-five states "to identify and validate essential practices needed by both general and special educators to successfully educate students with mild handicaps in general classrooms" (p. 300). Ninety-six essential teaching practices were validated for educating students with mild handicaps in general classrooms. Differences in ratings by the experts reflected differing emphases on the roles assigned to general and special educators. Of the six subcategories of teaching determined by the experts, Monitoring/Evaluation and Assessment/Diagnosis ranked first and third as essential categories for special educators, and fourth and last for general educators. Special educators were also seen to have greater responsibilities for mainstreamed students with mild handicaps for the categories Instructional Content and Instructional Practices. Managing Student Behavior ranked first for general educators and second for special educators, but the difference was not significant, nor were differences significant for ratings of Planning and Managing the Teaching and Learning Environment. Based on the results of the survey just described, Idol and West (1991) are developing a curriculum that "places particular emphasis on shared learning experiences that incorporate guided practice, structured and open-ended performance feedback, peer coaching, and practical application to the classroom" (p. 314). Cannon and associates also concluded that "a dual and complementary emphasis needs to be placed on (a) collaborative planning, decision-making, and problem-solving practices and (b) effective instructional practices by general and special educators who share responsibility for teaching students with mild handicaps" (p. 315).

Scruggs and Mastropieri (1992) have identified presenting characteristics of mildly handicapped students to include deficits in attention, memory, intelligence, language, social/emotional behavior, affect or motivation, basic skills, and organizational/study skills. They have also developed a model for the effective instruction of mildly handicapped students in regular classrooms. This model[1] is described briefly through eight general areas in which students must function acceptably.

1. Attention: Attention deficits, including hyperactivity and distractibility, have frequently been observed in mildly handicapped students. Interventions include first identifying the cause of the deficit to rule out especially that it does not lie in some other area such as lack of basic skills, that is, poor reading skills, or motivational/affective deficits.

Some suggested interventions or strategies to deal with attention-related deficits include (a) modifying the rate and presentation of the curriculum; (b) speaking to the student in private (making a direct appeal); (c) increasing proximity of student to teacher, also increasing rate of questions directed to the student; (d) reinforcing attending through use of a timer, such as an alarm clock or egg timer; and (e) teaching self-recording strategies of attending including cued tape-recorded beeps at random intervals, reinforced with various forms of positive recognition.

2. Memory: Attentional problems should be ruled out before memory deficits are determined to be present. Likewise, problems related to basic skills and organizational/study skills should also be ruled out.

Interventions/strategies suggested for memory deficits include (a) intensifying instructions for later recall, such as highlighting important points; (b) using external memory systems when appropriate, such as a calendar to locate the date rather than trying to remember each day's date; (c) using mnemonic instructions involving associating between new information and the learner's prior knowledge; and (d) promoting effective encoding through such methods as teachers questioning students on important concepts to be learned.

3. Intelligence: Although low intelligence is often the reason teachers refer students for special education, all students with low intelligence may not require special education classes. Some suggested interventions for students with low intelligence include (a) ensuring that presented information is similarly meaningful for all learners by, for example, teachers questioning students about their understanding of new information; (b) providing additional time to learn; (c) attending to developmental requirements of the content, such as content that is age related; (d) measuring achievement at later rather than earlier stages of acquisition; (e) using variables from the "effective teaching literature," such as teaching to prespecified objectives; and (f) employing "discovery learning," "inquiry," or "constructivist" approaches judicially.

[1]From Scruggs, T.E., and M.A. Mastropieri. "Effective mainstreaming strategies for mildly handicapped students." *The Elementary School Journal, 92*(3). Copyright 1992 by The University of Chicago Press. 0013-5984/92/9203-0010$01.00. Reproduced by permission.

4. Language Skills: There is considerable evidence that many students experience receptive or expressive language problems or both. Students with language problems can be assisted through the application of the following interventions: (a) Allow sufficient time for responding—"wait time"; (b) assist students in developing listening skills through such things as having students repeat important directions; (c) integrate language activities into regular instruction; and (d) support special services in language training such as from speech therapists.

5. Social/Emotional Behavior: Rule out that the behavior problems are not disguises for learning deficits. Often they are. Interventions for problems of withdrawal, aggression, disruptive behavior or social skills include (a) direct appeal/proximity, such as asking for student's help in improving the problem behavior; (b) reinforcing positive classroom behavior; (c) using peer mediation; (d) utilizing support personnel such as counselors; and (e) teaching social skills for those students who lack training in socially appropriate behavior.

6. Affect/Motivation: Lack of motivation and/or inappropriate affect may be the result of academic deficits; however, if the student is strong or adequate academically, the following interventions or strategies may be useful: (a) Create a positive, caring classroom atmosphere by letting students know that the teacher cares, and by using frequent encouragement and positive comments; (b) use attribution training such as helping students correctly attribute academic success to effort, perseverance, and the use of task-appropriate academic strategies; (c) establish goals for learning by helping students set short- and long-term goals and reward them for task completion; and (d) consult support personnel when necessary, such as a school psychologist if students show signs of depression or irrational behavior.

7. Basic Skills: "Mild" deficits of the basic skills of reading, writing, and math are potentially remediable in mainstreamed elementary classrooms. For pronounced deficits, or those appearing at the secondary level, special education classrooms and appropriate mainstream strategies can be used. Some recommended interventions or strategies include: (a) Employing parents as tutors with guidance for the parents; (b) employing peer mediation, such as through tutoring and cooperative learning; (c) using teacher effectiveness variables, such as teaching to clearly specified objectives and providing guided and independent practice; (d) tracking cognitive strategies such as self-monitoring or question generating; (e) de-emphasizing textbook approaches where appropriate; (f) modifying the demands of the class as necessary; and (g) intensifying special education by cooperating with special education teachers.

8. Study/Organizational Skills: According to Scruggs and Mastropieri, the failure of special education students in mainstream classes is to a large extent the result of poor or inadequate study and organizational skills. Deficits in this area interact with most of the seven other areas cited earlier in this summary of the Scruggs and Mastropieri (1992) model. The following strategies will benefit both regular education and special education students: (a) Provide structure—be explicit with all assignments, such as due dates for papers and criteria for acceptable performance; (b) teach general study techniques, such as how to study for tests and notetaking; and (c) teach test-taking skills, such as how to prepare for and take multiple choice or essay exams.

Scruggs and Mastropieri (1992) conclude their eight-part model with the following belief that is especially relevant to the purposes of this text.

> Finally, we would like to emphasize our overriding belief that sincerity and effective communication are at the heart of effective mainstreaming. . . . To the extent that positive communication is maximized, and effective techniques are utilized, mainstreaming efforts are likely to succeed. (pp. 405-406)

MAINSTREAMING STUDENTS WITH SEVERE HANDICAPS

Alper and Ryndak (1992) indicate that students with mild and moderate handicaps have been integrated into regular classes since the passage of Public Law 94-142, but students with severe handicaps have been the most segregated groups in American public schools. Segregating handicapped students early and then mainstreaming them with the expectation that they would catch up and maintain their rate of learning has not worked; therefore, educational reform recommended for regular students has also been recommended for handicapped students. Alper and Ryndak outline the learning characteristics of severely handicapped students and specify the values for both the severely handicapped and regular students in mainstreamed education.

First, the learning rate of severely handicapped students is much slower than regular students. Second, they have difficulty maintaining the skills that they have acquired. Third, they frequently have difficulty generalizing information and skills, and fourth, they have difficulty in combining skills learned in isolation.

Alper and Ryndak cite empirical studies to demonstrate that students with handicaps can be provided effective special services in regular classes. In addition, they concluded that the attitudes of nonhandicapped students toward their peers with severe handicaps improved as they had increased opportunities to interact. Some of the advantages for integration were that severely handicapped graduates were more successfully integrated into the adult community, they earned almost three times the pay of graduates from segregated programs, they had increased social interaction skills and friendships, they learned to model successful life skills, and they developed higher expectations. The advantages for nonhandicapped students in mainstreamed classes were that they had the opportunity to learn new skills, values, and attitudes about human differences that better prepared them for the realities of life after school. Especially important to both handicapped and non-handicapped was the development of reciprocal voluntary friendships.

The roles that special education teachers assume in regular classrooms include team teaching and sharing responsibility for curriculum and instruction; they engage in setting up cooperative learning strategies, and they serve as consultant teachers. Alper and Ryndak (1992) cite the McGill Action Planning System as one of the most successful programs for integrating handicapped and nonhandicapped students. The guiding philosophy of this school system is "'everyone belongs.' Every child's educational base is the regular classroom, with the necessary support provided to the child and the regular class teacher" (p. 383).

SPECIAL NEEDS AND THE HUMAN RELATIONS MODEL[2]

The human relations model presented in this text is essential in the formulation and follow-through of an effective treatment plan for the special needs child. Becoming a treatment team member and educating oneself in the various learning disabilities and attention problems will enhance classroom efficiency. Facilitative responding to the impulsive and short attention span presented by these children is a necessary ingredient to the success of both the child and the teacher.

Empathy is another essential characteristic that allows the teacher to avoid making an assumption that the child is "rebellious" and "uncaring," when in fact the short attention span is part of the disorder, and not necessarily a manipulation on the part of the student.

This model further allows the teacher to adapt to the student's needs by clarifying the requests from the student and helping simplify directions to strengthen the likelihood of compliance. Extending this model of communication skills to the treatment team approach utilized in many school programs will prove effective in furthering the communications with teachers, parents, and concerned others.

Practice in Responding to the Special Student

In the following exercises, use the cases of Adam and Tara described below. You may want to work in small groups in order to generate as many alterna-

---

[2]This exercise was contributed by and reproduced with permission of Michael Baltimore of Auburn University.

tives as possible. Apply the human relations communication model (Carkhuff model, as described in Chapter 1) in each of your interventions.

Case of Adam

Adam is a 10-year-old male who is having great difficulty controlling his behavior and his talking out in class. He is often impulsive and seems to get worse with any changes in the structure of the class. When the teacher asks a question, he is always the first to respond. He appears to be interested in school, but spends most of his time seeking attention from the others in class. He interrupts other students, and at times, the teacher. He can be quite inappropriate to others, but he is not physically abusive.

Reading comprehension is his most difficult subject. He loses his place when he reads and he shows difficulty concentrating. He appears to be very disorganized and cannot remember past lessons very well. Adam is easily distracted by every noise outside the classroom.

Adam is having great difficulty paying attention in class. He does not remain on task and requires eye contact in order to be attentive. He is more attentive to the other boys than to the teacher's instructions. He appears to be

---

EXERCISE 2-1   Addressing the Needs of These Students

You are the teacher. Your task is to formulate and list the problem(s) for Adam and Tara. You are to devise intervention strategies for managing their behavior in class.

1. List the problem(s) for Adam and Tara.
2. List the goals for these students and the objectives for each goal.
3. List the goals for teacher(s) (example: What interventions would you use?).

Example:

Problem(s): Easily distracted by other activities in the classroom.

Goal for the student: The student will remain on task.

Objectives for this goal: The student will demonstrate on-task behavior by sitting quietly at his or her desk and performing the task for ____ minutes.

Goal for teacher(s): Peer tutoring will be used to help focus the student's behavior on his or her own work.

(Hint: There may be other problems related to the ones mentioned. Discuss all possible trouble areas for the students.)

of average intelligence and does well on certain tasks. He makes unnecessary comments in the class and is often restless.

Case of Tara

Tara is a 16-year-old female who is often argumentative and has trouble complying with classroom instruction. She wants to be the center of attention in all activities. Her academic skills are lacking, and she states "I hate to read" in front of others in the class. Her moods are often unpredictable and she can appear very frustrated. Her anger outbursts in the past have disrupted class and caused everyone to get off task. Teachers have suspected that Tara has a drug problem because she displays behaviors that could be from alcohol or drug use. She denies this and resents the teachers' suspicions.

Tara displays an inability to pay attention; she has poor impulse control, is unable to sit still for very long, and is very disorganized. She is forgetful and demands a lot of attention and time.

Tara is very fidgety and appears restless. She shows some strength in academics, but with math she does not follow the necessary steps in problem solving.

REFERENCES

Alper, S., and D.L. Ryndak. 1992. "Educating students with severe handicaps in regular classes." *The Elementary School Journal* 93(3), 373–387.

Bredeson, P.V. 1992. "Responses to restructuring and empowerment initiatives: A study of teachers' and principals' perceptions of organizational leadership, decisionmaking and climate." Paper presented at the annual meeting of the American Educational Research Association, San Francisco. (ERIC Document No. ED 346 569)

Cannon, G.S., L. Idol, and J.F. West. 1992. "Educating students with mild handicaps in general classrooms: Essential teaching practices for general and special educators." *Journal of Learning Disabilities* 25(5), 300–317.

Collins, R.A, and M.K. Hanson. 1991. *Summative Evaluation Report, School-Based Management/Shared Decision-Making Project, 1987–88 Through 1989–90.* (Available from Dade County Public Schools, Office of Educational Accountability, 1444 Biscayne Blvd., Miami, FL 33132)

Cullinan, D., E.J. Sabornie, and C.L. Crossland. 1992. "Social mainstreaming of mildly handicapped students." *The Elementary School Journal* 92(3), 339–351.

Firestone, W.A., and B.D. Bader. 1991. "Restructuring teaching: An assessment of frequently considered options." *Educational Policy* 5(2), 119–136.

Greenbaum, S., and B. Turner. 1989. *Safe Schools Overview: NSSC Resource Paper.* Malibu, CA: U.S. Department of Justice, U.S. Department of Education, and Pepperdine University.

Hranitz, J.R., and E.A. Eddowes. 1990, Fall. "Violence: A crisis in homes and schools." *Childhood Education,* 4–7.

Idol, L., and J.F. West. 1991. "Effective instruction of difficult-to-teach students." Unpublished manuscript.

Koppich, J.E., P. Brown, and M. Amsler. 1990. *Redefining Teacher Work Roles: Prospects and Possibilities.* (Policy Briefs No. 13). San Francisco, CA: Far West Laboratory for Educational Research and Development. (ERIC Document Reproduction No. ED 326 930)

Meier, D. 1992. "Reinventing teaching." *Teachers College Record 93*(4), 594–609.

Passow, A.H. 1989. "Present and future directions in school reform." In T.J. Sergiovanni and J.H. Moore, *Schooling for Tomorrow* (pp. 311–329). Boston: Allyn and Bacon.

Peeler, T.H. 1992. *A Public-Private Partnership: South Pointe Elementary School.* (Available from SouthEastern Regional Vision for Education, 345 South Magnolia Drive, Suite D-23, Tallahassee, FL 32301-2950)

Sarason, S.B. 1971. *The Culture of the School and the Problem of Change.* Boston: Allyn and Bacon.

Scruggs, T.E., and M.A. Mastropieri. 1992. "Effective mainstreaming strategies for mildly handicapped students." *The Elementary School Journal 92*(3), 389–409.

Stephens, R. 1988, Spring. "Reaching out to our at-risk youth." *School Safety*, 2.

U. S. Department of Education. 1989. *Eleventh Annual Report to Congress on the Implementation of the Education of the Handicapped Act.* Washington, DC: Author.

Webster, R.E. 1986. "Use of the process interaction model for therapeutic intervention with behavior disordered adolescents." *Techniques: A Journal for Remedial Education and Counseling 2*, 156–166.

▶ 3

Multicultural Training Issues in Human Relations Development

As is the case with undertakings of this kind during the past few years, there is the recognition that the inclusion of multicultural information is a must. In this chapter, key multicultural training issues will be explored as they relate specifically to teacher education and generally to the helping professions (e.g., counseling, psychology, social work). It is important to understand that this chapter serves only as an overview to the area of multicultural training and education. Because of space limitations and the impossible task of covering the vast amount of information in this area that warrants attention, only a cursory examination is presented. With that in mind, the goals of this chapter are to increase awareness and stimulate thought about multicultural issues; to encourage further exploration and study of major multicultural concepts; and to challenge readers to behave, respond, and communicate in ways that indicate cultural sensitivity and understanding. While all of the issues and strategies presented in this chapter are applicable to all types of diversity, the primary focus will be on racial/ethnic diversity.

An examination of the education and mental health literature of the past two decades indicates that cultural diversity, multiculturalism, and multicultural training are topics that have received increased attention in the literature. This can be seen by the proliferation of books (Baruth and Manning 1992; Lynch and Hanson 1992; O'Hair and Odell 1993; Pedersen and Carey 1994), chapters, and articles addressing multiculturalism and diversity issues. The need to include racial/ethnic, cultural, gender, and class factors when discussing the philosophical, theoretical, empirical, and practical issues in education and mental health is paramount. Interestingly, the road embarked upon in bringing multicultural issues to the forefront has been similar in the field of education as well as in the mental health professions. In some instances there is overlap between the two areas, with much of the mental health literature in this area applicable to education.

In reviewing the work dealing with cultural diversity and multicultural issues in the areas of education and mental health, it is apparent that three rather distinct bodies of literature are well-represented. One body of literature focuses largely on philosophical issues (e.g., delineating the need for training in the area of multicultural education; addressing issues of specificity versus universality; attempting to define and clarify terms). The literature exploring multicultural training from various philosophical and theoretical frameworks has led to detailed explanations and justification for the inclusion of multicultural training in preparation programs. The need for multicultural training has been well-documented throughout the years. In 1972 teacher education recognized the importance of multiculturalism. The *Journal of Teacher Education* (Volume 24) contains a special section on multicultural education and addresses the issue quite directly and comprehensively. The Commission on Multicultural Education of the American Association of Colleges of Teacher Education (AACTE) developed a platform which was adopted by the AACTE Board of Directors in 1972. The result was "No One Model American," which elaborated on the importance of valuing and preserving diversity; the connection between cultural pluralism and the educational system; and the extent to which teacher preparation programs should be involved in multicultural endeavors (AACTE 1973).

Generally when discussing the need for multicultural training, several key factors are identified as germane to the discussion. One factor that is often cited is the changing demographics and rapidly increasing diversity in this country. It is predicted that during the twenty-first century our workforce, educational systems, and other institutions will be significantly different in terms of racial/ethnic make-up. Statistics indicate that this country is becoming more multicultural, multiethnic, and multilingual each day. *One-Third of a Nation* (ACE 1988) indicates that one-third of the American population will be made up of racial/ethnic minority group members. With this change has come a need to re-examine some of our basic values, beliefs, philosophies, and roles. This certainly holds true for educators and others involved in the education process. Locke (1992) asserts that "the role of teachers and counselors has been expanded to include the consideration of the cultural identities of students and clients" (p. xi). The effectiveness of educators and educational systems is of utmost concern because those people and systems are responsible for educating those individuals who represent the future of our country. As educators we must be prepared to work effectively with them. Much has been written about the need to move beyond a monocultural approach in our educational systems. Unfortunately, the future may be quite bleak if the trend found in *One-Third of a Nation* (ACE 1988) continues. This report, which was compiled by the Commission on Minority Participation in Education and American Life, points out quite poignantly the current educational status of racial/ethnic minorities in this country. According to the American Council on Education (1988), "America is moving backward—not forward—in its efforts to achieve the full participation of minority citizens in the life and prosperity of the nation" (p.1). The American Council on Education also projects that by the beginning of the next decade the school-age population will be one-third racial/ethnic minority students (African-American, Asian-American, Hispanics, and Native Americans). In many of the largest school districts in the United States, racial/ethnic students already make up the majority of students in the educational system. There is often a lack of success in communicating with and educating students from diverse racial/ethnic/cultural backgrounds. However, the future of our country greatly depends upon our success in this area.

A second factor that is often emphasized in the philosophical/theoretical discussions regarding multicultural training is the ethical, professional, and moral responsibilities that undergird our work as educators and mental health professionals. Many authors (Burn 1992; Goodlad 1990; Kurth-Schai 1991; Sue, Bernier, Durran, Feinberg, Pedersen, Smith, and Vasquez-Nuttall 1982) discuss multicultural training from this perspective. Central to this argument is the issue of competence, and the fact that educators and professionals must be competent in providing culturally appropriate services to racial/ethnic minority students. Educators play an extremely important role in the socialization process of students and have a tremendous impact through this process. Sometimes that influence is conscious and deliberate; at other times it is unconscious and subtle. It is incumbent upon educators and mental health professionals to aid in the socialization process in a culturally sensitive manner, without disrespecting or devaluing students. The goal of encouraging all students to reach their full potential is possible with cultural sensitivity and understanding.

Multicultural understanding within the school environment is important because it affects all areas within the school: school atmosphere and climate; race relations in the school; treatment of racial/ethnic minority students by teachers, administrators, and peers; type of curriculum taught; teaching methods utilized; transmission of values. It is important to recognize that multicultural understanding involves a self-examination process. It is a process whereby one learns about him- or herself in the process of learning about others. Multicultural understanding is often conceptualized solely as learning about other racial/ethnic groups. Thus, the aspect of learning about self is often overlooked when discussing multicultural issues. Increased cultural sensitivity and knowledge benefits everyone. It helps an individual grow, become more self-aware, and increases interpersonal skills. It helps others feel understood, valued, and respected. Multicultural understanding also provides an opportunity for honest and open dialogue to occur.

The body of literature that pertains to understanding the role and impact of diversity (racial/ethnic, cultural, gender, class) comprises the second distinct category found in the multicultural training area. Specific factors that are receiving empirical attention in this area include identity development (racial/ethnic, minority, gender), world views, learning styles, environmental issues, and biculturalism. Many of these factors have been examined between various racial/ethnic/cultural groups. While continuing to examine between-group differences, more attention is being focused on within-group differences. Often there is as much diversity within groups as there is between groups. It is also within this body of literature that we find discussions regarding the sociocultural and sociopolitical issues and their relationship to diversity issues. It is recognized that diversity issues are often intertwined with sociopolitical issues. Thus to address diversity issues effectively and honestly one must examine many of the sociopolitical issues—oppression, power issues, prejudice, discrimination, racism, monoculturalism versus pluralism—and their ramifications for culturally diverse populations in this society.

The third distinct area in the literature that has had a strong impact on multiculturalism is the conceptualization and development of multicultural training models. The development of cross-cultural/multicultural competencies in the mental health area has largely guided this movement and led to the emergence of various multicultural training models. Sue and colleagues (1982) delineated a minimum set of cross-cultural competencies necessary in providing culturally appropriate services to members of racial/ethnic populations. While these competencies were written specifically for counseling psychologists, the basic premises are quite relevant for educators and other mental health professionals. Three areas were identified as important in effective cross-cultural counseling. The first area addressed by Sue and colleagues (1982) is *beliefs/attitudes*. Four specific competencies within this area were delineated:

1. Movement from cultural unawareness to cultural awareness, including sensitivity to one's own culture and ability to appreciate differences.
2. An awareness of one's value system and biases, including their impact on racial/ethnic minority individuals.
3. Comfort with differences in race and beliefs that exist between the individual and others.
4. Sensitivity to factors (e.g., sociopolitical influences, racial/ethnic identity) that may necessitate referral of an individual to a member of his/her own racial/ethnic group.

Upon examination of the competencies in this area, it is clear that awareness is essential in providing effective services to culturally different individuals.

Included within the awareness arena is self-examination/understanding as well as an awareness and understanding of key issues and processes as they relate to members of racial/ethnic groups.

The second area of competencies identified by Sue and colleagues (1982) involves *types of knowledge*. Their four types of knowledge include:

1. Understanding of the sociopolitical system in the United States and its treatment of racial/ethnic groups.
2. Possession of culture-specific knowledge and information for the groups with which one is working.
3. Understanding and general knowledge of counseling and therapy.
4. Awareness of institutional barriers that prevent racial/ethnic populations from utilizing mental health services.

From these four knowledge-based competencies it is apparent that knowledge of several different domains is also another important aspect when working with culturally diverse populations.

The third area of cross-cultural competencies identified by Sue and colleagues (1982) involves *skills*. Their three skill-related competencies center around:

1. Flexibility in one's verbal and nonverbal responses.
2. Ability to communicate effectively.
3. Recognition of the need for institutional intervention skills and the ability to carry out such interventions on behalf of an individual when necessary.

The need to respond in ways that are acceptable and understandable to the individual is important. In some instances this may mean expanding one's repertoire to respond and communicate in ways that are different, nontraditional, and unfamiliar.

More recently, other culturally relevant counseling guidelines and competencies (APA 1991; Sue, Arredondo, and McDavis 1992; Sue, Carter, Casas, Fouad, Ivey, Jensen, LaFromboise, Manese, Ponterotto, and Vasquez-Nuttall 1992) have been developed. These guidelines also focus on the areas of awareness, knowledge, and skills as essential in providing culturally relevant services.

Pedersen (1988) discusses the relationship between cultural competencies for educators and counselors. He also elaborates on the similarity between the competencies of the two groups in providing culturally appropriate services. He calls to our attention that in several states—Minnesota, California, North Carolina—a requirement for teachers is the completion of a human relations training program in order to develop multicultural skills. This is further indication that multicultural skills and sensitivity undergird everything we do. Multiculturalism involves a philosophy, a level of awareness, knowledge, and skills that can be incorporated into all of our interactions and become a part of all that we do.

Efforts are also underway to evaluate the effectiveness of multicultural training in education. Bennett, Niggle, and Stage (1990) examine outcomes of a university preservice multicultural teacher education course. They found that students enrolled in the course did indeed benefit from multicultural training. Pedersen (1988) notes the importance of the demonstration of the following skills for educators:

1. An understanding of the contributions and life styles of various groups (racial, cultural, economic) in society.
2. Recognition and ability to deal with biases, discrimination, and prejudices.
3. Creation of learning environments that contribute to the self-esteem of all persons and to positive interpersonal relationships.
4. Respect for human diversity and personal rights.

Upon careful review of the competencies and guidelines that have guided multicultural training in education and mental health, it is clear that the areas of awareness, knowledge, and skills continually emerge as key areas of concentration. This has resulted in the development of various models of multicultural training that tend to incorporate one or more of these areas (Leong and Kim 1991). Depending upon the specific area(s) being addressed, each model has its own set of goals; underlying assumptions; philosophy; and techniques, activities, and intervention strategies. Adherence to a particular model or approach to training has had far-reaching effects on multicultural training. For a more detailed discussion of this issue see Leong and Kim (1991) and Valencia (1992).

It is clear that the need for multicultural training in education and mental health has been well-justified. This concept has been embraced at a philosophical/conceptual level. Various multicultural training models have also been developed. Many of these models are well-researched, comprehensive, conceptually sound, and practical. However, it seems that at one level strategies that allow individuals the opportunity to "put it all together" have been slower to emerge. One contributing factor to this might be the need for more working models (Egan and Cowan 1979).

EFFECTIVE COMMUNICATION

Apparent in all of the previous discussion is the importance of effective communication. In part, one aspect of the effectiveness of multicultural education seems to hinge on communication. By definition, communication involves the ability to send and receive verbal and nonverbal messages accurately and appropriately (Sue and Sue 1990). It serves as a foundation for multicultural understanding and provides a mechanism by which to incorporate multicultural awareness, knowledge, and skills in working with culturally diverse populations. For example, when communicating with an individual from a particular culture, culture-specific knowledge might be helpful in understanding some of the reactions of the individual. Cross-cultural communication is certainly not a new area. It has been a highly discussed topic in the fields of cross-cultural psychology and anthropology; and it has been studied extensively in relation to different countries/nations.

A brief discussion of the role of culture in communication and the relevance of effective communication to educators and helping professionals will be provided. Thus, a basic assumption being made here is that communication has a cultural component (i.e., culture has an impact on communication). With that in mind, one can identify cultural influences in both verbal and nonverbal communication. Often the role of culture has not been a consideration in the exploration of communication (Gudykunst and Ting-Toomey 1988). These authors suggest that additional factors (e.g., sociological, psychological) are also important in understanding communication. Their conceptualization of cultural, sociological, and psychological variables suggests that the use of psychological information allows interpersonal communication to take place, and the use of sociological and cultural information has direct impact upon intergroup communication.

Work has been done examining the interface between intergroup and interpersonal communication (Billig 1987; Gudykunst and Lim 1986; Stephenson 1981; cited in Gudykunst and Ting-Toomey 1988). Four quadrants are delineated: high interpersonal and high intergroup salience; high interpersonal and low intergroup salience; low interpersonal and high intergroup salience; and low interpersonal and low intergroup salience. There will be no attempt here to discuss in detail issues related to interpersonal or intergroup communication or to give detailed information on the theoretical underpinnings of communication. The reader is strongly encouraged, however, to study more thoroughly the general communication literature to understand more clearly the relationship of culture to communication.

COMMUNICATION STYLES

Communication styles is an area that has continued to receive attention. This aspect of communication focuses on those areas not related to communication content (e.g., processing of content, mode of delivery, resolution of conflict). Differences in communication style are often misinterpreted and/or misunderstood, thus leading to inaccurate attributions.

Gudykunst and Ting-Toomey (1988) have identified several verbal communication styles that differ for various cultural groups. These styles include direct versus indirect, elaborate versus succinct, personal versus contextual, and instrumental versus affective. The direct versus indirect dimension has been defined as "the extent speakers reveal their intentions through explicit verbal communication" (Gudykunst and Ting-Toomey 1988, p. 100). It involves the amount and degree to which people express verbally what is on their minds in regard to their objectives, needs, and wants. The elaborate versus succinct style refers to the amount of talk, including how much one talks. This dimension also includes the use of language (e.g., silences, metaphors). The personal versus contextual style, according to Gudykunst and Ting-Toomey (1988), is distinguished by the fact that "verbal personal style is individual-centered language, while contextual style is role-centered language" (p. 109). Differences in this dimension would be evident in individualistic versus collectivistic cultures. Instrumental versus affective style refers to a goal versus process orientation. "The instrumental verbal style is sender-oriented language usage and the affective verbal style is receiver-oriented language usage" (Gudykunst and Ting-Toomey 1988, p. 112).

An understanding of communication styles and other facets of communication, such as proxemics, kinesics, and paralanguage, in relationship to cultural influences can be beneficial in effectively working with culturally diverse populations. This understanding of cultural differences in language and communication can help the educator avoid making inappropriate attributions about students from other racial/ethnic/cultural backgrounds and can lead to greater multicultural understanding and sensitivity.

REFERENCES

American Council on Education. 1988. *One-Third of a Nation: A Report of the Commission on Minority Participation in Education and American Life*. Author.

American Association of Colleges for Teacher Education. 1973. *Journal of Teacher Education* 24(4).

American Association of Colleges for Teacher Education. 1973. "No one model American." *Journal of Teacher Education* 24(4), 264–265.

American Psychological Association. 1991. *Guidelines for Providers of Psychological Services to Ethnic, Linguistic, and Culturally Diverse Populations*. Washington, DC: Author.

Baruth, L.G., and M.L. Manning. 1992. *Multicultural Education of Children and Adolescents*. Boston: Allyn and Bacon.

Bennett, C., T. Niggle, and F. Stage. 1990. "Preservice multicultural teacher education: Predictors of student readiness." *Teaching and Teacher Education* 6(3), 243–254.

Billig, M. 1987. *Arguing and Thinking: A Rhetorical Approach to Social Psychology*. Cambridge, MA: Cambridge University Press.

Burn, D. 1992. "Ethical implications in cross-cultural counseling and training." *Journal of Counseling and Development 70*, 578–583.

Egan, G., and M. Cowan. 1979. *People in Systems: A Model for Development in the Human-Service Professions and Education.* Monterey, CA: Brooks/Cole.

Goodlad, J. 1990. *The Moral Dimensions of Teaching.* San Francisco, CA: Jossey-Bass.

Gudykunst, W., and T. Lim. 1986. "A perspective for the study of intergroup communication." In W. Gudykunst (Ed.), *Intergroup Communication.* London: Edward Arnold.

Gudykunst, W.B., S. Ting-Toomey, with E. Chua. 1988. *Culture and Interpersonal Communication.* Newbury Park, CA: Sage.

Kurth-Schai, R. 1991. "The peril and promise of childhood: Ethical implications for tomorrow's teachers." *Journal of Teacher Education 42*(3), 196–204.

Leong, F.T.L., and H.H.W. Kim. 1991. "Going beyond cultural sensitivity on the road to multiculturalism: Using the intercultural sensitizer as a counselor training tool." *Journal of Counseling and Development 70*, 112–118.

Locke, D.C. 1992. *Increasing Multicultural Understanding: A Comprehensive Model. Multicultural Aspects of Counseling Series 1.* Newbury Park, CA: Sage.

Lynch, E.W., and M.J. Hanson. 1992. *Developing Cross-Cultural Competence: A Guide for Working with Young Children and Their Families.* (Eds.). Baltimore: Paul H. Brookes.

O'Hair, M.J., and S.J. Odell. 1993. *Diversity and Teaching: Teacher Education Yearbook I.* (Eds.). Forth Worth, TX: Harcourt Brace Jovanovich.

Pedersen, P. 1988. *A Handbook for Developing Multicultural Awareness.* Alexandria, VA: American Association for Counseling and Development.

Pedersen, P., and J.C. Carey. 1994. *Multicultural Counseling in Schools: A Practical Handbook.* Boston: Allyn and Bacon.

Stephenson, G. 1981. "Intergroup bargaining and negotiation." In J. Turner & H. Giles (Eds.). *Intergroup Behavior.* Chicago: University of Chicago Press.

Sue, D.W., P. Arredondo, and R.J. McDavis. 1992. "Multicultural counseling competencies and standards: A call to the profession." *Journal of Multicultural Counseling and Development 20*, 64–68.

Sue, D.W., J.E. Bernier, A. Durran, L. Feinberg, P. Pedersen, E.J. Smith, and E. Vasquez-Nuttall. 1982. "Position paper: Cross-cultural counseling competencies." *The Counseling Psychologist 10*(2), 45–52.

Sue, D.W., R.T. Carter, J.M. Casas, N.A. Fouad, A.E. Ivey, M. Jensen, T. LaFromboise, J.E. Manese, J.G. Ponterotto, and E. Vasquez-Nuttall. 1992, August. "Multicultural counseling competencies: Revision, extension, and implementation." Paper presented at the meeting of the American Psychological Association, Washington, DC.

Sue, D.W., and D. Sue. 1990. *Counseling the Culturally Different: Theory and Practice* (2nd Ed.). New York: John Wiley and Sons.

Valencia, A.A. 1992. "Multicultural education: Contemporary perspectives and orientations for teachers and counselors." *Journal of Multicultural Counseling and Development 20*, 132–142.

▶ 4

Perceiving and Responding

THE ACT OF PERCEIVING

A universally accepted definition of perception is not available, but because we are emphasizing interpersonal relations in this manual we shall focus on interpersonal perception—the process whereby one person discerns both the overt and covert, or disguised, behavior of another. Carkhuff (1969a, 1969b) has referred to the same process as "discrimination." Hargrove and Porter (1971) contend that the process might better be labeled "discriminative learning." Discriminative learning is defined by English and English (1958) as "the learning to note those particular cues or clues in a situation needed to evoke one response rather than another" (p. 290).

To be interpersonally effective one must be able to perceive the behavior of others accurately. The ability to do this is influenced by several factors, such as one's own needs, preferences, expectations, defense mechanisms, prejudices, or fears, as well as the same factors operating in the other person. For example, people who feel "self-conscious" may well perceive that they are being "singled out" by others when in fact they are not. In this case feeling self-conscious hinders their accurate and objective perception. Faulty perceptions can cause considerable interpersonal conflict and create interpersonal barriers. When we fail to perceive accurately, we may miss an important part of the message (or the entire message) that others transmit.

While processing messages communicated by others, one generally begins to form beliefs concerning their personalities; that is, one begins to form *other-concepts*. However, because of the complexity of the perceptual process, it is often difficult to arrive at other-concepts that are free from distortion. As Jourard (1963) points out, "Other-concepts probably enjoy the unique advantage of being the last of the theories which an individual will test, much less abandon. By some curious quirk of vanity, each man believes he is an expert psychologist and that his other-concepts are accurate and irrefutable. Never has so much been believed about people, by people, on so little evidence" (p. 321).

LEARNING STYLE AND THE
SENSORY MODALITIES

One approach to improving one's perceptual skills centers on determining an individual's learning style. Being aware of the helpee's learning style can improve the accuracy of the helper's perception and thus the helpfulness of the interpersonal communication between the two. The sensory modalities are important variables in an individual's learning style. Most persons have a preferred "input channel"—visual, auditory, or kinesthetic—for learning. We can determine a person's favored channel by means of the Sensory Modality Checklist (Appendix E) or by listening carefully to the types of "predicates" that person uses. According to Bandler and Grinder (1975/1976) predicates (defined here as verbs, adjectives, and adverbs) represent the preferred sensory modalities. An individual who highly values the visual system will find self-expression in visual process predicates such as *clear, bright, see, perspective*. One who prefers the auditory mode will use auditory process words such as *sound, loud, hear, harmony*. Kinesthetic words such as *grasp, hard, handle, feel* are used by persons who prefer to learn through the kinesthetic system, either externally with tactile and muscle sensations or internally with emotions and gut feelings. Attention to these kinds of details can vastly improve one's perceptual skills as a helper.

SELF-EXAMINATION AND FEEDBACK

Another approach to improving perceptual skills is to achieve a more comprehensive understanding of oneself. This can be partially accomplished by introspection (observing and analyzing one's own behavior) and by participating in a counseling or training-group experience where self-exploration is emphasized. In such groups one may enter into relationships with others where feedback is given and received.

Nylen, Mitchell, and Stout (1967) define feedback as "communication which gives back to another individual information about how he has affected us and how he stands with us in relation to his goals or intentions" (p. 75). Feedback may be either positive or negative.

As stated earlier in Chapter 1, Jacobs (1975) reported that positive verbal feedback was found to be believable, desirable, and impactful for the recipient, but he found no evidence that negative feedback was advantageous to the recipient. Positive feedback delivered in a manner similar to *strength bombardment*, where each group member gives some positive feedback to a target person, was found to lead to increased group cohesion. He found similar results with intermittent positive feedback when, after the first group session, each member makes a positive statement to another, for example, the person in the next chair, at the beginning of a group session.

In an attempt to find a means of utilizing negative feedback, Jacobs (1975), based on preliminary research results, recommends detoxifying negative feedback. He suggests three methods of detoxification: (1) present information referring to desired improvement in a positive behavioral statement in association with positive affect; (2) increase the credibility of the feedback by emphasizing in its delivery its origin in and/or its repugnance to the deliverer; (3) give positive feedback just prior to the negative feedback.

Counseling or training groups can be viewed as feedback "loops" wherein, as within other social systems, one's behavior affects and is affected by the behavior of each other person (Watzlawick, Beavin, and Jackson 1967). We are constantly receiving information from others about the appropriateness of our behavior. Other individuals let us know either verbally or nonverbally how our behavior appears to them, and we thus learn how others are affected by it. Feedback helps us identify "blind spots," information that we ordinarily fail to see or hear. Self-awareness and enhanced understanding of others are potential results of appropriate feedback. One's perceptual skills improve in both cases.

CHANGE

Nylen and colleagues (1967) contend that our tendency to live by habit and to be comfortable with the familiar makes it difficult for us to adjust to new circumstances. We try to create a stable view of the world so that we will feel in control. We do this by "freezing" reality, denying that the world is full of change and that our mental and physical selves are constantly changing. Often, we simply fail to notice ourselves!

To live effectively one must be aware of changes in one's self and must incorporate these new meanings within the old framework, thus better comprehending and experiencing one's own person. But because our perceptual processes tend to work in a selective way, it is not easy to remain open to our own experiences. That is, we perceive that which favors our frame of reference and deny realities that are incongruent. Thus, we falsely perceive ourselves as functioning in ways that make sense and are reasonable. This kind of selective perception, while minimizing anxiety, can often be a barrier to learning more effective behaviors.

DEFENSE MECHANISMS

To perceive one's own and another's disguised feelings accurately, one must be aware of the nature of defense mechanisms and the most common types of patterns of defense. It may be helpful to remember that the more facilitative the environment, the less will be the need for such defensiveness.

Most of us suffer to some degree from feelings of inadequacy or guilt or from a fear of punishment that can cripple our effectiveness. Such feelings are sometimes disguised through our defense mechanisms which operate in an attempt to protect one's self-image and control the level of anxiety. "Defense mechanisms are not acquired deliberately. For the most part, they are unconscious and unverbalized. . . . Defensive behavior develops through blind learning and does not involve conscious choice. . . . The mechanisms offer useful descriptions of typical adjustments and valuable insights into the ways in which drives are reduced" (Shaffer and Shoben 1956, pp. 169–170). The reduction of drives (usually anxiety or tension) is the primary goal of any defense.

When defense mechanisms are used appropriately, they usually allay anxiety and promote a feeling of well-being. If these mechanisms fail to work, a person who is living effectively is capable of using other methods to achieve the same end. However, attempts to adjust or relieve tension through defense mechanisms are often nonintegrative because one drive is overemphasized at the expense of others, which results in unevenness of satisfaction. Also, the defense mechanisms employed may be harmful to other people and ultimately to the user if they are exaggerated. "A defensive person is so intensely engaged in proving his adequacy that he does not attend to the satisfaction of broader motives of self-realization. Another shortcoming of defensive behavior is that it limits social interaction. With the exception of identification, all defense mechanisms increase the social distance between a person and his fellow men" (Shaffer and Shoben 1956, pp. 184–185).

Although the mechanisms are generally defined as though they represent clear and distinct forms of behavior, they are not usually found in pure form. Often they overlap, or several may be involved in a given behavior. We now turn our attention to the basic defense mechanisms.

Identification

Identification involves anxiety reduction through ascribing to one's self the accomplishments and other valued characteristics of another person, group, or object. Identification typically occurs early in life between a child and the parent of the same sex. Individuals also identify with groups such as neighborhoods, professional organizations, teams or schools, and objects such as cars or homes. Identification is the result of trial-and-error learning, but for most people it is a constructive and integrative adjustment.

Some examples of identification are:

1. "Ms. Chin is my favorite teacher. I seldom disagree with positions that she takes."
2. "I want to be a counselor like Mr. Garza. He is so kind and understanding."
3. "Being a member of our varsity basketball team is the greatest thing that has happened to me."

Rationalization

Rationalization is a defense mechanism in which a person gives socially acceptable reasons for behavior that was motivated by socially unacceptable impulses. There are several types of rationalization. Blaming the incidental cause, sour grapes, and sweet lemon are common mechanisms.

Examples of each of these in the order cited above are:

1. "The only people who make the honor roll are wimps."
2. "If she goes out with Robbie, it just shows her bad taste."
3. "I would rather be on the plump side than look like I was anorexic like Sue Ann."

Compensation

A person who compensates reduces tension by accepting and developing a less preferred but more attainable objective for a more preferred but less attainable objective. Compensatory behavior also is often characterized by extreme preoccupation. The adjustment occurs because the substitute goal may be an adequate substitute for the preferred objective and because success in the achievement of the substitute goal diverts attention from other personal shortcomings.

Some examples of compensation are:

1. "Grading papers every evening suits me just fine."
2. "Nothing but perfection is acceptable to me in anything I do."
3. "James practices throwing a baseball every evening after school, but he rarely brings in completed homework."

Projection

Projection involves attributing one's own motives and characteristics to others, especially when these motives are a source of great anxiety.

Some examples of projection are:

1. "Climbing the career ladder is the only thing that interests our teachers."
2. "Everybody cheats on their taxes."
3. "I have no respect for those girls who spend all their time hanging on their boyfriends."

Reaction Formation

Reaction formation is the adoption of an exaggerated attitude that is the opposite of one that produces tension and anxiety. In effect, this reduces tension by concealing one's true motives from oneself and others.

Some examples of reaction formation are:

1. "I never lock my doors when I leave home."
2. "I love everyone equally, regardless of race, gender, or ethnicity."
3. "TV 'soaps' will be the ruin of mankind."

Repression

One who cannot bring material or thoughts to a conscious level is said to be repressing such thoughts or material. The material is kept at a level that is not easily reached. There can also be physical manifestations of repression, such as if one were afraid of achievement one might suffer paralysis in the hand with which one writes.

Some examples of repression are:

1. "I refuse to think about sexual topics of any kind."
2. "I can't remember anything about the night our house burned down."
3. "I don't remember anything about the summer I spent with my uncle when I was 8 years old."

Fixation

Instead of progressing through normal phases of human development, one stops at a certain phase and does not progress further. This is due to overwhelming anxiety regarding the next step in the progression.

Some examples of fixation are:

1. "Even though I'm 16 years old, I'm just not interested in the opposite sex."
2. "I'd really like to stop eating but it satisfies me like nothing else can."
3. "Smoking really fulfills a craving I have."

Regression

If one has an experience that is difficult to deal with, one might revert to a previous developmental phase.

Some examples of regression are:

1. "Even though I'm 6 years old, I want to sleep in my crib again."
2. "I wish Mom would cradle me the way she cradles the new baby."
3. "Everytime I get nervous, I wet my pants."

Displacement

The person who cannot get a need met one way will substitute another way to satisfy that need. Substitutions will continue to be made. They will stop when a substitute is found that can relieve the pressure built up in trying to find a substitute to relieve the ongoing tension.

An example of displacement is:

Teacher to Sue: "I told you not to do that!"
Sue to Carlos: "You're always mean to me!"
Sue to the family dog: "Get out of my way, you old mutt!"

Sublimation

This is a form of displacement in which one directs energy to an activity that is approved by society. It may also result in a "higher cultural achievement."

Some examples of sublimation are:

1. "When I get frustrated, I like to go exercise."
2. "I like to create clay sculptures."
3. "Drawing pictures provides a release for me."

The defense mechanisms have been described to assist trainees in perceiving and labeling responses that are unconsciously motivated to reduce anxiety. By being able to recognize these defensive behaviors, trainees will also be in a better position to time their responses to produce the least defensiveness and the greatest impact for positive change.

In Chapter 6 we describe and illustrate nine ineffective communication styles. Although there is no established validity for doing so, we believe they can be related to the defense mechanisms discussed in the next few paragraphs. Trainees can sharpen their perceptual skills and better understand situations like the ones in Chapter 6 if they can learn to relate ineffective behaviors and responses to particular defense mechanisms.

The ineffective communication style that may be related to *identification* is the *florist responder*. The florist responder tries to hide problems under flowery phrases and bouquets of optimism. This could be the result of overidentification with the helpee, leading to an overly protective attitude. Conversely, the ineffective *hangman responder* might respond to the negative feelings aroused through identification with the helpee and be quite critical of the helpee.

Rationalization may be expressed by *swami responders* who predict unhappy futures for themselves because of the behavior of someone else, or who account for predicted future failure because of some intervention over which they will have no control. The *guru responder* also may be illustrating the defense mechanism of rationalization. Gurus illustrate rationalization when they provide clichés to account for behavior: "You can lead a horse to water, but you can't make him drink."

The *magician responder* is another ineffective communication style that probably best illustrates *compensation*. Overcompensation would be the magician responder's attempt to have the problem ameliorated through denial of its seriousness: "It really can't be that bad." The *drill-sergeant responder* who "barks" orders and bosses others around may be responding (compensating) for feelings of inadequacy. The *foreman responder* who keeps everyone else busy with authoritative responses may also be compensating for a personal tendency to be nonproductive.

Projection is probably illustrated by several ineffective responder types. The *sign-painter responder* illustrates projection by putting certain kinds of labels on behaviors. The *hangman responders* may also be evaluating others based on projections of their own motives.

Reaction formation may be used to understand the *florist responder* who actually has an overriding fear that the worst will happen but responds as though everything will turn out fine. The opposite response may be conveyed by the *detective responders* who are very suspicious because they fear their own naiveté. The *hangman responders* could also be employing the defense mechanism of reaction formation by being either overly critical or very uncritical.

THE ACT OF RESPONDING

To respond means, among other things, to answer, reply, act, or behave. As used in this chapter and throughout the manual, it includes both verbal and nonverbal behavior as well as direct physical acts such as embracing, touching, striking, and so forth. We have chosen to substitute *responding* for Carkhuff's concept of *communication* because we feel it conveys a more complete interaction than that often inferred from the term communication. But for the most part we mean what Carkhuff (1969a, 1969b) means by "communication."

Just as gains or losses in a trainee's level of perception depend on the trainee and trainer, so it is with responding. If trainers are not capable of responding at high levels, they cannot provide the conditions in which trainees can reach high levels of responding and functioning. "The evidence is consistent, indicating that trainees of high-level communicating [responding] trainers improve while those of low-level communicators demonstrate negative change in communication [responding]" (Carkhuff 1969a, p. 197).

Carkhuff (1969a) found that training in interpersonal communication skills, in general, is best accomplished through a three-pronged approach: (1) experiential, (2) didactic, and (3) trainer modeling. A solid experiential base is developed when the circumstances surrounding the training are facilitative. Specifically, trainers must be perceiving and responding at high levels, and they must manage the group of trainees so that they provide experiences that are facilitative to one another. Trainees must experience an atmosphere where they are understood and accepted, and where they can practice extending themselves through experimenting with various behaviors.

If trainers are successful in creating a facilitative experiential base, they will be in a position to teach trainees in a didactic fashion also. There are many occasions where structured teaching is appropriate in this training model. Often when the trainees have experienced a facilitative base, trainers can best instruct by sharing their understandings of the constructs they use. In so doing, they also allow the trainees to question and search with them for more and more effective means of helping.

Regarding the importance of modeling by the trainer, Carkhuff is unequivocal. He states, "*Finally, the trainer is the key ingredient insofar as he offers a model of a person who is living effectively.* Without such a person there is no program" (Carkhuff 1969a, p. 201, emphasis Carkhuff's). In other words, the training can be only as good as the trainer. If the trainers have not been able to apply the core conditions to their own lives so that they are living effectively, they will be unable to teach or train others to do so.

Interpersonal Dynamics

The processes of perceiving and responding are closely related. When persons send messages, receivers respond to the messages as they perceive them. This manual is designed to aid persons in systematically increasing both the quality and the quantity of their perceptual and responsive skills. Along with this manual, the trainer will have access to a number of exercises in the *Instructor's Guide* that are designed to increase group feedback. This allows each person the opportunity to develop a more complete understanding of self, as we have described above. One may then wish to consider the possibility of behavioral changes that would result in greater interpersonal effectiveness.

But in order to improve understanding of self and others we must also understand the dynamics involved in communicating (responding). Some basic propositions should be understood:

Proposition 1. Both parties involved in an interaction are modified by the interaction. In this proposition, we are simply referring to a fundamental law of learning which, generally stated, means that the response produced by person A from person B will affect the next response of person A. That is to say that we are being influenced while we are influencing others.

Proposition 2. Responses may be nonverbal, verbal, or a combination of both.

Proposition 3. Nonverbal responses are more likely to transmit the real message, since they are often involuntary reactions transmitted from the autonomic nervous system. Mehrabian (1968) has shown that facial expression alone transmits over 55 percent of the meaning of a message. Often we communicate more than we intend to by our body posture, gestures, tone of voice, eye contact, and the like. Nonverbal communications may distort or even negate one's verbal messages. That is, one's nonverbal behavior may "speak" so loudly that one's verbal messages are scarcely heard.

Proposition 4. Verbal responses or messages are generally composed of two parts: content and affect. Content refers to the topic under discussion, whereas affect tells how one feels about the topic. For example, a child who has just been struck and hurt by a playmate says, "Sally hit me; I hate her!" The topic is Sally's hitting. The affect or feeling expressed is hurt combined with anger.

In the first chapter we presented the basic rationale for the practice exercises that are to follow in the remaining chapters. Our primary emphasis in the remaining chapters, then, will be to operationalize the theoretical model.

REFERENCES

Bandler, R., and J. Grinder. 1975/1976. *The Structure of Magic I/II*. Palo Alto, CA: Science & Behavior Books.

Carkhuff, R.R. 1969a. *Helping and Human Relations: A Primer for Lay and Professional Helpers*. Vol. 1: *Selection and Training*. New York: Holt, Rinehart and Winston.

Carkhuff, R.R. 1969b. *Helping and Human Relations: A Primer for Lay and Professional Helpers*. Vol. 2: *Practice and Research*. New York: Holt, Rinehart and Winston.

English, H.B., and A. English. 1958. *A Comprehensive Dictionary of Psychological and Psychoanalytical Terms.* New York: Longmans, Green.

Hargrove, D.S., and T.L. Porter. 1971. "Discrimination: An aspect of the helping process." *Journal of Research and Development in Education* 4(2), 28–35.

Jacobs, A. 1975. "Research on methods of social intervention: The study of the exchange of personal information in brief personal growth groups." Paper presented at the Invited Conference on Small Group Research, Indiana University, Bloomington, April, 1975.

Jourard, S.M. 1963. *Personal Adjustment: An Approach Through the Study of Healthy Personality.* New York: Macmillan.

Mehrabian, A. 1968. "Communication without words." *Psychology Today* 2, 52–55.

Nylen, D., J. Mitchell, and A. Stout. 1967. *Handbook of Staff Development and Human Relations Training: Materials Developed for Use in Africa.* Washington, DC: National Training Laboratories Institute for Applied Behavioral Science.

Shaffer, L.F., and J.J. Shoben, Jr. 1956. *The Psychology of Adjustment* (2nd Ed.). Boston: Houghton Mifflin.

Watzlawick, P.J., J. Beavin, and D.D. Jackson. 1967. *Pragmatics of Human Communication.* New York: W.W. Norton.

▶ 5

Helpee Statement Types

Throughout this text, we have included various exercises for the trainee. We also speak more directly to the trainee in an attempt to personalize the material.

Behavioral objective: The trainee will be able to classify helpee requests for assistance according to the four areas outlined in this chapter: (1) requests for information, (2) requests for action, (3) requests for inappropriate interaction, and (4) requests for understanding/involvement.

As soon as a helpee speaks to you, you begin to assess the situation. Even though you may not be aware of it, in your mind you seek answers to such questions as: "What does this person need? What does this person want from me? What can I do for this person?" Your answers to these questions determine the way you respond to the helpee.

When you assess the helpee's immediate needs, you draw on several kinds of expertise. Your professional training in your educational specialty is an important part of the process, you also draw on your own life experiences and "common sense," and on your grasp of interpersonal dynamics. Because you have considerable expertise in your field, this book does not attempt to provide more technical information about your specialty. Similarly, you already possess a wealth of life experience that can be utilized in helping other persons. The objective of this book is to help you understand the dynamics of interpersonal relationships and acquire communication skills that are essential in dealing effectively with others. When these are combined with your professional training, experience, and personal characteristics, you will be able to help other persons in the ways that research shows are productive and effective, as cited in Chapter 1.

Helpee statements can be classified into four categories based on what the helpee is seeking: (1) request for action, (2) request for information, (3) inappropriate interaction, and (4) request for understanding/involvement. For each type there is a helper response mode that has been shown to be effective (see Figure 5-1). While the helper's response differs for each kind of helpee statement, there are components of communication that are common to all, shown on the diagram as "facilitative dimensions used in all communications." Training in this manual covers responses to each type of helpee statement, with main emphasis on the "request for understanding/involvement." As the diagram indicates, the first task is for the helper to classify the helpee's statement into one of the four types, which are defined and illustrated below.

REQUEST FOR ACTION

Helpees often ask helpers to do something for them—to perform a physical act. For example, a teacher in the lounge might say, "Would you please hand me that test booklet next to your chair? I have my lap full of papers." This request is simple and straightforward; its meaning is obvious. An appropriate helper response would be to hand the test booklet to the teacher.

Requests for action may be as explicit as the example above, but often the request is only implied. The statement, "I don't have a ride home," may mean, "Would you please give me a ride?" In the latter case, the helpee may be *thinking*, "I have a favor to ask you, but I'm afraid you might not say yes. I wish I didn't have to ask. Maybe if I tell you my need, you will offer to help. That would be a lot easier than asking." As the helper, you must be aware of what is *not* said, and its significance, as well as what has been put into words. This is the skill part of responding to requests for action. Responding to overt and appropriate requests is easy; it is more challenging when the request is inappropriate or when you must "read between the lines."

Other requests, while simple to fulfill, require knowledge of the situation before they can be implemented. For example, a student might make a request that is in conflict with instructions from another teacher. When you are the helper, you must know whether or not *fulfilling* the requested action is in the best interest of the helpee. Helping sometimes means doing, and sometimes it means not doing, the things requested by the helpee. You use your professional training and other data to decide what is appropriate under the circumstances.

REQUEST FOR INFORMATION

This type of request is similar in dynamics to the request for action because the helpee is asking the helper for something. For example, a student might ask, "Will you give me some ideas about what subject I might use for my term

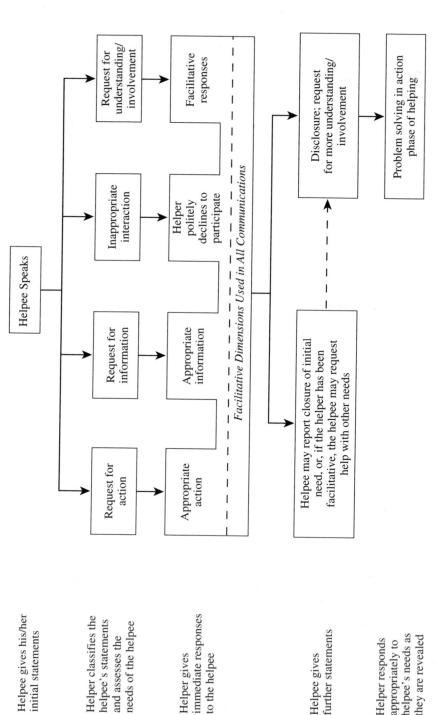

FIGURE 5-1   Helper Response Modes

56

paper?" Information involves a verbal response only, whereas action involves some physical movement on the part of the helper. Again, there are frequently underlying issues and implied concerns. With skill development the helper may begin to respond to the underlying issues. The neophyte helper should stay with the surface request and let the situation unfold as the helpee feels comfortable disclosing it.

REQUEST FOR UNDERSTANDING/INVOLVEMENT

This category represents conversations in which the helpee's feelings are of major importance. It is so called because the helpee is generally seeking a *relationship* with another person, rather than direct answers. A request for understanding/involvement may be explicit: "There's something that is really bothering me; I wonder if I could talk with you about it." Or, for example, a student might say, "I thought that I really had a great relationship with my parents, but recently I have started to wonder." This student has verbalized a real concern and the most appropriate response at this point is to listen fully and to respond to that concern with understanding and caring. The major part of this manual deals with communicating with persons about matters as intimate as the one in the latter example. In the process of learning to deal with such highly personal situations you will acquire skills that will help you in other kinds of interactions and relationships with other persons.

What may appear to be a simple request for action or for information may be the helpee's way of steering the conversation toward a substantive concern that the helpee is not willing to express directly. Most persons have occasions when they wish to talk with others about matters that are important to them. It is not uncommon for helpees to approach sensitive topics gradually, to avoid the possibly painful experience of being ignored or rebuffed by the helper. For example, a student might say, "Will basketball practice go past five o'clock this year?" Taken at face value, this is a request for information that can be answered with a word or two, but there may be much more on the helpee's mind than just the answer. The student may be wanting to say, "I can't work and be on the team at the same time." This example is just one of many that can be used to illustrate the importance of the categories of requests for information and action. These two kinds of requests are frequently used to "check out the helper," to see if the helper is any different from others who do not seem to understand. Therefore, it is important to be alert for needs that are not verbalized. To be fully effective as an educator, examine helpee statements to see if they are masking a need that goes beyond the literal message. Anyone can be ineffective. It takes a conscious effort to be truly effective in interpersonal relationships.

INAPPROPRIATE COMMUNICATION

There are several kinds of conversations that are potentially damaging to the persons talking, to persons not present, or to the organization. At best, such interactions are inappropriate, and they *can* become destructive and disruptive. Included in this category are (1) gossip, (2) chronic complaining, (3) inordinate griping, (4) rumor, (5) solicitation of a dependency relationship, and (6) encouragement of activities that are counter to the benefit of other persons or the organization, such as a student's attempts to turn one staff member against another.

For example, a tenth grader might say, "I'm always glad when fourth period rolls around. My teachers in the morning are pitiful!" Engaging in a conversation such as this could lead either to talking negatively about a person or persons not present, or to defending others, perhaps without firsthand knowledge. Either way of responding would be ineffective. To disparage your coworkers is to decrease the students' confidence in the organization or to encourage them to hold in their feelings about things they do not like. Attempting to defend the person or persons referred to in the inappropriate interaction is to deny prematurely the students' perception of the situation and possibly to lessen your credibility in the eyes of students.

Generally, then, the best response to an inappropriate helpee statement is to communicate your unwillingness to engage in that kind of conversation. This response must be given in a way that does not offend a friend and helpee. This is much more easily proposed than practiced! In the above example, the teacher might say, "I can tell you have some strong feelings about your other teachers, but I work with them and would feel uncomfortable talking about them in their absence."

When helpees' comments are inappropriate they usually know it, and when another person does anything but go along with them, the helpees are likely to feel some degree of embarrassment. Still, there is no basis for a helper to encourage inappropriate behavior, even by passivity. Even the act of listening without comment to inappropriate communication positively reinforces the behavior of the speaker who may infer that you are in agreement. *If you encourage inappropriate behaviors, even by silence, you may lose your opportunity to help and you could unwittingly become a model for negative or hurtful behavior.* An example of a response to a person who is trying to involve you in gossip is as follows: Helpee: "I'm sure glad to see that Gloria is getting chewed out for being late again. Did you know she's been slipping out to lunch with Mr. X and he's a married man with five children?" Helper: "I can see you've been irritated with Gloria for being late and for meeting with Mr. X, but I prefer not to get into a discussion about Gloria. I must admit that it sounds kind of juicy, but I've found I feel bad after I indulge in this kind of talk." A detailed discussion and training exercise in the skills for responding to inappropriate communication appears in Chapter 22.

EXERCISE 5-1   Classifying Communication Types

Behavioral objective: The trainee shall classify accurately 25 out of 30 exercises on communication types.

In this exercise you will practice classifying helpee statements. After carefully studying the examples of the four types of helpee statements, write in the space in front of each interaction the type of communication it illustrates. Use RA for request for action, RI for request for information, II for inappropriate interaction, and RUI for request for understanding/involvement. Check your answers with the Answer Key at the end of the chapter. Remember that written exercises are subject to various interpretations due to the absence of many of the nonverbal cues that would be available if the person were before you and also on the lack of background knowledge. Therefore, you may have legitimate disagreements with the categories given in the Answer Key.

Helpee Situations

_____ 1. Student to teacher: "I think I know how to do the homework, but would you help me with the first problem just to make sure?"

_____ 2. Student to teacher: "I want to apologize for making the class laugh today when you asked me the question about George Washington. I was being serious but everybody in class thought I was making a joke. It was really embarrassing."

_____ 3. Student to student: "I bet we could figure out a way to make Ms. Thompson lose her temper today like she did last semester when you set the trash can on fire—remember how funny that was!"

_____ 4. Student to teacher: "Sometimes I can study for hours and then when the test is passed out I just go blank—almost like I didn't study at all. I may never pass this course!"

_____ 5. Student to student: "Cover for me when I tell the music teacher that I have had laryngitis all day—I've got to get some of my homework done this period so I can go out tonight."

_____ 6. Student to student: "Would you help me with this student council poster? I've got to get it up before the next period."

_____ 7. Teacher to teacher: "You won't believe this! I was out at that new Mexican place last night and would you believe that Coach Anderson was sitting there drinking margaritas with his wife—and it was obvious that he had had more than one, if you know what I mean! What if a student had come in?"

Continued

EXERCISE 5-1   *Continued*

___ 8. Principal to teacher: "You know, when I became a principal fifteen years ago, things were different. The principal was respected by the teachers, students, and parents. Now, almost every decision I make is questioned by someone. I'm just counting the days until I can retire."

___ 9. Teacher to teacher: "Do you know what the student count is for this fall? Do we have more or fewer students than last year?"

___ 10. Student to student: "My parents are on my case all the time about college. I'm just concerned about getting out of high school right now—there's plenty of time to worry about college."

___ 11. Teacher to teacher: "I bet Julia's husband is really henpecked. Can you believe how she talks about him in the teachers' lounge? If she's half as bossy with him as she is with everybody here at school, his life must be miserable."

___ 12. Teacher to counselor: "I know you work with a lot of students who are having problems with their parents. I'm at my wit's end with a problem with my husband's parents—would it be appropriate for me to tell you about it?"

___ 13. Student to teacher: "Would you please write the test schedule on the board?"

___ 14. Teacher to teacher: "Do you know anything about the Robinson family? I know that they are divorced and he lives in Chicago, but I heard that he is black and she is white."

___ 15. Student to teacher: "Would you recommend a book I could read to find out more about the civil rights movement that you mentioned in class today?"

___ 16. Student to student: "Would you tell me where Mr. Littlejohn's office is?"

___ 17. Student to counselor: "I made 990 on my SAT. Would you recommend an in-state college I might be able to get into?"

___ 18. Teacher to teacher: "You know, we moved here from another part of the country, and the people there were really different from the people here. I keep getting the impression that the other teachers think I am too pushy—but I'm just being myself! Do you think I'm that bad?"

___ 19. Student to teacher: "My parents are having trouble paying all the bills since my dad got laid off at the plant, and I just got a job after school to try to help out. I may have to drop out of the Spanish Club, and I wanted you to know the reason."

___ 20. Teacher to custodian: "Can you get me a new chair for my desk? The one I have is just too short for me."

EXERCISE 5-1 *Continued*

_____ 21. Teacher to student: "Robert, do you have the extra work I asked you to do yesterday?"

_____ 22. Teacher to teacher: "When I taught in Illinois things were a lot different. We didn't have to put up with a nitpicking principal like we have here. I'm beginning to wonder if this guy has a brain in his head! Did you read the latest memo about lunch duty? Could you believe it?"

_____ 23. Student to teacher: "Would you grade my test now so I won't have to wait until tomorrow to find out how I did?"

_____ 24. Teacher to teacher: "There are going to be fireworks at the faculty meeting tomorrow afternoon. A group of us are getting together tonight at Mr. Stephen's house to plan it. We're going to catch Mr. Zeeland (principal) by surprise. Why don't you come over and join us?"

_____ 25. Student to teacher: "Do you think my nose is too big? Some boys were kidding me at lunch, and now I'm all confused."

_____ 26. Student to teacher: "Mrs. Yates, you asked me yesterday if I was going steady with Ralph. In fact, we are deeply in love. The problem is that his parents don't particularly like me. Ralph told me that they think I am a bad influence on him."

_____ 27. Custodian to teacher: "Would you ask your students to pick up the trash around their desks at the end of the day? It would make it a lot easier on me."

_____ 28. Student to counselor: "Do you have financial aid applications or do I need to get them from the colleges I am applying to?"

_____ 29. Teacher to teacher: "I know our students have suffered this year from all of the new curriculum materials we have had. I know I have had a lot of trouble keeping up and I'm sure the students have noticed the confusion and awkwardness. It was embarrassing."

_____ 30. Student to student: "You know the prom is coming up soon and I just know I won't get invited. I haven't had many dates, and the ones I have had have not worked out well. Maybe my parents will plan a trip that weekend so I will have an excuse for not going."

Chapter 6 presents examples of ineffective communication styles frequently employed by untrained individuals. Trainees are encouraged to compare their own responses with those in Chapter 6 and become consciously aware of any that might be in their own repertoire of responses. Awareness is the first step toward minimizing ineffective or hurtful responses.

The remainder of this chapter deals with practice in responding effectively to two of the communication types, appropriately giving information and appropriately providing action. These two categories appear simplistic, and in some ways perhaps they are, but the key to responding appropriately in these two dimensions is to determine whether granting the helpee's request is appropriate. This determination is based on (1) knowledge of the helpee, (2) the timing in the relationship, and (3) understanding the motives of the helpee. So providing action or giving information are not difficult concepts to understand, but proper implementation requires a conscious effort on the part of the helper.

RESPONDING WITH INFORMATION

As an educator, you are called upon daily to interact in a professional way with students and parents. Though these interactions may seem routine to you, the experience of talking with an educator is not routine to these individuals. Your attention, attitude, nonverbal behavior, and the information you provide are very important to them. In reading the next three paragraphs, try to understand the way in which the person speaking may look to you for information.

> I am a student. Being in school is, many times, an uncomfortable experience for me because I do not feel that I am a part of what is going on. I do know, however, that I know more about *me* than anyone else in the world. It is rare that another person can tell me something about me that I do not already know or understand. But in school I find myself in a situation in which others attempt to pass off information that is intended to help, but includes things that I either already know or things that are not true about myself. I believe that because of your position, your knowledge, and your years of education, there are many things that I can learn from you.
>
> I just ask that you take enough time to try to understand me and my situation. If that happens, when you speak I will listen to you; and I will probably remember a lot of what you say.
>
> I would like for this experience to be a very positive one, one in which both of us feel comfortable. Not only are your words important to me, but equally important are how you say those words and what you do while you talk to me. If you withhold yourself or your information about me from me, you make me feel like a child; I feel less secure. If you make decisions for me without any input from me or if you take me for granted, I feel powerless.

An essential task of all educators, then, is to help students feel less dependent and more like capable, worthwhile human beings. The educator has the capacity to do and say those things that will help students feel they have control over their lives, that they are not powerless, and that choices exist even when it appears there are none. This sounds like a lot to do, and it is more easily said than done, but it is an achievable task. This section on responding with information will deal with some familiar topics and describe the application of the basic principles of good communication to those situations.

In the following exercise, the helpee situations are, on the surface, requests for information. Many times a helpee will begin a verbal interaction by making a request for information. How the helper responds, both verbally and nonverbally, will in many cases determine whether or not the helpee will feel comfortable talking with the helper. If through this interaction the helpee feels good about the interaction with the helper, the likelihood is greater that the helpee will self-disclose at a more personally relevant level later.

The most appropriate helper response, at least early in the helping relationship, is to answer the information request without attempting to "read between the lines." By responding in this way helpers communicate respect for helpees by not probing into their life, and also, by responding to the "surface" inquiry, communicate that the person was heard. This way the pace of the interaction is determined by the helpee, a pace the helpee is comfortable with. The opposite approach, that is, to directly attack the hidden concern, would be premature and thus ineffective or hurtful. The helpee will generally resist a helper who "reads between the lines," resulting in a lack of rapport between helper and helpee. In this early stage the relationship is not strong enough to *assume* that the helpee will be willing to discuss personally relevant information with the helper. What frequently happens is that the helpee will deny the hidden concern that the helper has "read between the lines" and the helper has lost the opportunity to be helpful.

Before responding to each of the ten information requests that follow, contrast the responses below to better understand the idea.

A student you do not know well says to you, the teacher, after class: "Can you tell me if there are scholarships available for nursing school? I want to go but my parents can't afford to send me."

Appropriate response: "Nursing is a profession in great demand right now. There are several good sources of financial aid."

Discussion: Short, to the point response. Wait now for helpee's next question or statement.

Inappropriate response: "You sound discouraged because your parents can't afford to pay for your education after high school."

Discussion: A good facilitative response, but premature in focusing on the financial problem before dealing with the less emotionally charged issue of scholarships.

Inappropriate response: "Well, you could work your way through even if scholarships were not available."

Discussion: This is premature or inappropriate action. It is too early to give advice, and the helpee is not asking for any.

Inappropriate response: "You seem to be feeling sorry for yourself because you don't have a good supply of money for your education like a lot of your friends have."

Discussion: This is premature and reading between the lines. Even if you have a strong notion that this is the case, it is better to use confrontational techniques *later* in the interaction when you have earned the right to confront.

EXERCISE 5-2   Responding with Information

In the following situations, simply respond to the request—nothing more. Underneath each response, list possible underlying situations that might exist. Remember, though, that the "between-the-lines" issues are not for verbal use early in the interaction. In later discussions on facilitative interaction you will see ways in which these issues surface and can be dealt with interpersonally.

Helpee Situations

1. Student to teacher: "I'm planning on taking the SAT next fall and I was wondering if there was something I could do this summer to help me prepare for it?" _____

   _____

2. Teacher to teacher: "I was wondering how noticeable it was when I got embarrassed in the faculty meeting yesterday when I knocked the coffee cup on the floor right in the middle of the new superintendent's opening remarks. It felt like my whole face was on fire!"

   _____

3. Custodian to assistant principal: "Why do the halls need to be swept after *every* period?" _____

   _____

4. Student to teacher: "Did you work while you were in college?"

   _____

5. Student to counselor: "Do you have something I can read on depression?" _____

   _____

EXERCISE 5-2 *Continued*

6. Assistant principal to principal: "What do you think about the new dress code? Do you think we'll get much flak from the parents?"

   _____

7. Teacher to teacher: "Did you know that Mary Jane Smith is dating Manuel Gonzales?" _____

   _____

8. Student teacher to supervising teacher: "I know I have gotten good reports from you so far, but would you please tell me what you *really* think?" _____

9. Student to teacher: "You know yesterday you used an example in class of a father who walked out on his family . . . do you think that happens very often?" _____

   _____

10. Teacher to school secretary: "Are we *still* responsible for collecting all of the lunch money every day like last year?" _____

    _____

As an alternate exercise, with a partner pick a situation with which you can identify. Roleplay the same situation more than once using different ways of responding. Discuss and decide which seemed to be most effective for you. After 15 or 20 minutes, come back together as a group and try to reach some consensus concerning requests for information.

RESPONDING WITH ACTION

Most of what a teacher does in the classroom involves the transfer of information, and students are assisted in learning to become autonomous persons by being allowed to do as many things for themselves as possible. Still, there are occasions when the teacher will take direct action to do something for another person. This is what we mean by responding with action—*doing something for* helpees or intervening in their lives in some tangible, direct way. Facilitative communication is related to these activities and interventions because (1) facilitative communication is necessary in order to find out what the action should be and to establish acceptance of the action by the helpee, and (2) facilitative communication is supportive and restorative in its own right and in that sense is, itself, an "action."

In responding with action, it is important to watch for messages within messages. For example, a student says to you, "Would you mind helping me with this assignment for a few minutes? I'm not getting anywhere with it—but then I never do." All of that statement except for the last three words is a clear, straightforward request for help. Those last three words, however, give you a strong clue about the student's lack of confidence. The last three words are an important message hidden within the more obvious message. The student is probably desperately hoping for some understanding and involvement. In this case, the appropriate response would be to take the action of helping with the assignment but also to respond to the need for understanding/involvement when it seems appropriate to do so.

Attending to serious physical needs and protecting the welfare and safety of any person must always come first. In such a case to communicate facilitatively before taking action would only waste valuable time. Information, listening, and responding with understanding can follow the necessary action. Each situation or response is evaluated separately.

An important task is to evaluate the request in terms of what you should do personally and what should be referred to someone else. There are many reasons for referral, and the key for the helper is to be sensitive to the helpee's needs and aware enough of one's own skills and time constraints to recommend referral. Occasionally a situation may arise that requires your taking the initiative in protecting the best interests of the organization and other persons. In such a situation action often takes precedence over dialogue. Consider a couple of different kinds of situations.

Helpee Situation 1

Another teacher, returning from the playground, rushes into your room and says, "The maintenance men left a ladder against the side of the building and there is a small boy climbing it. I'm afraid he'll fall off!"

> *Response:* Take the action that will most quickly get a responsible person to the scene, at which time the situation is assessed for the best course of action.

Helpee Situation 2

A man in a gray work uniform says to the school secretary, "I'm from the pest control service. I'm supposed to spray in your storage room."

> *Response:* The secretary replies, "I would prefer to check with the principal about this first. Excuse me just a moment while I phone."

> *Discussion:* No employee should allow entrance to any nonpublic area containing valuable materials, confidential information, or equipment without authorization to do so from a supervisor. Posing as a maintenance service person or equipment repair person is a common method of deception used by unlawful persons today. If in doubt, check up.

EXERCISE 5-3 Weighing the Proper Response

In each of the following situations, write (1) what you would say and (2) what you would do. Would giving the appropriate action likely terminate the interaction, or do you think there is an underlying reason for the request?

Helpee Situations

1. First-year teacher to principal: "I'm mad as a hornet about the way the teachers smoke in the faculty lunchroom. Students can see them everytime the door opens. Can't you do something to stop that?"

2. Student to teacher: "Mr. Ricardo, since you pass right by my house on your way home, can I have a ride today? My car battery is dead."

3. Teacher to teacher: "You taught social studies last year, didn't you? Would you look over these lesson plans and tell me what you think? I have never taught this before."

4. Teacher to student: "I'm running behind schedule getting this bulletin board up. Would you give me a hand today during your study hall?"

5. Teacher to principal: "Do you have a copy of the teachers' parking lot rules you put out last fall? I lost mine."

6. Supervising teacher to student teacher: "I have developed a splitting headache. I know this may catch you unprepared, but you're going to have to teach my classes this afternoon."

7. Student to teacher: "I really like your class. Would you talk to Mr. Snow and see if I could switch homerooms after the Christmas break?"

8. As you are walking by the outside door to the gym, you notice that water from the rain has run into the building and onto the floor, making it very slippery. You know that classes will be dismissed in five minutes.

Continued

EXERCISE 5-3 *Continued*

9. Teacher to teacher: "I promised to get this test back to my class tomorrow. I know this is a lot to ask, but I have to go to a meeting tonight and won't have time to grade them. If you will help me, I'll do the same for you sometime." _____

10. Teacher to assistant principal: "When second period starts, I want you to just walk down the hall in front of Mr. Thompson's room. The noise is about to drive me crazy, and he just smiles every time I complain to him." _____

11. Student to teacher: "I work slower than most people, and all of the teachers in my other school gave me extra time for tests and special projects. My mom said she was sure that you would do the same."

_____

Answer Key or Exercise 5-1

1. RA	7. II	13. RA	19. RUI	25. RUI
2. RUI	8. RUI	14. II	20. RA	26. RUI
3. II	9. RI	15. RI	21. RI	27. RI
4. RUI	10. RUI	16. RI	22. II	28. RI
5. II	11. II	17. RA	23. RA	29. RUI
6. RA	12. RUI, RA	18. RUI	24. II	30. RUI

▶ 6

Ineffective Communication Styles

VERBAL VILLAINS

Behavioral objective: The trainee will become aware that many common ways of responding are not helpful and will recognize the major characteristics of good responses.

There are many ways to respond to a helpee situation and some are more effective than others. The ten "verbal villains" you will meet in the following pages are response styles that are generally not helpful, and may even be harmful. The verbal villains do not attend to the feelings or emotions of helpees. Instead, they keep the helpee at arm's length and put their own interests in the spotlight.

These "off-the-top-of-the-head" responses are usually not helpful, even when given with good intentions. It is not enough to *mean well*; we must also *do well*. We all use verbal villains sometimes, but we can be much more effective when aware of how we are coming across to others.

As you read through these situations, think of occasions when someone responded to you or you responded to someone else in these or similar ways that were not helpful Try to recall how you felt at the time. Each situation is followed by a helpful response that, following the model outlined in Chapter 1, illustrates a natural style that might be given in response to the situation.

Helpee Situation 1

High school student to teacher: "Every time at P.E. when we choose up sides, I'm the last one chosen. I don't think I'm that bad, but it's starting to get to me."

Helper Responses That Are not Helpful

1. *Detective:* "Who is involved in this? What happened? How many times has this happened? What? What? What? Let's get the facts of the case!"

> The detective is eager to track down the facts of the case and grills the helpee about the details of what happened and responds to this factual content instead of giving attention to feelings. The Detective controls the flow of the conversation, which often puts the helpee on the defensive.

2. *Magician:* "Basketball is just about over for the year, so it doesn't matter much now, does it?"

> The Magician tries to make the problem disappear by telling the helpee it isn't there. This illusion is not lasting. Denying the existence of a problem is not respectful because it denies helpees the validity of the helpee's own experience and perception.

3. *Foreman:* "Would you help me pass out these papers before the period starts?"

> The Foreman believes that if a person can be kept too busy to think about a problem, there will be no problem. Doing this has the effect of telling the helpees that the assigned task is more important than their problems, which is disrespectful even if true. Effective helpers communicate their awareness of the magnitude given by the helpee to any particular problem.

4. *Hangman:* "Remember last year when you kept losing your temper every time you played basketball? Of course they don't want you on their team! You're just reaping what you sowed."

> The Hangman likes to show the helpee that it was the past actions of the helpee that caused the present situation—that the helpee is guilty, and the Hangman is there to dish out the punishment. Although such responses may be accurate, they are rarely helpful because they are premature—given before the helpee is able to accept and use them. A helper may discipline and may give information that is painful for the helpee to learn, but a helper does not punish.

Helper Responses That Follow the Model

"I know it hurts to feel rejected every time teams are picked." Or, "That must really be embarrassing to be the last one chosen every time."

Helpee Situation 2

Teacher to another teacher: "Consultants! Consultants! They keep sending these people around with their impractical ideas!"

Helper Responses That Are not Helpful

1. *Swami:* "You better make them think you follow their suggestions. If you don't, it will get back to the principal. Then you'll be in real trouble!"

> The Swami knows and predicts exactly what is going to happen. By declaring the forecast, the Swami is relieved of responsibility and sits back to let the prophecy come true.

2. *Hangman:* "You're just not giving their ideas a fair chance. If you were more adaptable to progress, the consultants wouldn't have to spend so much time with you."

3. *Sign Painter:* "You're just a complainer! You don't seem to like anything that happens."

> The Sign Painter thinks a problem can be solved by being named. The Sign Painter has an unlimited inventory of labels to affix to persons and their problems.

4. *Drill Sergeant:* "You need to adapt their ideas to your own situations. Try thinking of it that way next time they come."

> Drill Sergeants give orders and expect them to be obeyed. Because they know just what the helpee should do, they see no need to give explanations or listen to the helpee's feelings, or to explain their commands to the helpee.

Helper Response That Follows the Model

> "It annoys you to get interrupted."

Helpee Situation 3

Eighth-grade student to teacher after class: "You asked me to be chairman of the panel discussion next week, but I can't do that. Please get somebody else. Anybody in the class would be better than me."

Helper Responses That Are not Helpful

1. *Drill Sergeant:* "When you get home tonight, figure out what each panel member will do. Give them assignments and make sure they work on it some each day. Get organized now and it will come out fine."

2. *Guru:* "You won't find out what you can do if you don't try new things. It's better to try and fail than not to try at all."

> Gurus dispense proverbs and cliches on every occasion as though they were the sole possessors of the accumulated wisdom of the ages. Unfortunately, their words are too impersonal and general to apply to any individual's situation with force or accuracy, and often are too trite to be noticed at all.

3. *Magician:* "You don't *really* mean that, do you?"
4. *Historian:* "I know exactly what you are thinking. I remember one time when I was in ninth grade, no, maybe it was eighth grade, well, anyway, I was asked to give a speech for somebody at school elections. I think that's what it was about. Anyway, I didn't think I could do it. So I went to the teacher, and she said . . ."

> Verbal villain historians dig up tired old stories about what happened to them. These "golden oldies" are unlikely to be entertaining or instructive early in a helping relationship.

Helper Response That Follows the Model

"You're sort of afraid to accept this responsibility—it looks like more than you can handle."

Helpee Situation 4

Parents to teacher: "You told us at our last meeting that if we worked with Johnny at home his grades should improve. We've spent more than enough time with him, but his grades aren't any better."

Helper Responses That Are not Helpful

1. *Detective:* "Let's talk about what happens at home. How do you go about helping Johnny? Do you do it for him? Do you do too much? Are you pushy? Do you threaten him? Is the emotional climate supportive? Are you getting along okay with the rest of the family?"
2. *Florist:* "Oh, you must be doing a lot of things right! I know you care a lot about Johnny! He says nice things about you! He is well behaved in class and that shows that he has a stable home life. These things take time, you know, but he has been trying harder in class. I think things are working out."

> The Florists are uncomfortable talking about anything unpleasant, so they gush flowery phrases to keep the helpee's problems at a safe distance. The Florist mistakenly thinks that the way to be helpful is to hide the problem under bouquets of optimism.

3. *Guru:* "Well, you know what they say about leading a horse to water. It could be that we're pushing Johnny too hard at this time. According to some developmental theories I've read. . . ."

Helper Response That Follows the Model

"All the extra work doesn't seem to be paying off—that discourages you!"

Helpee Situation 5

Teacher to another teacher: "Things today are all so confusing. My work seems to pile up and there's never enough time to get it done. I'm afraid I'm just getting so far behind that I'll never catch up."

Helper Responses That Are not Helpful

1. *Guru:* "Hard work never killed anybody. Just hang in there. Things could be worse."
2. *Detective:* "What do you mean? Do you have it more difficult than anyone else? Tell me exactly what is bothering you."
3. *Sign Painter:* "Come on now. You don't want to be known as a quitter. You're just discouraged. Be a go-getter."
4. *Swami:* "You're working yourself into a nervous breakdown if you take all this so seriously."
5. *Drill Sergeant:* "Stop complaining! Get organized and just plan to do one thing at a time."
6. *Hangman:* "Look, as I see it, you're the one responsible for this mess. You volunteered for the extra work."
7. *Magician:* "Things aren't that bad, you're just tired. Everything will be better tomorrow."
8. *Florist:* "Dedicated people such as you often feel this way. If we didn't have you people, nothing would ever be accomplished around here."
9. *Foreman:* "Look, we've got other things to worry about. This project we selected is right up your alley and I need your help."
10. *Historian:* "The same thing happened to me, except it was worse because it was my first year of teaching. Or it might have been the second. My principal was new that year and he didn't understand me at all, so when I told him that . . ."

Helper Response That Follows the Model

"You're confused and you feel discouraged because your work is piling up on you. And right now you don't see any way out."

THOUGHTS THAT LIE BEHIND
THE HELPEE'S WORDS

Behavioral objective: The trainee will learn the effect that nonverbal communication styles have upon persons.

Everything a helper says has an effect on the helpee. This effect can be for better or for worse. Sometimes we know what the effect of our communication is; often we do not. We do not get much feedback about our communication style. If we have been very helpful it may be hard for the other person to express appreciation. If we have been hurtful, they may be too angry to talk about it.

It is when we have been ineffective that we get the least feedback about our communication style. Most people are too polite or too timid to tell us when we have missed the mark in a conversation. The conversation will usually go on, but the helpee will probably play it safe. This is not good enough if we want to be fully helpful to others.

We often think that if we don't hear any negative remarks or if there is no obvious resistance by the helpee that our communication has been good, but the truth is that most helpees don't say as much as they would like to in those situations. And that makes sense, for, after all, if we have been ineffective in responding to what they have already said, why should they bother to say more? Most persons would rather close a conversation than continue with it if it does not benefit them.

The conversations below show what might be going through two helpees' minds as they reply to various helper responses. You will notice that what the students think is different from what they say. This often happens because of the social risk we take in expressing our feelings and attitudes fully. As you read these conversations ask yourself the question, "Is the helpee better off after this conversation?"

Helpee Situation 1

Student to teacher: "I know I'm behind in my work. It's because of the way people talk at my house and all over my neighborhood. Nobody I know except the teachers here at the school follow all these rules of grammar you want us to learn and use. This book talk is like a foreign language to me."

Helper Responses That Are not Helpful

1. *Instructor (Detective):* "Are there any rules in particular you don't understand? By the way, how much education does your mother have? And father? Do you have any brother and sisters who have been successful academically?"

Student says: "As to the rules, I don't know where to begin."

Student thinks: "And I don't like your other questions because they make me feel put down. My family is successful even if they didn't get to go to school much. The way they are is **different**, but you must think it's **worse**."

2. *Instructor (Swami):* "You'd better hit it pretty hard with the exam coming up next week. You know what happens if you fail that test."

Student says: "Oh, I **am** studying as much as I have time to!"

Student thinks: "Of course I know I should study. The thing is I have been, and I'm **still** having trouble. That's what's worrying me, and that's why I'm talking to you, but you're just not hearing me!"

3. *Instructor (Foreman):* "Say, I'm glad you stopped by. I know you're interested in the environment. Would you like to help out with a recycling project we're starting?"

Student says: "I guess so."

Student thinks: "I **came** for help, and now I'm **offering** help. Why are you jerking me around, and why do I put up with it?"

Helper Response That Follows the Model

4. *Instructor:* "Yes, there are a lot of variations in the way people talk in the United States. Right now, maybe it looks like it's not worth the effort to learn a more precise way to talk. Maybe it even seems impossible. If you want to, we can discuss why I think it's worth the effort, but I'm **most** interested in how the course is affecting you now."

Student says: "It seems like I learn it here, and unlearn it as soon as I get home."

Student thinks: "She knows **exactly** how I feel—that it seems impossible. I think she actually understands what I'm going through. Maybe I'm not the only person who has felt this way, and maybe I should learn what she wants to teach."

Helpee Situation 2

School secretary to principal: "I'm having a terrible time, financially. I may need to take another job, or find a better paying one just to feed my family."

Helper Responses That Are not Helpful

1. *Principal (Sign Painter):* "You're overreacting. You don't need to be such a worry-wart. Become a **confident** person. An **optimist!** Learn to be self-reliant. Your children aren't going to starve."

Secretary says, apologetically: "Well, I guess we've gotten along so far."

Secretary thinks: "Tell me I'm not self-reliant will he? I'll show him— by getting that better job!"

2. *Principal (Drill Sergeant):* "Do you budget your money? First, for a month, keep track of how you spend your money. Then, see where you can improve your habits. Next, make a good budget plan. Follow that to the letter."

Secretary says: "Yeah, that's good advice."

Secretary thinks: "With his fat salary, anybody could make it. I'd like to see him manage with what I make. By the time I pay the rent and buy food, there's nothing left! As if he cared."

3. *Principal (Magician):* "Oh, come on now, it couldn't be as bad as you say. I know how much you make. There are other people working here who make a lot less than you and are getting along fine. You're fortunate!"

Secretary says: "I don't know of anybody who's in a worse financial situation than I'm in."

Secretary thinks: "Why do I even bother to talk with him!"

Helper Response That Follows the Model

4. *Principal:* "It sounds like your situation is pretty difficult. You think you can't make ends meet without more money. That must be pretty heavy on your mind."

Secretary says: "I really hate to come to you like this, but I had to tell **somebody** about it. My money worries are keeping me awake at night and I'm afraid it will affect the quality of my work."

Secretary thinks: "It sounds like he cares about what's happening to me."

In the next chapter the trainee is provided with a rationale and need for training in attending behavior. Exercises for improving attending behavior are included.

▶ 7

Training in Attending Skills

Attending skills are the physical behaviors you use while listening to another person. These behaviors—such as posture, eye contact, and facial expression—carry messages to persons with whom you talk. They communicate without the use of words. This kind of communication is called nonverbal communication and you will learn more about it in Chapter 8. Here we consider the behaviors that are especially important in the facilitation phase.

Attending skills may be effective or ineffective. Effective attending skills communicate that you are interested in the other person. If attending skills are ineffective, it is unlikely that a helping relationship can develop.

There are no exact rules to follow in using attending skills. There are some general principles that will help you use behaviors that are effective and avoid those that are ineffective. Just as the communication model gives you general principles to follow and allows you to adapt those principles to your own personal style, the guidelines for attending skills will allow you to express your own uniqueness as a person.

Table 7-1 lists a number of modalities of communication and describes, in general terms, behaviors in those modalities that may be either effective or ineffective. The table is the result of review of some 200 research reports of nonverbal behaviors while listening. It describes behaviors upon which strong, clear-cut agreement was found. Styles of nonverbal communication vary among cultures, and, as noted by Sue (1990), it is an advantage to develop specific cross-cultural strategies. The information in Table 7-1 will help you show empathy, respect, and warmth in virtually all situations. There are several important benefits of using good attending skills:

1. They make it easier for you to listen and remember. Listening can be hard work. Good attending skills are behaviors that are physically comfortable. Being natural and comfortable makes it easier to stay emotionally and intellectually alert over a period of time.

2. They enhance the self-respect of helpees. They encourage helpees to feel better about themselves because you are giving fully of your own energy, time, and attention. This helps build a good base relationship.
3. They facilitate self-exploration. By making it worthwhile for the helpees to talk, they reinforce the helpees' openness and self-disclosure.
4. They model behavior that is appropriate. Your example teaches helpees useful skills.

Ineffective attending behaviors tend to close off conversation or prohibit a helping relationship from developing. If your attention begins to lapse after

TABLE 7-1   Attending Skills

Nonverbal modes of communication	Ineffective use	Effective use
	Doing any of these things will probably close off or slow down the conversation.	These behaviors encourage talk because they show acceptance and respect for the other person.
Space	distant; very close	approximate arm's length
Movement	away	toward
Posture	slouching; rigid; seated leaning away	relaxed, but attentive; seated leaning slightly toward
Eye contact	absent; defiant; jittery	regular
Time	you continue with what you are doing before responding; in a hurry	respond at first opportunity; share time with them
Feet and legs (in sitting)	used to keep distance between the persons	unobtrusive
Furniture	used as a barrier	used to draw persons together
Facial expression	does not match feelings; scowl; blank look	matches your own or other's feelings; smile
Gestures	compete for attention with your words	highlight your words; unobtrusive; smooth
Mannerisms	obvious; distracting	none, or unobtrusive
Voice: volume	very loud or very soft	clearly audible
Voice: rate	impatient or staccato; very slow or hesitant	average, or a bit slower
Energy level	apathetic; sleepy, jumpy; pushy	alert; stays alert throughout a long conversation

From *Amity: Friendship in Action, Part I: Basic Friendship Skills*, p. 31. Copyright 1980 by Richard P. Walters. Published by the author. Reproduced by permission.

EXERCISE 7-1　Attending Skills

Behavioral objective: The trainee will be able to demonstrate consistent use, as judged by the trainer and another trainee, of effective attending skills in a three-minute interaction.

Work in triads. One partner should talk freely for three minutes about any topic of interest. The other partner will mostly listen, although he or she may ask questions or otherwise encourage the speaker to continue. The third person will rate the helper (listener) on attending skills using the items in Table 7-1.

Each member of the triad will rotate through each of the three roles: speaker, helper-listener, and observer-rater. The observer-rater should give positive feedback before citing areas in need of improvement.

---

you have been listening to a person talk for a few minutes, you will probably notice some changes in the speaker's behavior. When the speaker suspects that your attention is beginning to drop, he or she is likely to try to recapture your attention, either by talking more loudly or in a more animated way, or by talking faster, or by changing the subject to something the speaker thinks may be of more interest to you. The speaker may move closer to you, or, if you are looking in another direction, may move into your field of view so you will be forced to look at him or her. These are signs that your attending skills are deficient at that time and indicate that the speaker is not satisfied with the level of attention that you are offering.

Wiens, Harper, and Matarazzo (1980) controlled the promptness of the interviewer's response and found that this affected the behavior of the interviewee. Hill and colleagues (Hill, Siegelman, Gronsky, Sturniolo, and Fretz 1981) also found that attending skills, better or worse, do make a difference.

REFERENCES

Hill, C.E., L. Siegelman, B.R. Gronsky, F. Sturniolo, and B.R. Fretz. 1981. "Nonverbal communication and counseling outcome." *Journal of Counseling Psychology 28,* 203–212.

Sue, D.W. 1990. "Culture-specific strategies in counseling: A conceptual framework." *Professional Psychology Research and Practice 21,* 424–433.

Wiens, A.N., R.G. Harper, and J.D. Matarazzo. 1980. "Personality correlates of nonverbal interview behavior." *Journal of Clinical Psychology 36,* 201–215.

▶ 8

Awareness of Nonverbal
Behaviors in Helping

You always communicate. You have been communicating since your first cry at birth and you never stop communicating. There is no way to not communicate. You can stop communicating in words, but there are many modes of communication that do not use words, and you use those whether you intend to or not: facial expression, the use of time, hand gestures, position taken in a room, eye contact, posture, style of dress, loudness of voice, touching, and many more.

Each of these modes, and the many ways in which each can be used, is potentially important in helping relationships. Each can communicate underlying feelings and motives of the helper and the helpee.

The study of nonverbal communication is fascinating. The diversity of modalities and range in expression that can be observed is almost endless. But, nonverbal communication can also be frustrating because the process of interpreting the meaning of nonverbal cues is imprecise. There are many things to see, but it is difficult to know the exact meaning of what you have seen.

Frequently, no single bit of nonverbal communication is meaningful. Still, the pieces add up, and for the perceptive helper, nonverbal cues add color, richness, and depth to the understanding of the other person. Trends can be detected, intensity of feelings may be more fully experienced, and conflicts and motives may be recognized before the helpee can express them in words.

We shall use a liberal definition of nonverbal communication: *any human behavior that is directly perceived by another person and that is informative about the sender*. This definition of "nonverbal" is liberal because it allows us to include an unlimited variety of behaviors if we find them useful. This definition of "communication" is liberal because it does not require that the sender has intended to communicate.

GENERAL CHARACTERISTICS OF NONVERBAL COMMUNICATION

Nonverbal behaviors include the attending skills described in Chapter 7 and the behaviors concerned with warmth discussed in Chapter 13. This section describes some general characteristics of nonverbal communication behaviors. Later sections will deal with behaviors related more specifically to the helper and the helpee.

Nonverbal Communication Uses Many Channels for Sending and Receiving

We receive through each of the senses: hearing, sight, touch, smell, and, rarely, even through taste. Messages may be sent in many ways, as Table 8-1 shows. This is a checklist that presents only a few specific nonverbal communication behaviors from among the thousands that may be observed in human interactions. Since it can only suggest the wide range of behaviors that exist, its purpose is to help you become more aware of the variety and complexity of nonverbal communication. With greater awareness you will develop greater understanding of the ways in which the nonverbal signals you send out are interpreted by others. Also, by improving your skills in reading the nonverbal responses other persons make to your communication, you will learn how you yourself are perceived.

The nonverbal behaviors below are categorized to assist the process of observation and awareness. Because meaning is so highly individual and dependent on context, only minimal information on possible interpretations has been included. Consult the recommended readings cited at the end of this chapter for further information about interpretations of nonverbal cues.

Nonverbal Communication Has Several Purposes

Nonverbal modes of communication are used for several purposes, usually intertwined, and the sender is usually not consciously aware of them.

1. To express emotion, for example, facial expressions, pounding the fist, or stamping a foot.
2. To modify verbal communication by accentuating, qualifying, or masking the meaning of the words, for example, the effect of inflection as demonstrated in Exercise 8-4 below, or a clenched fist that belies the accompanying words.
3. To regulate participation, for example, to frequently look at a watch as a way of saying, "I'm in a hurry" or "I would like to leave" or to remove sunglasses as a way of saying, "I'm willing to be myself and let you see

TABLE 8-1   Nonverbal Behaviors

I.   NONVERBAL COMMUNICATION BEHAVIORS USING TIME

Recognition

Promptness or delay in recognizing the presence of another or in responding to another's communication.

Priorities

Amount of time willing to communicate with another

Relative amounts of time spent on various topics

II.   NONVERBAL COMMUNICATION BEHAVIORS USING THE BODY

Eye contact (important in regulating the relationship)

Looking at a specific object
Looking down
Steady to other person
Defiantly at other person ("hard" eyes), glaring
Shifting eyes from object to object
Looking at other person but looking away when looked at
Covering eyes with hand(s)
Frequency of looking at another

Eyes

"Sparkling"
Tears
"Wide-eyed"
Position of eyelids

Skin

Pallor
Perspiration
Blushing
"Goose bumps"

Posture (often indicative of physical alertness or tiredness)

"Eager," as if ready for activity
Slouching, slovenly, tired looking, slumping
Arms crossed in front as if to protect self
Crossing legs
Sits facing the other person rather than sideways or away from
Hanging head, looking at floor; head down
Body position to exclude others from joining a group or dyad

Facial expression (primary site for display of affects; thought by researchers to be subject to involuntary responses)

No change
Wrinkled forehead (lines of worry), frown
Wrinkled nose
Smiling, laughing
"Sad" mouth
Biting lip

Hand and arm gestures

Symbolic hand and arm gestures
Literal hand and arm gestures to indicate size or shape
Demonstration of how something happened or how to do something

Self-inflicting behaviors

Nail biting
Scratching
Cracking knuckles
Tugging at hair
Rubbing or stroking

Repetitive behaviors (often interpreted as signs of nervousness or restlessness but may be organic in origin)

Tapping foot, drumming or thumping with fingers
Fidgeting, squirming
Trembling
Playing with button, hair, or clothing

TABLE 8-1 *Continued*

II. NONVERBAL COMMUNICATION BEHAVIORS USING THE BODY

Signals or commands

Snapping fingers
Holding finger to lips for silence
Pointing
Staring directly to indicate disapproval
Shrugging shoulders
Waving
Nodding in recognition
Winking
Nodding in agreement, shaking head in
  disagreement

Touching

To get attention, such as tapping on
  shoulder
Affectionate, tender
Sexual
Challenging, such as poking finger into
  chest
Symbols of camaraderie, such as
  slapping on the back
Belittling, such as a pat on top of head

III. NONVERBAL COMMUNICATION BEHAVIORS USING VOCAL MEDIA

Tone of voice

Flat, monotone, absence of feeling
Bright, vivid changes of inflection
Strong, confident, firm
Weak, hesitant, shaky
Broken, faltering

Rate of speech

Fast, medium, slow

Loudness of voice

Loud, medium, soft

Diction

Precise versus careless
Regional (colloquial) differences
Consistency of diction

IV. NONVERBAL COMMUNICATION BEHAVIORS USING
THE ENVIRONMENT

Distance

Moves away when the other moves
  toward
Moves toward when the other moves
  away
Takes initiative in moving toward or
  away from
Distance widens gradually
Distance narrows gradually

Arrangement of the physical setting

Neat, well-ordered, organized
Untidy, haphazard, careless
Casual versus formal
Warm versus cold colors
Soft versus hard materials
Slick versus varied textures
Cheerful and lively versus dull and drab
"Discriminating" taste versus tawdry
Expensive or luxurious versus shabby
  or spartan

Continued

TABLE 8-1 *Continued*

IV. NONVERBAL COMMUNICATION BEHAVIORS USING THE ENVIRONMENT

Clothing (often used to tell others what a person wants them to believe about him or her)

Bold versus unobtrusive
Stylish versus nondescript

Position in the room

Protects or fortifies self in position by having objects such as desk or table between self and other person
Takes an open or vulnerable position, such as in the center of the room, side by side on a sofa, or in simple chair, with nothing between self and other person
Takes an attacking or dominating position, may block exit from area, or may maneuver other person into boxed-in position
Moves about the room
Moves in and out of the other person's territory
Stands when other person sits, or gets in higher position than other person

---

me as I really am." Any of these signals can be done in ways that affirm or that insult or control the other.

4. To illustrate verbal communication, for example, to demonstrate size or shape of an object, or the motion of a tennis swing.
5. To make complete nonverbal statements, for example, to beckon by curling the index finger, or signals by athletic officials. These nonverbal behaviors have rather definite and widely understood meanings, much as a word has a dictionary definition.
6. To offer feedback about the relationship. As you watch two people standing and conversing, one person frequently yawns and edges backward. You interpret this as boredom. These same signals offer feedback to the

---

EXERCISE 8-1   Awareness of Behaviors

The first step in effective use of nonverbal signals is awareness. Using the checklist above, observe nonverbal communication used by others. Note examples of specific behaviors you particularly like or dislike. List nonverbal behaviors that seem to interfere with and/or terminate conversations between two persons. List other nonverbal behaviors that seem to cause a conversation to move ahead and that might indicate that the helpee is accepting the helper as a person and accepting what is being said.

EXERCISE 8-2   Self-Awareness

Observe your own nonverbal communication behaviors. List nonverbal behaviors that you wish to modify. List any that you think might be misinterpreted by others.

---

talker about the effect on the other person. Often, in our enthusiasm for talking, we ignore this valuable information.

We Are Usually Not Aware of Our Own Nonverbal Signals

Not only are we usually unaware of our own nonverbal signals, but we perceive little more than a fraction of the signals of others—signals that, if perceived, would help us understand them much better. Few persons have had much, if any, formal training in nonverbal communication. Our ability to help others increases greatly as we increase our own skills in nonverbal communication.

Nonverbal Behaviors Are Habits

As is true of other habits, nonverbal behaviors are automatic and you generally are not aware of them. Try this experiment to demonstrate the strength of habits: Place your hands in front of you, palms together, and clasp your hands with your fingers intertwined. Note how natural it feels. Notice which thumb is on top. Place the other thumb on top and reposition the fingers so they are again intertwined. This will probably feel quite awkward. The way you did it the first time is the way you always do it. You have a habit of clasping your hands together in a certain way. If you did it with equal frequency the two ways, they would feel equally natural. You may wish to repeat this experiment by folding your arms over your chest, then reversing the position.

Changing habituated nonverbal patterns is a long and difficult process. Even so, if you find yourself using nonverbal behaviors that reduce your ability to be helpful to others, it may be worth the effort required to change them.

Deception Leaks out Nonverbally

Since nonverbal behaviors are habits, it is difficult to deceive another person with words—your nonverbal gestures reveal your true feelings even though

---

EXERCISE 8-3   Improving Perception

To improve your perception of nonverbal signals, keep a list of examples of behaviors that fit each of these categories. Observe yourself as well as others.

EXERCISE 8-4   Vocal Emphasis

Vocal emphasis can change the meaning of the words of a sentence. Thelen (1960) points out that the tiny muscles of our vocal cords are extremely sensitive to the various states of tension in our body and reflect these changes in audible ways. Consider the following sentence and the various ways to say it:

"I WANT YOU TO STUDY THAT BOOK."

Notice that by simply changing the emphasis upon one of the principal words, as though the speaker were "pointing" to that word, the message of the sentence can be altered. There also is likely to be a change in the listener's perception of the speaker's attitude, as shown by the *possible*, though somewhat tongue-in-cheek, statements of attitude.

"I <u>want</u> you to study that book."

> *Message:* "It doesn't matter what others want you to do, this is what I want."
>
> *Attitude:* "This is me talking, your *teacher*, and you'd better respect my power!"

"I want <u>you</u> to study that book."

> *Message:* "It is your responsibility."
>
> *Attitude:* "It doesn't concern us now what the others do."

"I want you to study <u>that</u> book."

> *Message:* "Do what needs to be done, not just any old thing."
>
> *Attitude:* "*That book*, not the magazine you carry inside it."
>
> Note the dramatic difference a small emphasis here or there can make.

you seek to disguise those feelings with your words. Freud (1963) pointed out the complexity of deception and the interplay between verbal and nonverbal modes when he wrote: "He that has eyes to see and ears to hear may convince himself that no mortal can keep a secret. If his lips are silent, he chatters with his fingertips, betrayal oozes out of him at every pore."

Mehrabian (1971) and Ekman and Friesen (1969, 1972) have shown experimentally that persons cannot mask all signs of feeling from view. This certainly is a practical argument in favor of congruence on the part of the helper!

It can be useful and legitimate to mask or modify our displays of emotion. For example, it is better to not show anger to an angry person or fear to a frightened person during a crisis, not to avoid the realities, but to help them keep their emotions under control until the stressors are dealt with.

Behaviors that are frequently associated with deception are more speech errors, shorter responses, longer hesitations, less smiling, more eye contact, covering mouth with hand, and touching nose. This list was synthesized from reports by Heilveil and Muehleman (1981), Kraut (1976), Mehrabian (1971), Morris (1977), and Sitton and Griffin (1981).

Nonverbal Communication Is Given Greater Validity than Verbal Communication

For example, if a person sits with hands clasped white-knuckled, lips pinched tightly together, forehead wrinkled into a dark scowl and says to you, "Oh, things are fine, just fine. I'm cool. Not a care in the world," would you believe it? Of course not. When verbal and nonverbal messages are in contradiction, we usually believe the nonverbal message.

Nonverbal Channels Are the Primary Means of Expressing Emotion

There seems to be little doubt that the nonverbal component of communication is essential to full and adequate understanding of the person speaking. A research study by Haase and Tepper (1972) concluded that "to rely solely on the verbal content of the message reduces the accuracy of the judgment by 66 percent." Statistical analysis of communication in both verbal and nonverbal channels by Mehrabian and Ferris (1967) resulted in the following coefficients for each of the main effects: .07 for verbal components, .38 for vocal components, and .55 for facial components.

These data suggest that the impact of nonverbal behaviors is very great indeed. Unless the helper can receive the information carried through nonverbal behavior, whether it is intentional communication or not, essential information about the helpee will be missed.

Nonverbal Behaviors Vary Culturally

Nonverbal messages may have different or even opposite meanings from one culture to another. There are no truly universal meanings. For example, in our society a simple up-and-down head nod means "yes" and a side-to-side shake means "no," but in Bulgaria and among some Eskimos these signals mean the opposite. Helpers should be aware of the nonverbal language used by the persons with whom they interact.

Nonverbal Behaviors Vary with the Individual

Take, for example, the behavior of arms folded across the chest. This is often interpreted as a sign of defensiveness or rigidity. Indeed, some popular (but irresponsibly written) books state that if you see that behavior you can assume the person to have an underlying attitude of defensiveness. That's true *part of the time*. But, the behavior may also occur because: (1) it is comfortable, (2) the person is cold, (3) the person is covertly scratching, (4) the person is hiding a blemish or tattoo on the arm, (5) the person is hiding dirty hands, or (6) any of a number of other reasons. Similarly, tears may come from joy, relief, anguish, guilt, or self-pity.

Silence may be generated out of spite, embarrassment, confusion, feelings of being at an impasse, or overwhelming gratitude. Gottman (1980) found less consistency in the nonverbal communication of positive affect than negative. Making and acting on snap interpretations is likely to get you into trouble, so always set nonverbal behavior in context.

The Same Nonverbal Behaviors Vary from Person to Person

A given act or gesture may have opposite meanings for two persons. For example, a frown might mean concentration when displayed by one person, annoyance when displayed by another. Scheflen (1964) points out that variations may occur related to differences in personality, gender, age, status, position, and health.

Nonverbal Actions Anticipate the Words

Often, strong emotions can be observed in behavior before they are expressed verbally. Sometimes the behavior is symbolic, for example, you see a student's feet get jittery when you ask how things are at home. Later the student tells you about wanting desperately to get away from the bad situation there.

Consider these other examples and think about what they might mean: A girl's books frequently fall to the floor during history class. She honestly believes it is accidental. A boy who is usually alert closes his eyes any time the class discusses death or serious illness. In a discussion of drug abuse a student looks frequently at his watch and at the door. During a personal discussion a girl blushes when you mention that you teach part-time in an alternative high school for pregnant adolescents.

There are several possible meanings for each of these. We cannot be sure which is most likely to be accurate. Costanzo (1992) shows that correct interpretation of nonverbal behavior requires practice. We should observe all nonverbal behaviors but, before interpreting their meanings, we should collect more evidence that confirms or rejects our impressions.

Nonverbal Communication Offers Feedback about the Relationship

Persons may not put into words all we need to know about our relationship with them. Watch their nonverbal signals. Watch their attending skills. Watch for changes in their level of attending.

Simultaneous Nonverbal Behaviors May Contradict One Another

Have you ever been told by a person with a red face and bulging veins, "No! I'm not angry!"? Even facial expression can be in conflict, as in the person whose forehead is wrinkled in apparent concern but smiles saying, "Oh, everything is going to be all right." Part of the face shows optimism, part of it shows pessimism. This is not necessarily an effort to deceive, but is likely to be the actual state of the person—the familiar "mixed emotions." Our response might best be to listen so that we, *and the other person*, come to understand more completely the complex situation.

Nonverbal Vividness Increases Learning

Research by Schiefer (1986) found that nonverbal vividness had a positive impact on attention to lectures and recall of the information by students. Let's be more animated and energetic in the classroom!

THE HELPER'S NONVERBAL BEHAVIORS

Even though you do not consciously control many of your nonverbal behaviors, you can become consciously aware of them and control some of them. Table 8-2 summarizes some of the behaviors that are frequently associated with high or low levels of the core conditions. Several clusters of behavior are

TABLE 8-2   Nonverbal Communication of the Core Conditions

	Helper nonverbal behaviors likely to be associated with low levels	Helper nonverbal behaviors likely to be associated with high levels
Empathy	Frown resulting from lack of understanding	Positive head nods; facial expression congruent with content of conversation
Respect	Mumbling; patronizing tone of voice; engages in doodling or autistic behavior to the point of appearing more involved in that than with the helpee	Spends time with helpee; fully attentive
Warmth (see also Chapter 13)	Apathy; delay in responding to approach of helpee; insincere effusiveness; fidgeting; signs of wanting to leave	Smile; physical contact; proximity
Genuineness	Low or evasive eye contact; lack of congruence between verbal and nonverbal; less frequent movement; excessive smiling	Congruence between verbal and nonverbal behavior
Concreteness	Shrugs shoulders when helpee is vague instead of asking for clarification; vague gestures used as a substitute for gestures or words that carry specific meaning	Drawing diagram to clarify an abstract point; clear
Self-disclosure	Bragging gestures, points to self; covers eyes or mouth while talking	Gestures that keep references to self low-key, e.g., a shrug accompanying the words, "It was no big deal" when talking about a personal incident
Immediacy	Turning away or moving back when immediacy enters the conversation	Enthusiasm
Confrontation	Pointing finger or shaking fist at helpee; tone of voice that communicates blame or condemnation; loudness of voice may intimidate some helpees so that opportunity to help is lost; wavering quality of voice; unsure of self	Natural tone of voice

described by a common stereotype in place of a lengthy behavior description. Only those that are of unique importance to a particular condition are listed. These behaviors, along with good eye contact and the other behaviors described as attending skills, must usually be present to attain high levels of a given condition.

To adjust our nonverbal behavior so that the other person knows us more accurately raises the level of genuineness of our communication. To remove the ineffective patterns that intrude or distract increases the level of respect that we show. Let's do all we can to communicate helpfully, both verbally and nonverbally.

Some helper behaviors may be ambiguous. For example, the helper may show signs commonly associated with anxiety (excessive perspiration, wavering voice, trembling) when verbally communicating at high levels of the transition or action conditions. The helpee who notices these behaviors may interpret them as (1) inexperience or fear of failure, or (2) complete emotional involvement with a complex and difficult job at hand. Where there is no change in amount of eye contact, proximity, or degree of congruence during transition or action phases, this may be interpreted as (1) competence and comfort (which may or may not be true) or (2) lack of involvement. The interpretations made by helpees influence their perceptions of the helper's self-confidence or of the quality of the helper's involvement.

Webbink (1986) describes the importance of assertive eye contact in maintaining discipline in the classroom and in other leadership roles. Research by Van Houten and colleagues (Van Houten, Nau, Mackenzie-Keating, and Colanicchia 1972) showed that eye contact and a firm grasp of the student's shoulder enhanced the effectiveness of verbal reprimands.

Open posture communicates a sense of confidence (Ridley and Asbury 1988). Close proximity, to the point of invading personal space, can be used to convey warmth and humanness (Hillison 1983).

Rate of speech is another variable. A slow rate with a weak, faltering tone may be perceived as lack of confidence. Helpers who speak with the same slow rate but with a full, steady tone, show they are carefully thinking about what they are saying as they speak, something very respectful of the helpee. Persons who speak fluently and fairly fast, with variation in pitch and volume, are perceived as high in competence (Street and Brady 1982).

Appropriate touching conveys composure, immediacy, trust, and affection (Burgoon 1991), especially touching by high-status females (Storrs and Kleinke 1990). Hutchinson and Davidson (1990), replicating studies on touching done in the 1960s, 1970s and 1980s, found undergraduate men reporting less touching received from parents than reported in the earlier studies. Because humans seem to need to receive touch, consider expanding your use of this powerful mode of nonverbal communication.

Helpers should be aware of their nonverbal behaviors and seek to understand their bases. Exaggerated effusiveness may be motivated by a need to buy the friendship of the helpee. Other behaviors may result from a desire to dominate helpees or to communicate to them the helper's power, strength, or knowledge. Passive-aggressive helpers may use nonverbal means such as pouting to send messages that would be considered inappropriate or rude if put into words. Any of these circumstances would reduce the quality of the helping relationship.

Learn and use the most effective nonverbal behaviors. While we offer guidelines, there is flexibility; your nonverbal style can be individualized. Young (1980) shows that when the other person's attitude and overall impression of you are favorable, your nonverbal style can be less effective without harm to the relationship. You don't have to be perfect, or do things *our way*, to be effective! And remember that the essence of good communication lies in the quality of the message and not in the style of delivery. It is not necessary to be a silver-tongued orator to be effective as a helper. Tyler (1969) says, "One of the rewards of continuing counseling experience is the realization that what one says need not be fluent or elegantly phrased in order to be effective." If you give a person a nice present, he or she doesn't care how it's wrapped!

USING THE HELPEE'S NONVERBAL CUES

As a helper, you will observe the nonverbal behaviors of the helpee. These observations can assist you in understanding the helpee—they add to your perceptions of the helpee and the situation. If you always respond at the minimally helpful or higher levels of empathy and respect, and formulate interpretations in a tentative frame, perceptions of helpee nonverbal communication can be constructive to both helper and helpee.

Remember that nonverbal communication is highly idiosyncratic, or personalized; an act or gesture may have opposite meanings for two persons or for the same person on two different occasions. For example, a frown might mean concentration in one instance, annoyance in another. *Nonverbal behaviors must always be judged in context and their meanings considered tentative.* Use perceptions of the helpee's nonverbal behaviors as *clues* to possible underlying feelings or motives rather than as proof that such exist.

Johnson and Pancrazio (1973) propose "that overt indicators of pupil desire to communicate can easily be learned by observant teachers." They suggest that the way to learn these idiosyncratic indicators is by trial and error—to call on the student whenever you think he or she wants to communicate. Even if the student does not, to offer the opportunity shows respect, they contend.

The helpee's behavior is also a form of feedback that can help you better assess the relationship. The helpee's behavior is, in part, a product of the nature of your behavior. Table 8-3 outlines some clusters of helpee behavior

TABLE 8-3 Helpee Nonverbal Behaviors Frequently Associated with Attitude Toward Helper

	Relationship of mutual acceptance	Dependent quasi-courtship	Cautious, considering, evaluating	Rejecting, hostile
Head	affirmative nods			shakes head
Mouth	smile	mirroring	tightness	sneer; tightness
Level of arousal	alertness	passive	alertness	disinterest
Position	faces helper; moves toward	places self in sub-ordinate position	stationary; uses physical barriers	disinterest; moves or turns away; attacking moves or simulated attack
Eye contact	equal of helper's	much; seductive	little; looks down	avoids; defiant
Hands	palm open or up	reaching	fidgeting; rubbing face	clenched fists; gripping
General	spends time around helper; touches	"puppy dog" behaviors; mirroring of helper's mannerisms	locking up of emotions; uses great care over what is communicated; afraid to be fully open	unresponsive; passive-aggressive behavior; activity; noisy
Posture	open	courtship; seductive; helpless	protective	defensive
Proximity	normal	very close		distant

How to Use This Table: Each column lists behaviors that might be seen under certain conditions. If the helper-helpee relationship is characterized by the helpee attitude described in the column heading, you are likely to see at least several of the behaviors listed. But, you should not assume the attitude from the behaviors. The behaviors may be used as clues to the quality of the relationship and explored as appropriate.

that may allow the helper to confirm or reject a hunch about the helpee's attitude toward the helper. Table 8-4 summarizes clusters of helpee behavior often associated with four important emotional states. Both of these tables were synthesized from dozens of pieces of literature in scientific journals; they are very accurate when talking about people in general, but may not be at all accurate for any one person at a particular point in time, for the reasons given earlier in this chapter. Use this information with caution—as part of a total approach toward understanding the helpee.

When checking out your hunches, make it easy for the helpee to accept your observations and ideas. A simple remark, delivered with warmth, often results in helpee disclosure, for example, "You have been very quiet today," or "You seem to be pretty excited about something." If you are making an interpretation, phrase it tentatively, for example, "I notice you are staring at your desk instead of working. It makes me wonder if you might be worried about something."

There may be occasion to point out nonverbal behaviors used by the helpee that interfere with his or her functioning in society (e.g., poor eye contact, a tendency to intrude on the personal space of another, behaviors that are crude or obnoxious). To point these behaviors out is a didactic confrontation (see Chapter 19) and should be preceded by a strong base relationship.

You may see signals of resistance to your teaching. The behaviors of low eye contact, postural or muscular rigidity, and nonfunctional nervous movements are identified as signaling resistance by Fairbanks and colleagues (Fairbanks, McGuire, and Harris 1982) and Karpf (1980).

Because the meaning of nonverbal cues varies from one person to another and, for a single individual, from one instance to another (as well as the other characteristics of nonverbal communication that make it difficult), it is risky to present any "definitions" of nonverbal cues. At the same time, there are patterns that are *generally* consistent and therefore *likely* to be *somewhat* accurate. Keep these qualifications in mind as you consult Tables 8-3 and 8-4. They may help you formulate hunches about the attitudes and feelings of other persons.

EXERCISE 8-5   Interpreting Nonverbal Behavior

With a partner, talk about anything of interest to you or a stressful situation in the past that is now resolved. Have an observer make notes of nonverbal behaviors and give feedback at the end. The observer should notice the listener's attending skills and the talker's behaviors that precede verbal disclosure or that in any way indicate feelings that were mentioned or that might not have been put into words. Then discuss the observer's style in giving feedback. Switch tasks and repeat.

TABLE 8-4 Nonverbal Behaviors Frequently Associated with Four Emotional States

	Depression often shows in	Anxiety often shows in
Head	down	stiff movement; chin down
Face	frown	flushed; pale
Mouth	downturned; tightness	tightness; clenching teeth
Eye contact	little or none	darting glances, vigilant
Hands	rubbing; clutching	tightness; gripping; sweaty palms
Posture	hunches while sitting	frequent movement; crouching; hunches shoulders
Position	moves	angled away; protective
Distance	more than usual	moderately away
Energy	low	may be high
General	lack of interest; avoids people or activities	jerky movements; tics; guards "territory"

	Anger often shows in	Low self-worth often shows in
Head	forward or tilted upward	downward
Face	angry frown (eyebrows down at center)	half-smile; quickly follows your expressions
Mouth	lips tensed; pushed forward	quivering; halting speech
Eye contact	excessive; defiant	low; peeking
Hands	clenching; fist thumping (symbolic hitting)	restless
Posture	edge of chair	way back as if to be invisible, or on edge as if to run; protective
Distance	moves into others' space	more than usual or, if they trust you, extra close
Energy	high	low
General	acting out such as slamming door, jerking or shoving objects, extra noisy	watching for signs of approval or disapproval from others

These lists appear in more detailed form in "Nonverbal Communication in Group Counseling" by R.P. Walters, a chapter in *Group Counseling: A Developmental Approach.* 4th Ed. by G.M. Gazda, Newton, MA: Allyn and Bacon, 1989.

Paul Ekman and Joseph Hager (cited by Goleman 1981) caution against drawing conclusions from just one or two nonverbal cues, as well as the person's
subjective reports. Perhaps we are overly cautious about presenting this information, but during the last few years there have been so many oversimplified
statements made in the popular literature about interpreting nonverbal signals
that we must clearly point out the risks in careless interpretation.

In the chapters that follow and in your exercises associated with them,
you will combine the facilitative conditions of empathy, respect, and warmth.
You will also be giving close attention to both the verbal and the nonverbal
components of your communication and of the other person's communication. It gets more complex, but also more interesting as you discover how to
increase your effectiveness in helping other persons learn and live.

REFERENCES

Burgoon, J.K. 1991. "Relational message interpretations of touch, conversational distance, and posture." *Journal of Nonverbal Behavior 15*, 233–259.

Costanzo, M. 1992. "Training students to decode verbal and nonverbal cues: Effects on
confidence and performance." *Journal of Educational Psychology 84*, 308–313.

Ekman, P., and W.V. Friesen. 1969. "Nonverbal leakage and clues to deception," *Psychiatry 32*, 88–105.

Ekman, P., and W.V. Friesen. 1972. "Handmovements." *The Journal of Communication
22*, 353–374.

Fairbanks, L.A., M.T. McGuire, and C.J. Harris. 1982. "Nonverbal interaction of pa-
tients and therapists during psychiatric interview." *Journal of Abnormal Psychology
91*, 109–119.

Freud, S. 1963. "Fragment of an analysis of a case of hysteria (1905)." *Dora: An Analysis
of a Case of Hysteria*. New York: Collier Books, p. 96.

Goleman, D. 1981. "The 7,000 faces of Dr. Ekman." *Psychology Today 15*(2), 43–49.

Gottman, J.M. 1980. "Consistency of nonverbal affect and affect reciprocity in marital
interaction." *Journal of Consulting and Clinical Psychology 48*, 711–717.

Haase, R.F., and D.T. Tepper. 1972. "Nonverbal components of empathic communication. *Journal of Counseling Psychology 19*, 417–424.

Heilveil, I., and Muehleman, J.T. (1981). "Nonverbal clues to deception in a psychotherapy analogue. *Psychotherapy: Theory Research and Practice 18*(3), 329–335.

Herring, R.D. 1990. "Nonverbal communication: A necessary component of cross-
cultural counseling." *Journal of Multicultural Counseling and Development 18*, 172–
179.

Hillison, J. 1983. "Communicating humanism nonverbally." *Journal of Humanistic Education and Development 22*, 25–29.

Hutchinson, K.L., and Davidson, C.A. 1990. "Body accessibility re-revisited: The 60s,
70s and 80s." *Journal of Social Behavior and Personality 5*, 341–352.

Johnson, W.D., and S.B. Pancrazio. 1973. "Promoting effective pupil thinking through
nonverbal communication." *College Student Journal 7*, 92–96.

Karpf, R.J. 1980. "Nonverbal components of the interpretive process in psychoanalytic psychotherapy." *American Journal of Psychotherapy 34*, 477–486.

Kraut, R.R. 1976. "Verbal and nonverbal cues in the perception of lying." Paper presented at the annual meeting of the American Psychological Association, Washington, DC.

Lee, D.Y., M.E. McGill, and M.R. Uhlemann. 1988. "Counsellor and client reliance on verbal and nonverbal cues in judging competency, trustworthiness, and attractiveness." *Canadian Journal of Counselling 22*, 35–43.

Mehrabian, A. 1971. "Nonverbal betrayal of feeling." *Journal of Experimental Research in Personality 5*, 64–73.

Mehrabian, A., and S.R. Ferris. 1967. "Inference of attitude from nonverbal communication in two channels." *Journal of Consulting Psychology 6*, 109–114.

Morris, D. 1977. "Nonverbal leakage: How can you tell if someone's lying?" *New York 10*, 43–46.

Ridley, N.L., and F.R. Asbury. 1988. "Does counselor body posture make a difference?" *School Counselor 35*, 253–258.

Scheflen, A.E. 1964. "The significance of posture in communication systems." *Psychiatry 27*, 316–331.

Schiefer, H.J. 1986. "Effect of verbal and nonverbal vividness on students' information-processing." *Perceptual and Motor Skills 63*, 1106.

Sitton, S.C., and S.T. Griffin. 1981. "Detection of deception from clients' eye contact patterns." *Journal of Counseling Psychology 28*, 269–271.

Storrs, D., and C.L. Kleinke. 1990. "Evaluation of high and equal status male and female touchers. *Journal of Nonverbal Behavior 14*, 87–95.

Street, R.L., Jr., and R.M. Brady. 1982. "Speech rate acceptance ranges as a function of evaluative domain, listener speech rate, and communication context." *Communication Monographs 49*, 290–308.

Thelen, H.A. 1960. *Education and the Human Quest.* New York: Harper.

Tyler, L.E. 1969. *The Work of the Counselor* (3rd Ed.). New York: Appleton-Century-Crofts, p. 41.

Van Houten, R., P.A. Nau, S.E. Mackenzie-Keating, and B. Colanicchia. 1972. "An analysis of some variables influencing the effectiveness of reprimands." *Journal of Applied Behavioral Analysis 15*, 65–83.

Walters, R.P. 1989. "Nonverbal communication in group counseling." in G.M. Gazda, *Group Counseling: A Developmental Approach* (4th Ed.). Newton, MA: Allyn and Bacon.

Webbink, P.G. 1986. *The Power of the Eyes.* New York: Springer Publishing Co., p. 45.

Wright, W. 1975. "Counselor dogmatism, willingness to disclose, and clients' empathy ratings." *Journal of Counseling Psychology 22*, 390–395.

Young, D.W. 1980. "Meanings of counselor nonverbal gestures: Fixed or interpretive?" *Journal of Counseling Psychology 27*, 447–452.

RECOMMENDED READING FOR FURTHER STUDY

The books below contain interesting and reliable general reviews of the topic of nonverbal communication.

Harper, R.G., Wiens, A.N., and Matarazzo, J.D. 1978. *Nonverbal Communication: The State of the Art.* New York: Wiley.

Katz, Albert M. and Virginia T. Katz (Eds.). 1983. *Foundations of Nonverbal Communication.* Carbondale: Southern Illinois University Press.

Leathers, Dale G. 1986. *Successful Nonverbal Communication.* New York: Macmillan.

Melandro, Loretta A., and Larry Barker. 1983. *Nonverbal Communication.* Reading, MA: Addison-Wesley.

Weitz, Shirley. 1979. *Nonverbal Communication* (2nd Ed.). New York: Oxford University Press.

For application to counseling, see:

Walters, R.P. 1989. "Nonverbal communication in group counseling." In G.M. Gazda, *Group Counseling: A Developmental Approach* (4th Ed.). Newton, MA: Allyn and Bacon.

▶ 9

Training in Perceiving Feelings

Behavioral objective: The trainee will learn to perceive accurately surface and underlying feelings from written helpee situations.

The first step in communicating helpfully is identifying the helpee's feelings, a process we call *perceiving*. The examples of "not helpful" communication in Chapter 6 were characterized by ignoring or denying the helpees' feelings; the helpers seemed to be unaware of how the helpees felt.

In this manual instruction is given for responding to feelings as well as to the content of the helpee's situation. Before we respond, we must perceive; that is, we must decide what the helpee is feeling and think of words to express those feelings.

This chapter provides practice in perceiving feelings. Examine Helpee Situation 1 which has already been completed. Notice that there are many words that can be used to describe the feelings of the helpee. Often, no single word will summarize all the feelings the helpee has expressed. Also, there is not necessarily a "right" and "wrong" response to the question, "What is this person feeling?" The more possibilities you can think of, the more likely you are to be accurate in responding to others.

This exercise will help build the repertoire of words you can use to describe emotions, and it will sharpen your analysis of helpee feelings so that you can be more accurate in responding. To be effective, a helper must be accurate in perceiving feelings and spontaneous in responding. This involves judgment and practice. Helpee Situation 1 is offered as an example. For Helpee Situations 2 through 11, write several words to describe how the helpee might have been feeling in that situation.

In order to assist you in selecting the most appropriate feeling word, the following five steps proposed by Cash, Scherba, and Mills (1975) are recommended.

1. Identify the general category/mood—positive or negative.
2. Identify the specific kind of feeling—unhappy, fearful, elated, and so forth.
3. Decide on the intensity level of the feeling—high, moderate, low.
4. Select a word that means the same as those feeling words used by the helpee.
5. Verbalize (write) the word that would be meaningful to the helpee, that is, in the helpee's vocabulary range.

After you have listed as many words as you can think of, refer to Appendix B, Vocabulary of Affective Adjectives, and add any additional words that seem appropriate.

Some of the feelings a helpee experiences are obvious from the words used and the way they are said. These feelings are clearly related to the situation being discussed. We call these *surface feelings*.

Other feelings must be inferred from the helpee's statements. For example, in Helpee Situation 1, that the teacher is feeling insecure or embarrassed is less obvious than his feeling mad or angry. We inferred that the helpee may be ashamed for blowing up for no reason, or that the helpee may feel embarrassed after the incident.

We also determine feelings by interpreting the way portions of the conversation are put together—the familiar "reading between the lines." We will call these inferred and interpreted feelings, *underlying feelings*. These feelings are more abstract than surface feelings and may not relate directly to the content of the situation being discussed.

When we begin responding, we will use only words that refer to the surface feelings, but we want to be aware of the underlying feelings and keep them in mind for possible use later. We form tentative ideas about the helpee and the nature of the helpee's situation from the underlying feelings, but we keep these words in reserve. Later sections will discuss the appropriate use of underlying feelings.

Look over the feelings you have perceived in Helpee Situations 2 through 5 and classify them as surface or underlying. Then, for Situations 6 through 11, circle the words that describe the helpee's underlying feelings.

In Helpee Situations 12 through 18, list as many surface and underlying feeling words as you can think of for each situation. Use the five-step process described for use with situations 2 through 11.

When you exhaust your supply of feeling words, turn to Appendix B and locate and record additional feeling words from this list.

EXERCISE 9-1   Perceiving Feelings

Helpee Situation 1

Teacher to teacher: "It makes me want to just give up. This ringleader in 6th period tries to get me to lose my temper just about every day. Then when I get mad everybody starts giggling *at me.* Feelings present: *frustration, anger, discouragement, powerlessness, embarrassment, defeat, picked on, insecure, worthless, ashamed*

Helpee Situation 2

Student to teacher: "My parents are really old-fashioned. They just don't understand why I don't like the country music that they listen to all the time!"

FEELINGS PRESENT _____

Helpee Situation 3

Student to teacher: "My parents don't trust me. When I have friends over in my room, they keep coming in and checking on us. They always think I am up to something."

FEELINGS PRESENT _____

Helpee Situation 4

Student to history teacher: "When I graduate I'm just going to get a job, and probably buy a new car. What good is learning about the past going to do me?"

FEELINGS PRESENT _____

Helpee Situation 5

Student to student: "I know I can make A's and B's if I study every day. My problem is I don't *like* to study, so I *don't* most of the time.

FEELINGS PRESENT _____

Helpee Situation 6

Student to homeroom teacher: "I feel on top of the world. I worked real heard on my science project and I found out a minute ago that I got an A."

FEELINGS PRESENT _____

Helpee Situation 7

Student to student: "Learning to diagram sentences has nothing to do with being a fitness instructor. This school stuff is for the birds."

FEELINGS PRESENT _____

Continued

EXERCISE 9-1   *Continued*

Helpee Situation 8

Student to teacher: "I just found out yesterday that I was accepted at Duke. I bet I didn't get two hours' sleep I was so excited!"

FEELINGS PRESENT _____

Helpee Situation 9

Student to teacher: "My sisters were both straight A students. And the worst part of it all is that at least half of the teachers here remember one or both of my sisters and that's the first thing they mention—how smart they were. You talk about pressure!"

FEELINGS PRESENT _____

Helpee Situation 10

Teacher to teacher: "You wouldn't believe this new student who came in mid-year. I thought I had a lot of insight into behavioral problems, but nothing I have tried has worked—in fact I think he is getting worse instead of better."

FEELINGS PRESENT _____

Helpee Situation 11

Parent to teacher: "We work with Henry every night, just like you advised the last time we had a conference. He reads just fine at home, and for some reason every time he has a test at school, he messes up. We don't know what to do."   ·

FEELINGS PRESENT _____

Helpee Situation 12

Student to teacher: "I think my weight problem is genetic and there is nothing I can do about it. At a family reunion in West Virginia last summer I noticed that all of my relatives are overweight."

SURFACE _____

UNDERLYING _____

Helpee Situation 13

Student to student: "I can't wait until the football game Friday night. All of my friends are going to meet before the game at Mike's house because his parents are out of town until Sunday."

SURFACE _____

UNDERLYING _____

EXERCISE 9-1 *Continued*

Helpee Situation 14

Student to teacher: "I'd really like to make an A in your class, but I think the C that I have now is about the best I can do."

SURFACE _____

UNDERLYING _____

Helpee Situation 15

Teacher to teacher: "I may ask for a transfer to a school across town for next year. The composition of this neighborhood bothers me more and more. And I don't feel safe any more leaving school late."

SURFACE _____

UNDERLYING _____

Helpee Situation 16

Student to teacher: "Trouble seems to follow me everywhere I go. Now I can't even get along with my best friend."

SURFACE _____

UNDERLYING _____

Helpee Situation 17

Teacher to teacher: "I was hoping that Mr. Zeeland (Principal) would have at least mentioned that I finished my master's this summer. He couldn't say enough about his own workshop at Harvard, and the trip to Europe that Ms. Mendez took with the honors group."

SURFACE _____

UNDERLYING _____

Helpee Situation 18

Teacher to teacher: "I'm thinking about having this new eye surgery so I won't have to wear glasses all the time. They say it only takes 15 minutes and can be done in the doctor's office. But I don't know . . ."

SURFACE _____

UNDERLYING _____

Beginning with Chapter 10, and including Chapters 11, 13, 16, 17, 18, 19, and 20, the trainee will be introduced to each of the core conditions of the helping relationship. Chapter 10 includes exercises in perceiving and responding with empathy. Each chapter focusing on a core condition is arranged similarly to Chapter 10.

REFERENCE

Cash, R.W., Scherba, D.S., and Mills, S.S. 1975. *Human Resources Development: A Competency Based Training Program* [Teachers Manual]. Long Beach: CA: Authors.

▶ 10

Perceiving and Responding with Empathy

Empathy was shown in Chapter 1 to be the key condition in developing helpful communication with another person. The degree to which empathy is communicated in an interpersonal interaction can be measured on the Empathy Scale presented in Table 10-1. The Empathy Scale is the first of nine scales that will be presented in the manual. Eight of the scales deal with the extent to which a particular dimension, like empathy, is communicated in a response. One scale, the Global Scale, in Chapter 14, involves assimilation of all dimensions into one scale.

It is helpful during the training process to examine each dimension individually, so that deficits and strengths can be discovered. With practice, and with conscious awareness of performance on individual dimensions of the model, strengths can be enhanced and deficits can become strengths. The Global Scale is helpful at the point in training when facilitative responding is being practiced. At this point dimensions are being combined in a way that enhances the response, and the Global Scale allows a single number to represent the extent to which the response is effective or appropriate.

EMPATHY—ITS MEANING AND VALUE

Not only must helpees' feelings be understood, but this understanding must be put into words. The first step in communicating with empathy is to listen carefully to what helpees are saying about how they feel as a result of what is happening to them. The second step is thinking of words that represent the helpees' feelings and the helpees' situations. The third step is to use those words to tell helpees that you are *attempting* to understand their feelings and their situation. This process is not easy, but with practice it can become "auto-matic." The challenge for helpers is to stick with the process through the "awkward" or "this is just not me" phase until responding with empathy feels comfortable.

Empathy and sympathy are different. Sympathy means that the helper experiences the same emotions as the helpee. If the helpee is sad, the helper feels sad; if the helpee is afraid, the helper also experiences fear and perhaps also the physical sensations that may accompany fear (such as trembling, sweaty palms, and upset stomach). Fortunately, it is not necessary to experi-ence the helpee's feelings to be helpful. You can help if you approach under-standing of the other person's feelings, and that is what is meant by empathy.

All persons have, at one time or another, experienced the same emotions, even though it may have been under different circumstances. I have been afraid and you have been afraid. The thing that made me afraid may not cause you to be afraid, but if I talk about fear and if I describe how I feel when I am afraid, you can understand that because you can remember how it felt when you were afraid. Feelings are universal—they are the same among all peoples throughout the world—even though the things that cause us to expe-rience a particular emotion may be quite different from one culture to an-other. It is possible, therefore, to communicate empathy without having had the particular life experience of the helpee.

When we respond with empathy we prove that we understand, as best we can, what someone is saying about his or her feelings. Some people try to take a shortcut and say, "I know what you mean," or "I understand." Prob-ably someone has said that to you, and when that person did, you may have realized he or she actually had no idea what you were talking about. Those phrases are overused, and as a result, they lose their meaning and become mechanical. If helpers really do understand, they can go beyond the "I know how you feel" stage and put a label on the feeling. This is a concrete expres-sion by helpers that they are attempting to empathize.

What is the effect on helpees when you respond to them with empathy? Helpees will realize that you are listening to them with full attention and that you are attempting to understand what they wish you to understand about them. Giving another person your full attention is the greatest compliment you can give, because it shows that person that you think he or she is important and worth your time. This is a compliment that is made all the more meaningful because there is no way that giving time and attention can be faked.

The helpfulness of empathic responding knows no bounds. It can be a part of everyday life that will help bring about more meaningful relation-ships. If your response shows others that you are seeking to understand their points of view, they will, over time, become more attracted to you and will seek to understand your needs, interests, and feelings. Helpful responses be-get helpful interaction.

TABLE 10-1   Empathy Scale

Helpful/Not Harmful	Minimally Helpful	Very Helpful
Uses helpee's feelings against helpee.	Communicates surface feelings indirectly.	Communicates surface feelings and content directly.
Denies helpee's feelings.		Communicates underlying feelings and related content.
Inaccurately identifies content and affect.		

Table 10-1 sets the requirements for each level of empathy. This revised Empathy Scale has been simplified for ease in training and application. The more complex version of this scale used in research is included in Appendix A. All other "core condition" research scales are also included in Appendix A.

ILLUSTRATION OF THE EMPATHY SCALE

The helpee situation below will define each individual definition given in the three levels of the Empathy Scale. Remember that these are rated solely on the dimension of empathy and no other conditions.

Teacher to teacher: "My students come into class in the mornings discussing television shows that they have no business watching. Most of the trash on TV is not appropriate for adults, much less seventh graders! I wonder if their parents know what they are watching."

Harmful/Not Helpful

"Frances, I think that you're all wrong. Children today know a lot more than you give them credit for. Besides, you're getting mad about something you have no control over."

> This response punishes the helpee for stating the opinion. Even if you do not agree with what someone is saying, if you are in a helper role your first responsibility is to help the other person explore the situation. The first teacher is missing an opportunity to help the second teacher understand her anger. This type of response usually leads either to an argument or the conversation terminates with a residue of bad feelings on both sides.

"Frances, calm down! You shouldn't get so worked up over this."

In this response the helper is not allowing the teacher to express the negative feelings. She writes off the importance of the communication by simply saying that her coworker should "calm down." This almost never works because the emotion is already there and by simply telling someone they should or should not feel a particular way will not alter their emotional state at the moment.

"I can tell that you're frustrated."

This is an attempt to empathize with the teacher, but the word chosen, "frustrated," does not relate the affect (emotion) of the other person.

Listen to how the teacher responds to this: "No, I'm not frustrated, I'm MAD. The children shouldn't watch that trash!" As a helper, your job is to think about the emotional or affective state of the other person and attempt to match it. When you miss, as this helper did, you communicate that you do not understand.

Minimally Helpful

"So, you wish the parents would be more vigilant."

This response communicates some attempt to understand, but it is indirect and also incomplete. This would probably not terminate the interaction, and it is more effective than the preceding responses, but it lacks key elements of an empathic response, namely the accurate feeling word and the essence of the content.

Very Helpful

"You seem angry that the parents of seventh graders let them watch TV shows that you consider nothing but trash."

When you communicate the accurate feeling word (anger, in this case), and the essence of the content in a situation, the other person will feel listened to. It does not matter whether you agree or disagree, the main thing is to communicate two things: (1) I heard what you said, and (2) I'm attempting to understand how you feel. If you do these two things, you have done about all you can do in an initial response. The response does not solve the problem, but it opens the issue up for discussion and encourages the other person to begin a self-exploratory process.

"Besides being angry, you almost seem to be personally offended—like maybe the TV programs violate your value system."

Responses like this are risky at best, especially when they are used early in a relationship. The reason they are risky is that you have a good chance of being wrong when you go beyond what the person has told you and essentially guess about what is going on. In this case, you suspect that the surface anger goes much deeper to a personal value system that is being violated. You may be right, but on the other hand, you may be wrong. Also, you may be right and the other person will not wish to discuss anything this personal with you. At any rate, the safe response is the first response above, but as the relationship develops, or in certain cases to speed the interaction along, a response like the second response might be used effectively.

EXERCISE 10-1   Perceiving Empathy

Behavioral objective: The trainee will be able to rate helper responses on the Empathy Scale with an average discrepancy score of 0.5 or less. (The discrepancy score is obtained by subtracting the trainee score and the Answer Key score, adding the absolute differences and dividing by the number of items for the following situations.)

Several helper responses are given to each helpee situation below. Rate each on the Empathy Scale. Place the number (1, 2, or 3) in the blank to the left of the helper response.

Harmful/Not Helpful	Helpful	Very Helpful
1	2	3

Helpee Situation 1

Teacher to teacher: "I would never say this to anybody around here but you, but I feel like I can talk to you since we work so closely together every day. I have had this very uncomfortable feeling every time I am around our new principal. I get the distinct feeling that she is prejudiced against blacks."

Helper Responses

_____ **1.** "Racial prejudice is resurfacing all over the country. Have you been reading about that big restaurant chain that was accused of seating whites ahead of blacks and hispanics?"

_____ **2.** "I think the best way to deal with a situation like that is to face it head-on. Ask her for a meeting after school and just lay the cards on the table."

Continued

EXERCISE 10-1 *Continued*

_____ 3. "That's just plain foolishness. You know she wouldn't be where she is today if she were racially prejudiced."

_____ 4. "I know that must be disturbing to think that her reactions to you might be affected by your race."

_____ 5. "You know what I think? I think that she has a deep-seated feeling of inferiority. She is threatened by anyone who might perceive her weaknesses. I know what you're saying because I have even felt it toward myself—and I'm white!"

_____ 6. "You seem confused about the principal's reaction to you and think that it could be related to your race."

_____ 7. "That's a really serious accusation. I don't feel comfortable discussing that because she and I are becoming pretty good friends outside of school—we are in an aerobics class together at the Y every afternoon."

_____ 8. "You are naturally concerned about this uncomfortable feeling—and I sense that beyond that you may be worried about your upcoming evaluation for that administrative job at the school board."

Check the Answer Key at the end of the chapter for the correct ratings and calculate your average discrepancy scores by dividing the sum of the scores by eight. Review the ones you missed to learn why they are rated as they are, then proceed to Helpee Situation 2.

Helpee Situation 2

Student to teacher: "Everybody thinks Tommy and I spend a lot of time together. Between his baseball practice, church activities, and weekend job I hardly ever see him except at school."

_____ 9. "Just be thankful that you have a boyfriend. Many girls would change places with you in a heartbeat."

_____ 10. "I can tell that you feel left out—and maybe a little angry—that everything seems to be more important than, and comes before, your relationship with Tommy."

_____ 11. "You seem to be disappointed that Tommy doesn't have a lot of time left to spend with you."

_____ 12. "Where did you say he worked?"

_____ 13. "I know how you feel. I had a relationship like that once, and let me tell you, it can be extremely frustrating. I finally had to call it quits one day when we were supposed to go to the movies and he called to say that his boss wanted him to work overtime on Saturday night. Life is too short to be waiting around for someone like that!"

EXERCISE 10-1 *Continued*

___ **14.** "You really seem to be a little annoyed that Tommy has so many activities that the two of you have very little time together."

___ **15.** "I knew he played baseball, but I didn't know about the other things."

Check the Answer Key at the end of the chapter for the correct ratings and calculate your average discrepancy score by dividing the sum of the individual discrepancy scores by seven. Review the ones you missed and learn why they are rated as they are.

EXERCISE 10-2 Responding with Empathy

Behavioral objective: The trainee will be able to write helper responses in a natural style at levels Helpful or Very Helpful on the Empathy Scale.

In this exercise you will apply the principles of responding empathically by writing responses to helpee statements. When responding, attempt to reflect back to the helpee the *feelings* and *content* the helpee has expressed. This shows the helpee that you have attempted to hear and understand what he or she said. Read each stimulus situation carefully, perceiving the surface and underlying feelings. Choose a word or two that best summarizes the feelings and content, and fill in the blanks in the formula sentences below each situation. Responses written in this fashion tend to sound mechanical, but beginning this way will help you concentrate on choosing words that accurately reflect the feelings and content. With practice, it then becomes easier to state the response with spontaneity and freshness. The formula response and the natural response would *technically* get the same rating, but with practice your responses will sound more and more natural as you combine empathic responding with your own style of being with people.

When you have written formula responses for each situation, write a natural response for each. The natural response should contain the same elements as the formula response but should express them in good conversational style. You may use Appendix B, Vocabulary of Affective Adjectives, to find a variety of words to express the feeling you perceived in the helpee's statement.

Continued

EXERCISE 10-2   *Continued*

Helpee Situation 1

Student to student: "After dating Rich for two weeks I don't think I will ever be able to just go back to doing the same old things on the weekends."

Helper Responses

Formula: You feel _____ because _____

Natural: _____

Helpee Situation 2

Student to teacher: "In art blues and greens seem to look alike. Mrs. Abercorn seems to think I might be colorblind. That sounds scary."

Helper Responses

Formula: You feel _____ because _____

Natural: _____

Helpee Situation 3

Teacher to teacher: "My husband said he noticed that I don't seem excited about teaching like I used to. I don't know; maybe I need a year off."

Helper Responses

Formula: You feel _____ because _____

Natural: _____

Helpee Situation 4

Student to teacher: "I don't know much about football rules, and the other guys kid me about it. They think I'm a nerd just because I don't play football."

Helper Responses

Formula: You feel _____ because _____

Natural: _____

EXERCISE 10-2 *Continued*

Helpee Situation 5

Teacher to school counselor: "I need some help with some students in my class who feel like they are better than the other students. They run around in a group and make fun of the other kids who don't have as much as they have. I've tried to help, but they don't seem to take me seriously."

Helper Responses

Formula: You feel _____ because _____

_____

Natural: _____

_____

Helpee Situation 6

Teacher to teacher: "These other teachers just kill me when they say that they treat everyone the same regardless of who they are, what color they are, who their parents are, and on and on. Everybody has biases that they learn growing up and it affects how they respond to others."

Helper Responses

Formula: You feel _____ because _____

_____

Natural: _____

_____

Helpee Situation 7

Teacher to teacher: "I feel real guilty at times when I don't practice what I preach in the classroom."

Helper Responses

Formula: You feel _____ because _____

_____

Natural: _____

_____

Helpee Situation 8

Parent to teacher: "Emily complains about how much homework she has, but when I talk to the other mothers they say their children seldom have more than 30–45 minutes worth. Now I wonder if something is wrong with my child."

Continued

EXERCISE 10-2   *Continued*

Helper Responses

Formula: You feel _____ because _____

Natural: _____

Helpee Situation 9

Parent to teacher: "Rudolph had black and blue spots all over his back when he got home from school yesterday. I don't know if he plays that rough on the playground, or if someone has been slapping him on the back, or if he has something else more serious wrong with him. It's distressing."

Helper Responses

Formula: You feel _____ because _____

Natural: _____

Helpee Situation 10

Student to student: "I've got big-time problems. My dad said if I made a C this term that I couldn't play soccer. There's no way I can pull my math grade up in the next three weeks."

Helper Responses

Formula: You feel _____ because _____

Natural: _____

Answer Key for Exercise 10-1

Helpee Situation 1

1. 1 (distances self from the helpee and does not reflect helpee's "uncomfortable" feeling)
2. 1 (premature advice without attending first to helpee's feelings)
3. 1 (denies helpee's feelings and uses them against her)
4. 3 (surface feelings and content are communicated)
5. 2 (communicates empathy indirectly through self-disclosure)
6. 3 (surface feelings and content are communicated)
7. 1 (uses helpee's feelings against her)
8. 3 (attempts to communicate underlying feelings and content)

Helpee Situation 2

9. 1 (uses helpee's feeling against her)
10. 3 (communicates underlying feelings and content directly)
11. 3 (communicates surface feelings directly)
12. 1 (ignores helpee's feelings and focuses on unimportant content)
13. 2 (communicates surface feelings indirectly through self-disclosure)
14. 3 (communicates surface feelings and content directly)
15. 1 (does not focus on helpee's feelings but rather on the boyfriend who is not present)

▶ 11

Perceiving and Responding with Respect

In this chapter you will learn to use the dimension of respect. As you will recall from the discussion in Chapter 1, respect involves having faith in the helpees' ability to solve their own problems. We develop respect for helpees as we learn about their uniqueness and their capabilities. We demonstrate respect by good attending behavior and by showing our belief in helpees' capacities to help themselves. We do this by supporting their efforts rather than by doing things for them which they can do for themselves. The Respect Scale (Table 11-1) is provided to help you better understand this dimension. As with the Empathy Scale there is a Not Helpful/Harmful category, a Minimally Helpful category, and a Helpful/Very Helpful Category.

TABLE 11-1   Respect Scale

Not Helpful/ Harmful	Minimally Helpful	Helpful/Very Helpful
Overtly communicates disrespect	Helper is open to involvement with the helpee	Helper is open to or will consider entering a helping relationship
Helper attempts to impose his or her beliefs and values on to helpee		Helper suspends acting on his or her own situation
Helper dominates the conversation		Helper willing to make sacrifices and risk being hurt in order to further the helping relationship
Communicates that helpee is not able to function on his or her own		

Examples of Respect Scale Responses

Parent to teacher: "I just frankly don't believe that Julie got a good foundation last year in Mr. Mahoney's class. He seemed to be more interested in his coaching duties than in teaching math!"

The following responses correspond to the scale definitions above. The responses are ordered to correspond to the scale descriptors in order from upper left to lower right.

"I've known Mr. Mahoney for years and I know for a fact that his first priority is teaching."

"That's horrible. I think that teaching academic subjects and sports should be kept separate for that very reason. You can't do both well at the same time."

"When my children were growing up the coaches could teach anything in the curriculum. They were usually given the easiest courses to teach so that they could spend most of their time thinking about sports. But I remember one year my oldest child had an American history class from a coach during football season, if you can believe that. Needless to say when he got to college he had the most trouble with history. I still blame that on a poor foundation in high school."

"Unfortunately it won't help Julie, but for the sake of the students who come after her I think you should go all the way to the top with this complaint—but don't quote me on that."

"Mr. Mahoney and his wife are both good friends of mine and I simply would not feel comfortable talking about them. I hope you understand."

"You're concerned that Julie might have problems with math this year as a result of her experience in Mr. Mahoney's class."

"It's upsetting to think that Julie might have gotten less than she deserved in math class last year."

(Early in the relationship, before a base is established) "Mrs. Camp, I can see how frustrated you are about this, and I'll be happy to talk with you about it further if you want."

(Later in the relationship, a firm base has been established) "Mrs. Camp, I just want you to know that I am committed to backing you up on this if you decide to take it any further."

ILLUSTRATION OF THE RESPECT SCALE

The helpee situation below illustrates the three categories of the Respect Scale. Ratings are based on the Respect Scale alone; they might be rated differently on other dimensions or on the Global Scale.

Senior student to teacher: "Some of the kids don't seem to care at all about keeping the cafeteria clean. It's not our class; we really care about the school. It's mostly the freshman class."

Not Helpful/Harmful

"Well, John, what more can we do? I think you should just leave that problem up to the cafeteria monitors and the janitors."

> The helper seems to assume that: "What I think, you should think also." This is not respectful because it imposes the helper's beliefs onto the helpee. Also, it ignores the helpee's concern and closes the conversation by saying, in effect, "It's none of your business."

"I'm a teacher, not a cop. I have to put all of my attention on the classroom."

> This response is rated Not Helpful/Harmful because it devaluates the worth of the helpee as a person. It communicates, "I am more important than you. Leave me alone. If it were important, I'd already be interested in that." This sets up a definite dichotomy of more knowing/less knowing that separates two persons.

"Oh, come on, John, it can't be as bad as you say!"

> This response is rated Not Helpful/Harmful because it challenges the accuracy of the helpee's perception of the situation. This kind of response communicates to the helpee, "I know more about you and what you believe than you know about yourself." The helpee is very unlikely to accept your assessment when it is in conflict with a real feeling he is having. As a consequence, the response is hurtful. It will have a tendency to terminate the relationship.

"Please don't ask me to get mixed up in this—I'd like to help you but I can't. I've had to work very hard this year to get along with the freshmen. If I mention this, it might undo all that I've done."

> In this response, the helper declines to help, offering regrets and a rational reason for withholding from the helping relationship. Though intended to be a neutral response so as not to lose face with

the helpee, in practice this kind of response discourages the helpee from seeking help in the future.

Minimally Helpful

"It makes you mad to see other kids messing up the cafeteria. Let's talk about what we might be able to do."

This response represents an openness to involvement with the helpee, which is the minimally helpful level of respect. The experienced helper enters a helping relationship cautiously, with the knowledge that involvement takes a commitment, can be time-consuming, and has the potential of bringing hurt and disappointment to the helper. It is respectful of the helper, then, to weigh carefully the decision to help, and not to enter into it half-heartedly or carelessly, or to enter a situation in which he cannot be effective.

Helpful/Very Helpful

"It hurts you very much to see a school you like very much to be abused. I'll do what I can to help and I'll start by talking to the principal about the supervision in the cafeteria."

This response is rated Helpful/Very Helpful because it is a commitment to involvement by the helper. Timing is important in making this kind of commitment, and a good relationship between helper and helpee is essential.

EXERCISE 11-1   Perceiving Respect

Behavioral objective: The trainee will be able to rate helper responses on the Respect Scale with an average discrepancy score of 0.5 or less. (To compute the discrepancy score see, on page 109 in Chapter 10, the behavioral objective for perceiving empathy.)

Several helper responses are given to each helpee situation below. Rate each on the Respect Scale. Place the number (1, 2, or 3) in the blank to the left of the helper response.

Harmful/Not Helpful	Helpful	Very Helpful
1	2	3

Helpee Situation 1

Parent to teacher: "Our seventh grader wants to have a boy/girl party at our house next week. I don't know exactly how to respond since this is the first time the subject has come up."

Continued

EXERCISE 11-1   *Continued*

Helper Responses

____ **1.** "Since I don't really know all the parents involved, I would be hesitant to say one way or the other."

____ **2.** "You're really uncertain about what to do since this has never come up before."

____ **3.** "I would absolutely put my foot down on that one. They have plenty of time to date—let them wait until they are at least 14 or 15."

____ **4.** "That's a tough one! I'll be happy to discuss it with you if you'd like."

____ **5.** "The decision is difficult when children start pushing the limits."

____ **6.** "I remember those times well. My situation was complicated by the fact that I was a single parent and had no one to discuss it with."

Check the Answer Key at the end of the chapter for the correct ratings and calculate your average discrepancy score by dividing the sum of the scores by six. Review the ones you missed to learn why they are rated as they are, then proceed to Helpee Situation 2.

Helpee Situation 2

Teenager to parent: "Dad, have I ever given you any trouble? I mean, you would think I was a juvenile delinquent or something the way I am treated. Give me a break—all I want to do is stay out a little later than usual next weekend!"

Helper Responses

____ **7.** "Let me tell you something, son, and I want you to hear it loud and clear. As long as you live under my roof and I support you, you are not going to make the rules."

____ **8.** "Son, I want to discuss that with you. Let me finish up here in the kitchen so I can give you my full attention. I'll just be a minute."

____ **9.** "James, I think you *do* deserve to stay out a little later. Why don't we discuss it as a family when your mother gets home from work?"

____ **10.** "James, when I was your age there was no such thing as talking back to parents the way you just talked to me. 'No' meant 'no' and 'yes' meant 'yes' and that was that."

____ **11.** "You really do feel mistreated and think that you are right on this issue of staying out late at night."

EXERCISE 11-1 *Continued*

____ 12. "James, I've said all I'm going to say about this. I'm leaving the decision up to your mother."

Check the Answer Key at the end of the chapter for the correct ratings and calculate your average discrepancy score by dividing the sum of the scores by six. Review the ones you missed to learn why they are rated as they are, then proceed to Helpee Situation 3.

Helpee Situation 3

Parent to principal: "It seems like the emphasis in this school is always on the better students. The average student gets lost in the shuffle."

Helper Responses

____ 13. "Ms. Koch, I don't mean to be disrespectful, but I get sick and tired of hearing about discrimination. If it's not black/white its black/hispanic, or white/hispanic, or male/female. Now you come to me with gifted/average. I wish you would sit in my seat for one day and try to make everything come out exactly even."

____ 14. "Last year I set up a parent committee to deal with accusations about the management of our school. I think instead of responding to this I will try to reconvene this committee."

____ 15. "You're worried that your child may not be getting the attention he deserves."

____ 16. "Let me have Ms. Marsh, the assistant principal, give you a call. She is attending a continuing education class today, but I'll have her call you first thing tomorrow."

____ 17. "You know I've heard that about athletics in the past, but this is the first time anyone has mentioned our gifted program. We are proud of our total curriculum, from gifted to special education. All of our teachers are committed to the total child concept, and everyone is given maximum attention within the constraints of time and financial resources."

____ 18. "You're upset because it seems that we discriminate against the average student—that maybe a little too much attention is given to other groups of students."

Check the Answer Key at the end of the chapter for the correct ratings and calculate your average discrepancy score by dividing the sum of the scores by six. Review the ones you missed to learn why they are rated as they are.

EXERCISE 11-2   Responding with Respect

Read each helpee situation and develop your response as though you were speaking to the helpee. Write it down as quickly as possible to retain the conversational style. Check your response with the criteria of a Helpful/Very Helpful response on the Respect Scale. If it falls below this level, rework the response to meet the criteria.

Helpee Situation 1

Teacher to teacher: "It's funny how every year it seems that one class is overloaded with problem children. My fourth period this year is a dumping ground for big-time problems."

HELPER RESPONSE _____

_____

Helpee Situation 2

Teacher to teacher: "You wouldn't believe the difference between this school and where I was last year! Last year I spent half my time trying to keep order. With the great disciplinarians we have here in the office, I can tell that this year is going to be a pleasure."

HELPER RESPONSE _____

_____

Helpee Situation 3

Parent to teacher: "I don't know quite how to say this, but my daughter has been coming home from school every day and talking about you. It seems to be an infatuation, but it worries me just the same."

HELPER RESPONSE _____

_____

Helpee Situation 4

Parent to counselor: "I really don't think enough is being done to discourage our children from drinking. When I talk to parents in other school systems they are always talking about workshops and other activities that they are involved in. All I have seen here is this booklet that was published six years ago."

HELPER RESPONSE _____

_____

EXERCISE 11-2   *Continued*

Helpee Situation 5

Student to teacher: "Jewelry seems to be *the thing* now for kids my age. I wanted to get one ear pierced, and you wouldn't believe the fit my dad pitched. He as much as accused me of being gay!"

HELPER RESPONSE _____

_____

Answer Key for Exercise 11-1

Helpee Situation 1

1. 2 (withholds self from involvement because of insufficient data)
2. 3 (suspends acting on helper's own situation)
3. 1 (imposes helper's values)
4. 3 (open to entering a helping relationship)
5. 2 (withholds self from direct involvement)
6. 1 (focuses on self—dominates)

Helpee Situation 2

7. 1 (communicates helpee cannot function on his own)
8. 3 (open to entering a helping relationship)
9. 3 (suspends acting on his own)
10. 1 (imposes his own values and beliefs)
11. 3 (open to entering a helping relationship)
12. 2 (withholds self from involvement)

Helpee Situation 3

13. 1 (communicates disrespect and dominates conversation)
14. 2 (withholds self from involvement)
15. 3 (open to entering a helping relationship)
16. 2 (withholds self from involvement)
17. 1 (dominates conversation)
18. 3 (open to entering a helping relationship)

▶ 12

Combining Empathy and Respect in Responding

The responses that are rated effective on the Empathy Scale and the Respect Scale often look and sound similar. When a person is being effective interpersonally, the respect that is shown in the relationship is characterized as much by what the helper *does not do* as by what the helper actually says or does. This is sometimes difficult to conceptualize, so this chapter attempts to demonstrate the two dimensions and indicate how they are used together to communicate effectively.

Sometimes respect is put into words directly (such as telling the helpee that you are willing to help, or by declining to participate), but more often it is implied and "rides along" with the other core conditions, especially empathy. For example, when a helper listens in a nonjudgmental way, it is judged effective on both the Empathy and Respect Scales.

COMBINING EMPATHY AND RESPECT EFFECTIVELY

In the following example, Tom, a fourth-grade student, is in his first semester at a private school. Although Tom lives in a working class neighborhood, his family has always valued education and his parents want him to be better educated and ultimately have a better lifestyle than they have had. Crime and violence in the public school prompted his parents to make the decision to send him to private school. Although it is a financial strain, Tom's parents have made the commitment for both of them to work, and for Tom's father to work quite a bit of overtime on the weekends in order to pay the tuition and other expenses of the private school. Tom left the majority of his friends when he transferred, and has to take a city bus across town every morning to get to school. He is a likable child, but compared to the other children in his class he is "rough around the edges" and his academic background is somewhat lacking. Tom makes up for some of this by being outgoing and athletic. The other kids like him, and he has been included while at school. The problem that is being addressed in the following scenario is one of exclusion from afterschool activities such as birthday parties, trips to amusement parks, and invitations to other children's homes to play, spend the night, and other such activities. Tom feels this, takes it personally, and is pulled down emotionally by it. The scene opens when Mr. Larkins, the science teacher, is walking home on Friday afternoon and runs into Tom at the bus stop. Tom looks dejected, so Mr. Larkins, who is familiar with the situation, stops to talk.

Mr. Larkins: "Hi Tom, is everything okay? You look a little down in the dumps."

> Pleasant greeting, includes recognition of an affective state. Encourages helpee self-exploration.

Tom: "Well, I missed my bus. But did you know that almost everybody is going to Sid's house tonight, and then they are going as a group to the skating rink?"

Mr. Larkins: "Yes, I heard about that."

> Request for information was made by Tom and responded to by Mr. Larkins. Mr. Larkins also knew that there was more to the issue than that, so he stopped with a short response and waited for more information. Respect is communicated by pausing to listen to the other person.

Tom: "Well, I know they didn't mean to, but everybody talked about it all day in front of me."

Mr. Larkins: "I know it hurts to be left out, and it's embarrassing to have them discuss it in front of you when you were not included."

> Empathy is communicated by identifying the affective states of being hurt and embarrassed. Respect is communicated by *not* trying to smooth things over, explain the situation away, or give advice. The important thing at this point in a personally relevant situation is simply to listen, a skill that encourages the other person to self-explore.

Tom: "Yes. I wish I had never come here. I need to be back home with my real friends."

Mr. Larkins: "Even though you seem to get along with everyone at school, you really don't think that they consider you to be a friend."

Mr. Larkins focuses in on the friendship issue at school, and does not mention the friends at home. He wants to hear more from Tom about this. Again, respect is communicated more by what he is not doing that what he is doing.

Tom: "I don't know what it is, I just feel it."
Mr. Larkins: "This whole thing is confusing to you."

Again, empathy and respect to continue to help Tom clarify the issue.

Tom: "All of my friends here have a lot more money than I have. Their mothers don't work, and they get picked up in big, nice cars. I wish my parents wouldn't put me though this."
Mr. Larkins: "You really feel different from the other kids. I wonder if that might explain some of what you are experiencing?"

Mr. Larkins is using Tom's own conclusion to help him understand his situation. The respectful part is that there are no lectures, or explanations, other than clarification.

Tom: "Well, one nice thing is that I still have a lot of friends in my neighborhood. When I get home I kind of forget about this, and we still have a good time."
Mr. Larkins: "Tom, I'm glad that you do have a lot of good friends in your neighborhood, and I can understand how you feel about not being included in afterschool activities. I appreciate your sharing this with me, and I want you to know that I will be happy to talk with you at any time. Just let me know."

Mr. Larkins has gone about as far as he can go at the bus stop. He communicates a high level of respect by offering to continue to talk with Tom at school. Notice that at no time during this interaction did Mr. Larkins give Tom advice, or suggest strategies, or offer explanations. Tom felt understood as a unique individual as a result, and the stage has been set for further discussion.

Tom: "Thanks, Mr. Larkins."

**EXERCISE 12-1 Combining Empathy and Respect
in Responding**

Example 1

In this example, Ralph, an urban junior high student, has spent the summer in an out-of-state camp for boys. This was a very unusual experience shared by few, if any, of his classmates. Their community is a blue-collar area with very high unemployment due to the closing of the plant that was the largest employer in town. Ralph attended the camp as a gift from his well-to-do aunt in Chicago. He had experiences in camp that most of his classmates had only read about or dreamed about. They went whitewater rafting, hiked on the Appalachian Trail, confronted wild animals close up, slid down long rockslides into mountain pools surrounded by waterfalls, and many, many other unique activities. When Ralph returned to school in the fall he felt estranged from his classmates. He was still living the summer experience. He has been distracted in class to the point that his teacher finally asks the school counselor to talk with him. The interaction begins as follows:

> Ralph: "I don't really belong here. Everybody thinks that living here is all there is to life. I tried to tell my friends about the camp, but they don't seem to want to listen. Then to top things off, my teacher told me not to *brag*. I wasn't bragging; I was just trying to tell them about the world that lies beyond the city limits!"

The counselor's job is to understand Ralph from his point of view. Empathizing is appropriate as well as respecting Ralph's right to be himself in the situation. Remember that the counselor does not have to agree in order to have empathy and respect. Put yourself in the counselor's chair and write what you would say in the space provided.

Example 2

Tim is a fifth grader whose ambition in life seems to be to play baseball. He talks about baseball incessantly and spends most of his free time with a bat and glove in hand looking for someone to play with him. As his teacher, you worry that he puts baseball ahead of schoolwork, and that his grades are suffering as a result. You ask Tim to stay behind after

Continued

EXERCISE 12-1 *Continued*

class and your goal is to empathize with him, respect his right to set priorities, and at the same time communicate your concern about his schoolwork. Write what you would say in the words you would use in the space below.

_____

_____

_____

Example 3

Tonya is in her first year of high school and has transferred in from a nearby town as a result of her father's changing jobs. She has been despondent during the first three weeks of school, and her parents have been driving her back and forth between her old neighborhood and her new home. This seems to make matters worse because it delays her transition to the new school. You understand how difficult it is to leave old friends, but you also feel that Tonya needs to begin making friends in her new school. You decide to initiate a conversation with her. Develop a script of four interactions that shows you care, you understand, and you respect Tonya. Remember your goal is not to convince Tonya of something, but to begin developing rapport with her so that you can influence her later through the strength of the relationship.

You say: _____

_____

Tonya says: _____

_____

You say: _____

_____

Tonya says: _____

_____

You say: _____

_____

Tonya says: _____

_____

You say: _____

_____

Tonya says: _____

_____

▶ 13

Perceiving and Responding with Warmth

The dimension of warmth, to be considered in this chapter, is the third of the facilitative conditions that are essential for establishing a helping relationship. Warmth is the degree to which helpers communicate their caring about helpees. Warmth is seldom communicated by itself; it is most often included in communications of empathy and respect. Warmth alone is insufficient for relationship building, for the development of mutual respect, or for problem solving, but appropriate communication of warmth enhances these processes.

Sherer and Rogers (1980) found counselors whose nonverbal behaviors communicate warmth to be rated as more effective. Many other studies have shown that when a teacher or other leader expresses warmth it perpetuates itself and spreads, increases disclosure by group members, encourages greater responsiveness to the leader, and improves healthy group processes. See LaCrosse (1975), Gibb (1972), and Neidigh (1991).

Warmth is communicated primarily through a wide variety of behaviors such as gestures, posture, tone of voice, touch, or facial expression. These behaviors, for the most part, do not include words, so they are referred to as "nonverbal communication." These nonverbal messages are received by others and given meaning, just as words are, and their impact can be just as strong as that of verbal messages. Consider common expressions about the use of the eyes: "an icy look, a piercing stare, a look that could kill." Or think about the rage that can be expressed by a shaking fist. These examples only suggest the powerful impact nonverbal behaviors can have. This chapter presents the nonverbal mode of communication as it relates to warmth. A more general treatment of nonverbal communication appeared in Chapter 8.

It is chiefly through nonverbal messages that the helper's caring for the helpee is communicated. But warmth can also be expressed in words, such as,

"If this is important to you, it's important to me. Let's talk about it some more." Or, "You're in a bind, and I'd like to help out if there's any way I can."

The level of warmth the helper communicates can be rated (see Table 13-1), just as you have rated helpers on their empathy and respect. Examples of nonverbal behaviors at different levels of the scale follow the scale.

A high rating on nonverbal warmth does not automatically follow high levels of empathy or respect. A helper may *have* high levels of empathy and respect, and may try to communicate that, but by being unexpressive nonverbally, may be perceived by the helpee as uncaring. This type of helper may find that it takes more time to build a base than would a helper whose nonverbal behaviors are more clearly warm.

Helpers who do not nonverbally communicate warmth must first be careful that their nonverbal behaviors are not harmful to the development of relationships, and then learn how to demonstrate their caring through words and deeds.

High-level warmth behavior may occur with low-level empathy or respect, as in a person who uses effective attending skills but doesn't care about the helpee or who is seeking to manipulate the helpee. Warmth that is not genuine can usually be detected by the helpee. When verbal and nonverbal messages do not agree, the helpee usually believes the nonverbal message, even though he or she may not be consciously aware of having received it. For example, the helper who states an interest in talking, but frequently glances at the clock, will probably not be trusted by the helpee.

The way warmth is expressed varies. When a helper with low-level warmth talks with a helpee who has been accustomed to high-level warmth, the base-building process will probably be lengthened. On the other hand,

TABLE 13-1   Warmth Scale

Not Helpful/Harmful	Minimally Helpful	Helpful/Very Helpful*
Shows disapproval or is disrespectful	Most of the helper's attending skills are effective; uses ineffective attending skills only occasionally	Gives and shows caring by using effective attending skills
Seems disinterested		Enters the helpee's personal space
The helper's affect is not congruent with helpee's affect	Authentic encouragement	
	Sounds interested, but mechanical	Congruence
Other ineffective attending skills		

*References for items in the Helpful/Very Helpful column: Bayes 1972; D'Augelli 1974; Duncan, Rice, and Butler 1968; Solomon 1982; Glick, DeMarest, and Hotze 1988; Hill 1990; Kelly 1972; LaCrosse 1975; Mansfield 1973; Mehrabian 1969; Shapiro 1972; Strong, Taylor, Bratten, and Loper 1971.

Examples of Warmth Scale Responses

The examples are ordered to correspond to the scale descriptors from upper left through lower right. See Table 8-2.

A frown, stare, sharp or growling tone of voice; compliments and encouragement are stereotypic or based on incomplete information

The helper looks through a magazine while the helpee talks; does not respond when approached or spoken to; mumbles or does not speak loudly enough to be heard; appears impatient for helpee to go away, as communicated by fidgeting, frequently looking at watch, drumming fingers on desk, etc.; faces helpee, but slouches; compliments and praise are based on incomplete informa-tion; smiles while the helpee describes personal pain; does not change behavior with changes in helpee's affect, for example, does not laugh out loud

Offers compliments that have been earned, and about which the helper has information.

Helpers in training, when concentrating on saying the right words, may not be very fluent.

General positive affect, especially as communicated through facial expression. Verbal fluency and absence of filled pauses such as "um" or ah."

Movement, with greater movement being interpreted as alertness.

Posture in which helper's trunk is leaning forward. Voice tones that are normal to soft in loudness, open, and normal to low in pitch. Vocal quality would be described as relaxed, serious, and concerned.

A high level of alertness.

Maintaining eye contact.

Absence of fidgeting.

Face-to-face orientation.

May be physically close (39" vs. 55" or more). May make physical contact in a way acceptable to helpee.

Facial expression is congruent with helpee's affect; encouragement is shown by vertical head nods.

warmth and intimacy cannot be forced. Helpers should allow helpees to exercise their right to maintain distance in the relationship if this is their preference. High levels of warmth during the early stages of a relationship can harm the base-building process with helpees who have received little or no warmth in the past, or who have been misled by phony expressions of warmth.

TOUCH

Touch—we can't get along without it. Yet touching between adults in our culture is risky because of the wide range of attitudes and reactions.

We have a preference, based on the extensive literature on the value of touch as well as more personal reasons, and the preference is to encourage nonsexual touching when the helpee is comfortable with that. The overwhelming trend of literature is that, especially in times of emotional stress, most persons not only welcome but *need* the strong bond that touch can communicate so much more completely than can words (Gazda, Childers, and Walters 1982). Research by Willis and Hamm (1980) found touching to increase effectiveness in persuading another person. Major (1980) regards it as an appropriate means of expressing warmth, and especially valuable with those who need comfort and reassurance. Burgoon's (1991) research showed that touching conveyed affection and these other elements related to warmth: trust, receptivity, and informality.

The two most important factors to consider in using the communication modality of touch are: (1) the level of trust between the two persons and (2) whether or not the touch is perceived as sexual. It is the other person's perception, not your intent, that determines this. The entire context affects the level of trust and the perception, and there are many variables: the other person's attitudes and practices, the relationship between the persons, the level of other communication past and present, and the physical setting.

Research by Steward and Lupfer (1987) found that teachers who touched students lightly on the arm for no more than five seconds during an evaluation conference were rated more effective, and students showed superior performance on the next course examination. Steward and Lupfer concluded that touching conducted in a conference situation to help students improve class performance can be an effective teaching tool. However, touching calls for sensitivity to one's own motives and to ethical implications, points carefully made by Holub and Lee (1991).

To help you evaluate the situation and monitor your own behavior, you might ask yourself questions such as these:

1. How does the other person perceive this? Is it seen as genuine or as a superficial technique?

2. Is the other person uncomfortable? If the other person draws back from being touched, adjust your behavior accordingly.
3. Am I interested in the person, or in touching the person? Who is it for— me, the other person, or to impress those who observe?

The reassurance of physical touch can be appropriate and very helpful in education, teaching, and friendship. Use it well; use it often.

EXERCISE 13-1 Perceiving and Responding with Warmth

Behavioral objective: The trainee will be able to rate the communication of warmth in agreement with the majority of trainees 80% of the time and respond with warmth at the level of helpful or very helpful.

Because the communication of warmth is primarily nonverbal, written exercises are almost without value. Use the group exercise below to learn and practice communication of warmth at helpful levels. You may find it useful to reread Chapter 8 before doing this exercise.

For each of the following stimulus situations, choose a helper and a helpee. The helpee will read the statement and the helper will respond, attempting to attain high levels of warmth. Continue the dialogue in a role-playing fashion for as long as you wish. After each stimulus situation, the other group members should discuss specific aspects of the helpee's nonverbal behaviors and assign a rating on the Warmth Scale. They should then determine the consensus rating for that stimulus situation. Continue this exercise until all members of the group have a chance to play the role of the helper and communicate at the level of Helpful/Very Helpful.

Helpee Situations

1. Student to teacher: "There's no way I can get all your work done this week. This is one of my dad's bad weeks. He drinks like crazy, and when he does, there's no peace in the house. He bothers everyone in sight as long as he's awake."
2. Teacher to teacher: "These kids are just getting to be too much for me. I've been teaching for twenty years, and it looks like I just can't keep up with the pace of things. Especially the kids from other cultures. I don't understand them. I guess that means I should quit, but I don't want to."
3. Student to teacher: "I'm glad you're going to be teaching us about biology soon. I really love animals—all kinds—and I hope I can get a job working with animals when I'm older."

Continued

EXERCISE 13-1 *Continued*

4. Student to teacher: "My attitude about drugs, even crack, used to be pretty laid back. Then one of my brother's friends OD'd. That got my attention! Since then I've done some serious thinking; even some reading in the library about it."

5. Teacher to teacher: "The neighborhood where I live is in a racial transition. My husband says 'Let's move out while we can.' I think that's wrong and foolish, but if I try to talk with him about it he leaves the house."

6. Teacher to teacher: "My heart attack was a real scare to me, but it woke me up to a lot of the real value of life. I have more appreciation of the little things that students and teachers do for me. I plan to make a few changes in my life now."

7. Student to teacher: "I don't know why some people can't be satisfied with what they have. There are kids around here who have all kinds of money, a good car, they make grades easy and all that—everything—but all I hear them do is cry and moan about what they don't have. I'd trade problems with them in a minute!"

REFERENCES

Bayes, M.A. 1972. "Behavioral cues of interpersonal warmth." *Journal of Consulting and Clinical Psychology 39*, 333–339.

Burgoon, J. K. 1991. "Relational message interpretations of touch, conversational distance, and posture." *Journal of Nonverbal Behavior 15*, 233–259.

D'Augelli, A.R. 1974. "Nonverbal behavior of helpers in initial interactions." *Journal of Counseling Psychology 16*, 647–655.

Duncan, S.D., Jr., L.N. Rice, and J.M. Butler. 1968. "Therapists' paralanguage in peak and poor psychotherapy hours." *Journal of Abnormal Psychology 73*, 566–570.

Gazda, G.M., W.C. Childers, and R.P. Walters. 1982. *Interpersonal Communication: A Handbook for Health Professionals.* Rockville, MD: Aspen Systems.

Gibb, J.R. 1972. "TORI theory: Nonverbal behavior and the experience of community." *Comparative Group Studies 3*, 461–472.

Glick, P., J.A. DeMarest, and C.A. Hotze. 1988. "Keeping your distance: Group membership, personal space and requests for small favors." *Journal of Applied Social Psychology, 18*(4), 315–330.

Hill, C.E., and A. Stephany. 1990. "Relation of nonverbal behavior to client reactions." *Journal of Counseling Psychology 37*, 22–26.

Holub, E.A., and S.S. Lee. 1991. "Therapist's use of nonerotic physical contact: Ethical concerns." *Professional Psychology, Research and Practice 21*, 115–117.

Kelly, F.D. 1972. "Communicational significance of therapist proxemic cues." *Journal of Consulting and Clinical Psychology 39*, 345.

LaCrosse, M.B. 1975. "Nonverbal behavior and perceived counselor attractiveness and persuasiveness." *Journal of Counseling Psychology 22*, 563–566.

Major, B. 1980. "Gender patterns in touching behavior." in C. May and N.M. Henley (Eds.), *Gender and Nonverbal Behavior*. New York: Springer-Verlag.

Mansfield, E. 1973. "Empathy: Concept and identified psychiatric nursing behavior." *Nursing Research 22*, 525–530.

Mehrabian, A. 1969. "Significance of posture and position in the communication of attitude and status relationships." *Psychological Bulletin 71*, 359–372.

Neidigh, L.W. 1991. "An experimental analogue examining effects of facilitative behaviors and subjects' warmth on students' perceptions of a counseling relationship." *Psychological Reports 68*, 1099–1106.

Shapiro, J.G. 1972. "Variability and usefulness of facial and body cues." *Comparative Group Studies 3*, 437–442.

Sherer, M., and R.W. Rogers. 1980. "Effects of therapist's nonverbal communication on rates skill and effectiveness." *Journal of Clinical Psychology 36*, 696–700.

Solomon, H. 1982. "There are smiles that make you helpful." *Psychology Today 16*, 12.

Steward, A.L., and M. Lupfer. 1987. "Touching as teaching: The effect of touch on students' perceptions and performance." *Journal of Applied Social Psychology 17*, 800–809.

Strong, S.R., R.G. Taylor, J.C. Bratten, and R.G. Loper. 1971. "Nonverbal behavior and perceived counselor characteristics." *Journal of Counseling Psychology 18*, 554–561.

Willis, F.N., Jr., and H.K. Hamm. 1980. "The use of interpersonal touch in securing compliance." *Journal of Nonverbal Behavior 1*, 49–55.

▶ 14

Scale for Global Ratings of Responding

The Global Scale presented in this chapter was designed to allow an overall assessment of communication. Like the other scales in the manual it is a 4-point scale. Helpful responses on the Global Scale are those at levels 3.0 and 4.0, while those at levels 1.0 and 2.0 are either hurtful or at least ineffective. *Facilitative responding*, which combines empathy, respect, and warmth at minimally helpful levels, occurs at level 3.0. A Global Scale 3.0 response is strictly helpee-centered and encourages the helpee to self-explore. That is, the helper, basically an anonymous entity at this point in the interaction, primarily listens to the helpee, allowing the helpee to explore the situation. Therefore, problems are not necessarily resolved here, but facts are developed that aid in problem solving later.

There are two primary factors that determine how fast a helper and a helpee can successfully move through the facilitation phase of the helping process. One is the relationship or rapport extant between helper and helpee. If the helper is talking with someone familiar, facilitation may progress very rapidly, and in some cases may not be necessary at all. In cases where there is little or no rapport, extended facilitation will aid in rapport development. The second determining factor is the willingness of the helpee to self-explore. Many other factors, both related and unrelated to the helper, determine the helpee's pace of facilitation: the setting, any past experiences with helpers, the value system of the helpee, the seriousness of the problem, and so on. If the helper respects the pace of the helpee, it increases the probability that the helpee will successfully pass through the facilitation process. (Appendix D includes three scales for rating the helpee's desire for and commitment to the helping relationship.)

Following the facilitation phase, helpers have at their disposal five transi-

TABLE 14-1   Global Scale Summarized

Level	Key word	Results	Helper actions characterized by	Helper's goal
1.0	Harmful	Not helpful	Criticism or inaccuracy	Inappropriate; to gratify self by dominating the helpee
2.0	Ineffective	Not helpful	Unsuitable advice	Inappropriate; stated goal to help; real goal is to be important in the eyes of the helpee
3.0	Facilitative	Helpful	Relationship building	To earn the right to help
4.0	Additive	Helpful	Problem solving	To help

tion and action dimensions (introduced in following chapters) that allow them more involvement in the problem-solving process. Helpers shed anonymity at this point and become active participants in option development and exploration and in problem solving. Timing is the important variable involved in moving into the transition and action phases.

Table 14-1 summarizes the characteristics of communication at each level of the Global Scale that follows. Study this summary before reading further in order to get an idea of the process of helping developed in the model used in this manual. Communication at levels 1.0 and 2.0 includes the styles given in Chapter 6 as examples of damaging and ineffective communication. Level 3.0 involves facilitative responding, the subject of Chapter 15. Level 4.0 will be introduced in this chapter, and studied and used in the following chapters.

GLOBAL SCALE FOR RATING HELPER RESPONSES

Level 1.0   Harmful: Not Helpful

A response in which the helper:

> ignores what the helpee is saying,
> ridicules the helpee's feelings,
> seeks to impose own beliefs and values on the helpee,
> dominates the conversation,
> challenges the accuracy of the helpee's perception, or
> uses problem-solving dimensions in a way that damages the relationship.

Level 2.0   Ineffective: Not Helpful

A response in which the helper:

> communicates a partial awareness of the helpee's surface feelings,
> gives premature or superficial advice,
> responds in a casual, mechanical, or questioning way,
> reflects content but ignores the feelings of the helpee,
> uses problem-solving dimensions in way that impedes the relationship, or
> offers rational excuses for withholding involvement.

Level 3.0   Facilitative: Helpful

A response in which the helper:

> reflects accurately and completely the helpee's surface feelings,
> communicates acceptance of the helpee as a person of worth, and
> clearly communicates caring.

Level 4.0   Additive: Helpful

A response in which the helper:

> demonstrates willingness to help and accurately perceives and responds
> to the helpee's underlying feelings (empathy),
> appropriately uses one or more of the problem-solving dimensions to:
>
> > assist the helpee to move from vagueness to clarity (concreteness),
> >
> > reveal perceptions of the helpee in their entirety (genuineness),
> >
> > share similar experiences (self-disclosure),
> >
> > suggest things the helpee might do (expertise),
> >
> > point out discrepancies in the helpee's words and/or actions (confrontation),
> >
> > talk about present feelings between the helpee and helper (immediacy).

The following illustrates the four levels of responding of the Global Scale. Even though *all* the responses listed under a particular level are not necessarily of that level, most are, and the interaction taken as a whole represents a particular level. The problem situation is described below:

> Arnold Desney is a fourteen-year-old junior high school student who is an only child and comes from a low socioeconomic home. He lives with both parents. Arnold's verbalized problem seems to be under-

socialization, although he is comfortable around adults and children younger than himself. His parents are away from home a lot, and when they are home there is a great deal of arguing in the household. When they are out of town, Arnold stays with his grandmother. Arnold's parents think he is old enough to take care of himself; thus, he is reluctant to discuss school problems with them. At school, Arnold seems to have a severe problem with children his own age. His peers make fun of him, tease him, and ridicule him. No one in his class seems particularly close to him. At home, Arnold plays with two ten-year-old boys. Arnold's teacher notices the rejection by other students in the class and sees Arnold being bullied by his peers.

LEVEL 1.0

"Arnold, please wait, I need to talk to you for a few minutes." The teacher waits until the room is empty and says, "The reason I wanted you to stay is because I would like to talk to you about the incident outside the building this morning."

Arnold	Teacher	Discussion
Oh, you saw that, huh?	Did I ever! You know I thought to myself, Arnold is out there getting into trouble again. I'll bet he's starting a fight. Then I thought about how my children used to fight when they were your age and then I thought that maybe there was nothing to it. But somehow I get the idea that in your case it's different. After all, my children were always big for their ages and could protect themselves pretty well against all the kids in school. I was worried that maybe you would hurt one of them.	This response is Level 1 because it is dominating the interaction. Arnold did not request the meeting, much less a review of the teacher's family history. This kind of interaction is confusing to the helpee. He is thinking, "Why is she sticking her nose in?"
Those guys are really bullies. They pick on everybody.	Bullies pick on people who let themselves get picked on.	This response is ridiculing and thus hurtful. The helpee is thinking, "You just don't understand."

LEVEL 1.0 *Continued*

Arnold	Teacher	Discussion
Yeah, but they were ganging up on me. One of them gets behind me, the other one gets in front of me and they play jokes on me; they kick me. There's two of them and one of me.	Are you sure you aren't making it worse than it really is?	This response challenges the accuracy of the helpee's perception of his own situation and the teacher thinks maybe it is not so bad. This is analogous to your saying to your friend, "I have a stomachache," and the friend replies, "No, you don't."
You just saw them this one day. It's happened lots of times. Today was nothing compared to sometimes.	There was a rumor that your family was going to move next year. Is that true?	This response ignores what the helpee has said. Many times, ignoring takes the form of changing the subject. Usually not done intentionally, the negative effect is almost always felt by the helpee.
No, we're not moving. I'll have to put up with them again next year.	If I were you, I would stay away from them, even if I had to change my route going home.	This response seeks to impose the helper's beliefs and values onto the helpee. It is irrational to expect that what is right for one person is necessarily right for another person; yet this response has that flavor. It fails to allow for individuality by exploring what is possible for the helpee.
They would think that I was afraid of them if I did that.	What you need is to be a little more afraid, Arnold. Your attitude provokes others to bully you.	This response uses the dimension of confrontation inappropriately. It is pointing out a deficit in a way that will surely be perceived as punishing by the helpee.

O.K., Can I go now?

LEVEL 2.0

"Arnold, please wait, I need to talk to you for a few minutes." The teacher waits until the room is empty and says, "The reason I wanted you to stay is because I would like to talk to you about the incident outside the building this morning."

Arnold	Teacher	Discussion
Oh, you saw that, huh?	Were you scared?	This response picks up partially on the helpee's surface feelings. There is much more that could have been communicated. Also the question gives the response a tentative flavor. There is enough information from the observation of the incident to make an affirmative statement of surface feelings.
I was scared okay, but what really bothers me is that all the other kids just laughed.	Many children are insensitive to others. You'll just have to grin and bear it.	The first response is a casual, general response that has virtually no personal meaning. Instead of tuning in to where the helpee is, this helper is generalizing. The second sentence, of course, is a cliché that is very mechanical and impersonal. Statistics do not matter at this point in the helping relationship. The key is to establish a personal relationship, not to relate the helpee's concerns to others in a general way.
Yeah, but it really makes me feel bad. I wish somebody would help me out.	You wish someone would help you out?	This response picks up on a part of the content and ignores the feelings. This type of response tends to direct the interaction by choosing only part of the content to reflect instead of communicating completely, thus leaving the direction open to the helpee.

LEVEL 2.0 *Continued*

Arnold	Teacher	Discussion
Yeah, well I think I need some help. I don't know if you know it or not but those boys have been picking on me all year. They slip up behind me, play jokes on me . . .	If all that is true, I think what you should do is report them to the principal.	This response represents premature use of the action dimensions. The helper is giving advice that the helpee has probably already considered. After all, advice off the top of your head is probably something that the helpee has already considered. For some reason, this is not an option for him. It is more important to explore with the helpee what he considers to be his options before offering such advice.
I would never do that. They would really get me then! I could never go around them any more.	Well, Arnold, I can remember when I was your age that's the way I handled tough situations at school. The principal seemed to appreciate the information.	This response is considered inappropriate use of the self-disclosure dimension. The helpee has already rejected this strategy for problem solving, yet the helper seems to be trying, through self-disclosure, to convince the helpee that he is wrong.
I still don't think that I want to tell the principal.	I'm sorry, Arnold, but that's about all I can offer. I don't want to get involved personally in this matter since the other boys are also in my class, and I have to try to get along with as many students as possible.	This response is level 2.0 since the helper has given a rational excuse for declining to enter the helper relationship.
O.K., can I go now?		

LEVEL 3.0

"Arnold, please wait. I need to talk with you for a few minutes." The teacher waits until the room is empty before continuing.

Arnold	Teacher	Discussion
	I overheard some conversation between you and a couple of other guys outside the building this morning and I wondered if that was anything that would be worthwhile to talk about?	This is level 3.0 response, openness to involvement, and it leaves further interaction as a helpee decision. The teacher simply communicates concern for the helpee and leaves it there.
Well, I really don't know what you could do about it. Those guys have been picking on me all year—since school started this year—and I haven't been able to do anything about it.	That must be a pretty frustrating thing to put up with. I don't know for sure if there is anything I can do about it, but I certainly hope that things change, and maybe the way to begin would be just talking about it. I would be glad to listen.	This response is rated level 3.0 because the helper communicates the surface feelings and is open to involvement.
Yeah, I don't mind talking about it, because it's gotten to the point that if things don't change, then something's just gotta give because, like I say, it's been going on all year, and it seems like the last couple of weeks it's gotten worse.	It's something that has just kind of been building up, and right now it's to the point where you're not sure if you are going to be able to put up with it any longer. You're at the end of your rope.	Level 3.0. This response encourages further helpee self-exploration.
Yeah, that's right. You see, they always pick the time to pull a practical joke on me when there are other kids around. The other kids always laugh.	So, that makes it embarrassing on top of just being pretty hard to take.	Level 3.0. The helper is doing neither more nor less than listening and communicating that he or she heard and is trying to understand.
Oh, it's really, really embarrassing. I want to just—you know—I just want to run and hide somewhere.	Just disappear and not be seen.	Level 3.0. The helper is staying with the helpee in his exploration.

LEVEL 3.0   *Continued*

Arnold	Teacher	Discussion
I get up in the morning and I don't want to come to school. I just hate walking down the hall because those guys—you know—they usually just slip up behind me when I'm not looking.	So that is spoiling the whole thing. They're interfering with more than just your time here at school, but it's something you kind of live with all during the day, even when you're not around here. That sucks.	Level 3.0. Facilitative.
That's right and—you know—the kids at school don't want to associate with me and I guess they figure if they associate with me then those guys will probably pull tricks on them, too. So most kids really just don't want to be friends with me.	So, they deal with it by leaving—by not having anything to do with you and that leaves you pretty lonely, I guess.	Level 3.0. Facilitative.
Yeah, it is lonely. It *is* lonely at school. Now, I have friends at home who don't go to my school because they're younger than I am, but boy, at school it really does get lonely. I usually wind up having lunch by myself. I usually go home by myself after school.	So, around here you're just pretty much isolated from all the other kids. You do, though, have friends that you see around home.	Level 3.0. Facilitative. Notice that through good listening the helpee feels comfortable self-exploring and becoming more and more personally relevant.
Yes. They are both ten years old, but they're the best friends I have.	That gives you someone to play with when you're home. It's really nice to have other people in your life whom you get along with, that you can do things with.	Level 3.0. Facilitative.

Arnold	Teacher	Discussion
Well, it's all I have right now. You know, I really don't have any friends at school and these people, these kids at home are neighbors and they're always around and we usually get together most every day after school.	And that is a pretty good thing, at least as far as it goes. That kind of takes care of after school for having things to do.	Level 3.0. Facilitative.
But I would really like to have some friends at school. It's a matter of just kind of being embarrassed, you know, when you're kind of made fun of you want to just go hide rather than try to be friends with the kids. That's why I just kind of stay to myself.	You'd rather just stay out of everyone's way than be given more attention and just end up being embarrassed because of it.	Level 3.0. Facilitative.
That's right. You know, the less attention I attract the better because it seems like it never works out.	At least it isn't working out right now.	Level 3.0. Facilitative.
Uh huh.	You'd like for things to be different now.	Level 3.0. Facilitative.
Well yeah, if I could start over again.	If you could start over, then you could do things differently and they might work out better for you.	Level 3.0. Facilitative.
Before the kids got the bad impression of me I think I could have made some friends.	But the way it looks now, they've kind of got an idea about what you're like and as you see it, there's no way to change their bad impression of you.	Level 3.0. Facilitative.

LEVEL 3.0 *Continued*

Arnold	Teacher	Discussion
Let's just put it this way, I haven't been able to . . . I don't know what to do. I just know that something's got to give.	It can't go on like this very much longer.	The helper has at this point helped the student move to a point of discussing some of the action strategies that are available to him. By listening, the helper has established rapport with the helpee and also has a better idea of the helpee's life situation.
That's right.		

LEVEL 4.0

The bell has rung and the students are leaving the class. The teacher moves toward Arnold and says: "Arnold, I need to see you for a minute if you have time." They wait until the other students leave.

Arnold	Teacher	Discussion
	I saw what happened outside the building this morning. It looked pretty unpleasant for you. I wondered if it really was.	This response is a global level 3.0 and is an openness to involvement with the helpee. The helpee has the decision of whether or not to talk with the teacher.
Yes, it was bad, but I don't know what I can do about it. I tried to ignore them but the last couple of weeks it's been worse and I can't ignore it any more.	This is something that has been going on for a while and it looks like it's not going away by itself. It must be pretty unpleasant for you at school.	Level 3.0. Facilitative.
It's gotten to be a terrible problem for me. It's more than just what happened this morning.	Sounds like it is pretty important to you and if you want to talk about it I'd be glad to listen. If there's any way I can help you with it, I'll be glad to.	This is a global level 4.0 response that involves a commitment on the part of the helper. This goes beyond an openness for involvement and actually makes a commitment for involvement with the helpee.

Arnold	Teacher	Discussion
Well, I appreciate the offer to help. One of the worst things is that they always pick a time when other kids are around. Then everybody always laughs. I want to just run and hide.	That must be terribly embarrassing for you. It sounds like you're pretty helpless to do anything about this.	Level 4.0. This response accurately hits on the underlying feelings of helplessness.
I'm really at the end of my rope. I don't have any friends here and the future doesn't look any brighter.	You've tried some things to solve the problem but so far nothing has worked.	This is a global level 4.0 concreteness response. The helper is attempting to elicit specificity from the helpee. This kind of response will usually elicit information concerning what the helpee has tried up to this point.
I tried to ignore them, but that hasn't worked. Also, I've tried to be friendly to some of the kids, but they don't seem to want to associate with me. I'll try anything to solve this problem.	I've noticed some things that might be affecting the way people react to you, Arnold. I think maybe you are sending some messages to the other kids that you don't really mean to send.	This is the beginning of helper genuineness. It is continued in the next helper response.
I'm not following you.	Well, sometimes at lunch I notice that you go out of your way to sit by yourself. The other kids *may* think that you're really a snob and don't want to associate with them. I think you have a lot going for you and a lot you can offer to the other kids.	This is a global level 4.0 genuineness response. The helper is communicating his or her feelings about the helpee, both positive and negative.
The reason I try to stay away from the other kids is because I'm embarrassed to be around them.	I can remember moving to a new town when I was in school. Since it was to a different part of the country the kids used to make fun of the way I talked. I can remember the embarrassment I felt every time I opened my mouth. My teacher helped me get over that.	This is a global level 4.0 self-disclosure response. The helper shares personal information that relates to the helpee's problem.

LEVEL 4.0 *Continued*

Arnold	Teacher	Discussion
Really! Well I guess you know how it feels, then. Do you have any ideas about what I could do?	I think a start might be to look at some of the little things that you are doing which may be turning the other kids off. Maybe we could start with lunch and just try doing some things differently at lunchtime.	This is a global level 4.0 expertise response. The helper has made a suggestion after hearing the things that Arnold has tried for himself. If this course of action is followed, there will be considerable discussion concerning *how* the changes will be implemented, keeping in mind what is possible for the helpee.
Well, I don't know if I could.	You said a few minutes ago you would try anything; now you're about to back off from taking a risk. I won't push you into anything that's going to be too threatening for you.	This is a global level 4.0 confrontation response. The helper points out the discrepancy here in order to encourage the helpee to follow through on an action strategy.
I guess at this point I don't have much to lose since I don't have any friends here now.	I'm really happy you're going to work on this problem. Knowing you as I do, I don't have any doubt that things are going to be better. The changes might be slow at first, but the important thing is that you stick with the plan.	This is a global level 4.0 genuineness response. The helper again has taken a stand concerning his or her faith in Arnold. Genuineness takes form in the expression of the helper's own feelings about the helpee.
I really appreciate what you're doing for me. My parents don't understand and since I don't have many friends, I was really desperate.	Thank you for the compliment. I *am* interested in helping you, and it makes it worthwhile to know that you really appreciate it.	This response is a global 4.0 immediacy response. The helpee has brought up the subject of the relationship between the two of them and the helper responded accordingly.

At this point in the helping relationship, the helper and helpee can begin an action plan. There are many ways to do this, and aspects of many different theories of helping can be incorporated into the plan. Some of these strategies, and references to others, will be discussed in Chapter 21, Strategies for Change—Problem Solving.

EXERCISE 14-1 Rating Helper Responses on the Global Scale

After carefully studying the levels of the Global Scale, rate the helper responses in Helpee Situation 1. Write the rating number in the blank to the left of the response number. If you rate any response at 3.5 or 4.0, underline the portion that is additive, that is, goes beyond facilitative responding.

> *Behavioral objective: The trainee will be able to rate 75 percent of the responses correctly (within 0.5 of the rating shown in the Answer Key is considered accurate).*

Helpee Situation 1

Teacher to teacher: "Talk about a shock! In my last job I had total freedom in the classroom. Now the principal insists on knowing every move we make."

Helper Responses

____ 1. "You resent his method of supervision."
____ 2. "Being treated like that makes you mad. When you aren't given credit for being able to handle the class by yourself, it really is a put-down."
____ 3. "Why don't you get a petition together and send it to the school board?"
____ 4. "What is it he watches you do?"
____ 5. "If you think this is bad, you should have been here before he came."
____ 6. "He will get off your back if you insist on it. You just haven't been forceful enough."
____ 7. "It's a real put-down when people don't treat you like a professional."

Helpee Situation 2

Student to teacher: "My feeling is that I am not as smart as the other kids in class. That's why I'm not doing very well."

Continued

EXERCISE 14-1 *Continued*

Helper Responses

_____ **8.** "We are here to talk about your grades, not your excuses."

_____ **9.** "You seem pretty sure that your ability to do well is not as great as the other kids'."

_____ **10.** "You seem concerned by the fact you are not doing well in class."

_____ **11.** "I think if you hang in there, your grades will improve."

Helpee Situation 3

Teacher to teacher: "We'd be better off without those school psychologists! I sent one of my problem students up there for discipline last week, and she's been worse since she got back. Now I have reason to think the psychologist told her I'm just a poor teacher."

Helper Responses

_____ **12.** "You're angry and a little suspicious about the psychologists. As far as you can tell, they aren't doing much of a job."

_____ **13.** "You're paranoid."

_____ **14.** "You feel that all they do is sit up there in the office while we put up with the kids all day."

_____ **15.** "Why don't you go talk to her about it?"

_____ **16.** "You think we should just get rid of the psychologists."

_____ **17.** "You felt a little unsure about how to handle the situation yourself, so you sent her upstairs. That didn't help either, and now you're stuck with a bigger problem. You're asking yourself 'What do I do now?'"

Helpee Situation 4

Student to student: "Since I took that part-time job, I've gotten behind in school. I don't know how I will catch up."

Helper Responses

_____ **18.** "What courses are you taking?"

_____ **19.** "I know what you mean. The same thing happened to me last year."

_____ **20.** "It's discouraging when you get in such a bind and can't see any way out."

_____ **21.** "When I get behind I make it a point to study in the library. That way I get more done."

_____ **22.** "You feel frustrated because you can't seem to get caught up."

EXERCISE 14-2 Global Responding

Behavioral objective: The trainee will be able to write helper responses at level 3.0 on the Global Scale.

Read each helpee situation and try to understand where the helpee is in terms of affect and content. Formulate your response and write it down as quickly as possible in order to retain the conversational style. Attempt to match predicates as much as possible. Check your response against the criteria of a level 3.0 response on the Global Scale. If your response is not at least a level 3.0, rework it to meet level 3.0 criteria.

Helpee Situations

Black student to teacher: "Those counselors seem to always talk to white students. They never talk to me and I really need some help with my plans for college. I heard Mr. Moore say, 'You people who need financial aid for college better come and see me.' I think he is prejudiced against blacks."

RESPONSE _____

_____

Teacher to teacher: "What do you think about a parent who calls about twice a week? We want our parents to be concerned, but this family seems to be going overboard."

RESPONSE _____

_____

High school student to teacher: "What do you think is a good time to be in on the weekends? I think my parents are unreasonable."

RESPONSE _____

_____

Teacher to teacher: "Our new neighbors are a lot of fun, but they don't think they can socialize without drinking. I'm afraid that it's a bad influence on our children."

RESPONSE _____

_____

Student to student: "My parents are paranoid like you wouldn't believe! They stop just short of smelling my breath every time I come in at night."

RESPONSE _____

_____

Continued

EXERCISE 14-2 *Continued*

Student to student: "I like Tom, and we have fun together, but I never know how he feels. He just keeps everything to himself."

RESPONSE _____

_____

Teacher to teacher: "There seems to be a morale problem here at school. No one seems friendly any more."

RESPONSE _____

_____

Student to teacher: "I don't want to complain, but everything we have done in this class has been a waste of time. Is there any way to make it a little more challenging?"

RESPONSE _____

_____

Student to teacher: "I want to make up my own mind about college, but my parents insist on telling me what I should do!"

RESPONSE _____

_____

Student to student: "Do you think I should try to work part-time after school to make spending money for my car? My parents are against it, but I know I could keep up with my schoolwork and have a part-time job."

RESPONSE _____

_____

Answer Key for Exercise 14-1

Helpee Situation 1   *Helpee Situation 2*

1. 3.0   **8.** 1.0
2. 3.5   **9.** 2.0
3. 2.0   **10.** 3.5
4. 1.5   **11.** 2.0
5. 1.0
6. 1.0
7. 3.0

Helpee Situation 3   *Helpee Situation 4*

12. 3.0   **18.** 1.0
13. 1.0   **19.** 1.5
14. 2.5   **20.** 3.0
15. 2.0   **21.** 2.0
16. 2.0   **22.** 3.0
17. 3.5

▶ 15

Facilitative Responding

Facilitative responding during the early stages of a helping relationship allows helpees to be comfortable being themselves and revealing themselves to the helper. The following points review what facilitative responding is and does, and summarizes the major reasons why it is effective.

1. A facilitative response is one in which the helper verbally and nonverbally communicates that he or she has heard what the helpee has said and is attempting to understand how the helpee feels.
2. The necessary components of a facilitative response are: (1) empathy—reflecting accurately and fully the helpee's surface feelings; (2) respect—communicating acceptance of the helpee as a person of worth; and (3) warmth—showing attentiveness and caring through appropriate nonverbal behaviors.
3. A facilitative response restates the helpee's statement, communicating its content and affect with accuracy and equal intensity. Nothing is added to what the helpee has said, nor is anything left out.
4. Facilitative responding begins with careful listening. But merely listening and restating the message is not sufficient. It is equally essential to read the helpee's nonverbal messages, to send appropriate nonverbal messages while listening, to synthesize the communication received from the helpee, and to make mental notes of important items or hunches for possible future use. The complexity of these tasks demands the most intense, conscious involvement and participation of which the helper is capable.
5. Facilitative responding provides a nonthreatening atmosphere in which the helpee feels accepted and free to express him- or herself in any manner. In this atmosphere a relationship of mutual trust and caring can develop between helper and helpee. This relationship is referred to as a

"base relationship" because it provides a foundation on which to build meaningful dialogue on significant personal matters.

6. Facilitative responding defines the helper's role. The helper knows what is effective and thereby what is ineffective. He or she knows that it is best to avoid inappropriate or premature behaviors such as judging, advising, imposing, criticizing, confronting, dominating, ridiculing, or belittling.

7. Facilitative responses assist the helpee in getting a complete and accurate picture of him- or herself. Just as a mirror reflects our physical self, a facilitative response reflects the helpee's psychic self, allowing the helpee to see things that usually remain hidden.

   When the helpee's statements are reflected back, which is what an empathic response does, views become more clear in his or her own minds and he or she can test the validity of perceptions, memories, and judgments. The helpee asks him- or herself, "Is that really true? Really how I feel? Really what I believe?" He or she may discover omissions within his or her statements or contradictions in what he or she has said or believes. The helpee may decide that some of his or her assumptions or expectations are unrealistic, while others may be quite appropriate. Facilitative responding gives the helpee an opportunity to correct misstatements and to clarify matters not sufficiently explained to the helper. The experience of self-exploration leads to better and more complete understanding of the situation and of self, both necessary prerequisites to growth and problem solving.

8. Most of us rarely feel we are really understood by others. (How often can we be sure that we are talking to someone who is really listening?) Facilitative responding is a way of demonstrating to other people that they have your full attention; it is one of the greatest compliments you can give.

LANGUAGE DISTORTION

As a helper you need to be aware of the impact of the language used by both you and the helpee in facilitative interactions. We are not speaking here of your avoiding profanity and clichés (although you should certainly be cautious with these), but about the structure of the language itself. Many times a helper will nominalize a response, or a helpee will consciously or unconsciously generalize the meaning of a statement or delete a portion of it. Learning how to identify and correct such transformations will improve your ability to understand what the helpee is really saying and to respond in a more helpful way.

Nominalization is the transformation of a verb (action word) into a noun (event word). When the vital action of an experience is changed to a passive unmoving event, much of the impact of the communication is lost. For example, an emotional feeling expression would be: "You are feeling angry and afraid of what you might do." A nominalization of his expression might be: "You have some anger and fear about the situation." The affective energy becomes neutralized and almost static. Positive words can also be nominalized. "You had a lot of pleasure and happiness with them," is a less dynamic way of saying, "You seem pleased and happy with them." The active verbs that express most fully the vitality of the experience have been changed to the passive nouns that set you (and the helpee) apart from your real feelings.

Generalization hides the richness and detail found in the specific statement. The specific statement of a painful experience becomes one of general misery. The helpee is generalizing when "Tom (or Sue) doesn't like me," becomes "Men (or women) don't like me," which becomes "Nobody likes me." Generalization words are universal qualifiers like *all, each, every,* and *any* and such negative qualifiers as *never, nowhere, none, no one, nothing,* and *nobody.* These sets of words are not specific and do not contribute to effective communication when used without further explanation.

Deletion means that portions of the original experience have been omitted. This prevents full expression of the underlying meaning. The sentences are incomplete because the full explanation of the communication has been left out. By "reading between the lines" the helper can often supply the missing data. When a helpee says, "I don't know what to do," the helper knows the helpee is in a stressful situation but wonders: *do* about what?, *do* to whom?, *do* when or where? By responding, "You seem upset and confused about what to do now to help yourself make some good decisions," the helper tries to improve the communication with some reasonable guesses. These guesses must be meaningful to the helpee, however, who verifies through feedback that they are. By being alert to communication distortions like these, helpers can respond more accurately and can conceptualize the helpee's problem more rapidly.

NONFACILITATIVE VERSUS FACILITATIVE RESPONDING

Behavioral objective: The trainee will recognize specific hazards in responding without the facilitative conditions or with premature use of the action dimensions, and will understand the advantages of responding facilitatively.

The two dialogues below illustrate two different ways of responding to the same helpee situation. The first dialogue exemplifies the helper responding in nonfacilitative ways; the second shows the helper responding in the manner of the helping model.

Read both dialogues carefully and study the discussion of them. In both dialogues, which concern the same helpee and problem, the helper is a teacher who knows the helpee. The helpee is a potential high school dropout.

DIALOGUE 1: NONFACILITATIVE HELPER

Dana (helpee)	Pat (helper)	Discussion
Hi, Pat!	Hi! Well, school starts tomorrow. Ready for it?	Regular small talk. So far, so good.
No way! Ready to forget about it, is all. High school is a waste of time. I got better things to do.	Oh, sure. Like you got a big job waiting for you as a TV star. Or maybe you know you're going to win the lottery.	Sarcasm is *always* insensitive. Here it tramples on clues that the helpee needs to talk about something.
You can laugh, but the fact is, I got a job; and the money will be big—really big—soon enough.	Yeah, all kinds of jobs for people with no education. I saw your last job. After work your shoes were so greasy you couldn't stand up. If this is another one of those, you'll wish you were back in school.	More harsh sarcasm (which many people mistakenly think is humorous because TV sitcoms give it a laugh track). Closes with the cheap advice of a Verbal Villain "Swami."
This is a job where I dress good. It's with some big-time people.	Like who? Or can't you say? Because it's illegal? Drug deals? Is that it? Huh?	The conversation becomes very competitive as the Verbal Villain "Detective" arrives.
Well, maybe there is some risk in it, but look— what else can a person like me do, when my grades all the way up to now are so bad because I never tried? So, I gotta do what I gotta do. It's all there is for somebody like me.	Look, you oughta go to school tomorrow, get started, then talk to the career counselor about a real career. You got the brains to do about anything. You'd be crazy to waste yourself on the streets.	First the Verbal Villain "Drill Sergeant" gives orders, then the "Florist" says a few nice things. The real problem is that Pat ignores Dana's sense of hopelessness, missing an opportunity to help.
Wrong! Going down a dead-end street is the crazy thing. Like working for minimum. Money is all that counts, so get it any way you can.	What you say, how you say it, and especially what you *don't* say, tells me the whole story. So, I've got you figured out. But I understand, because I've been through it all myself.	The conversation has become a contest between Pat and Dana—no understanding, just conflict.

DIALOGUE 1 *Continued*

Dana (helpee)	Pat (helper)	Discussion
Sure you have. Except both your parents work, and my one parent just got laid off from her job. You have one brother; I have two brothers and three sisters. You understand perfectly, 'cause we're *exactly* alike.	I know your life can't get better by doing something stupid.	Is this Dana's desperate cry for help? Maybe. If so, it was lost on Pat who was defensive and combative instead of seeking to understand Dana.
Now you're calling me "stupid." Thanks a lot, *former friend*. Now you're my newest stranger. See you around, *never*!	Hey, wait . . . uh, goodbye.	Opportunity lost.

DIALOGUE 2: FACILITATIVE HELPER

Dana (helpee)	Pat (helper)	Discussion
Hi, Pat!	Hi! Well, school starts tomorrow. Ready for it?	*Small talk* is valuable because it can lead to *important talk*.
No way! Ready to forget about it, is all. High school is a waste of time. I got better things to do.	Wow, you said a mouth-ful there! If I hear you right, you're sick of school, but are you actually planning to do something else?	Reflects the feeling about school and seeks to clarify the remark about "better things to do."
You better believe it, I am. I'm through with school and moving on to better things.	So . . . you have a *definite* plan for what you're going to do? A job or something?	A routine question for clarification. In this context, not demanding or too personal, like the "Detective."
Sure, a job. A *good* job. With some big-time people.	Hey, that must be exciting for you. A good job is hard to get, especially at our age. I'm curious, you know, about what . . . or maybe I shouldn't ask.	Reflects content and feelings, showing that the helpee has been heard accurately, with the effect of encourag-ing Dana to say more. Politely says it's okay if you don't want to talk about it.

Dana (helpee)	Pat (helper)	Discussion
Well, you can ask, but I can't tell. Not exactly, that is, well, *nothing* actually, except that I could be making some *very big* money in quite a short period of time. So, it would be worth the risk.	When the word "risk" comes into a conversation it sort of stands out like it's painted red, so naturally, because you're my friend, it makes me a little uneasy. Is this "risk" like possibly hazardous to your health, or something?	Reaffirms friendship; shows concern, even as it shows interest in knowing more.
Oh, maybe. I *hope* not. But, even so, sometimes a person's gotta do what they gotta do, know what I mean? You know, like for me, with my grades all the way up to now being so bad because I never tried, maybe this is the only chance I'll ever have to make some good money. So I have to go for it even if . . .	So you're pretty sure you're on the right track. And yet, after you said "even if" you were real quiet all of a sudden, like your thoughts got super heavy. Maybe I'm way off base saying this, but it makes me wonder if there is something about your plan, or that job, that doesn't seem good to you.	Reflects the surface feelings, and then suggests that Dana's underlying feelings may be a little different than the surface feelings. Leaves it up to Dana to decide whether to talk about those feelings.
Okay, okay! So maybe I'm a little bit scared. You would be, too! It's all going to be new. But I'm trapped. If I thought I could make it at school, I would, but it's too late. I'm a year behind for my age, even if I am as smart as anybody over there, which the counselor told me I am.	Maybe the plan is not so good, but that's not all there is to it. There have been some frustrations at school, for a long time. Some options *seem* closed to you now, even though you have a *lot* of natural ability, as we know.	As suspected, Dana has other things to talk about, and wants to. Pat's responses continue to be facilitative. They are supportive, show careful listening, do not offer opinions, and have a basis for affirmation (in contrast a "Florist's" cheap flattery).
Yeah, college could be easy for me, the counselor said, except I can't read for nothing, because I never have. All brains and no education, no matter that I been in schools all my life.	I guess a college education looks good to you, but doing it seems impossible. You feel cheated out of it, maybe—sort of bitter about not being prepared to go.	Again, reflects content and feeling. This always assists the helper to understand the helpee accurately.

DIALOGUE 2 *Continued*

Dana (helpee)	Pat (helper)	Discussion
Right all the way. But it's my fault. I'm one of the Smart Stupid People. The brains to power through school like a Corvette, too air-headed to do it. I could kick myself. Brains enough to be a doctor, the counselor told me. Grades enough to be a dropout. So what am I gonna do?	Maybe you've thought of this, but I'll suggest it anyway. There is evening high school, where all the students are older. And they have a lot of courses to help people catch up on what they missed. Especially reading skills. A lot of people have laid back in their early years, and get caught up later.	The suggestion is offered respectfully.
Yeah, I know. But it would mean giving up an opportunity.	Giving up the opportunity that you have mixed feelings about, and the opportunity that makes you at least a little bit scared. But gaining the chance to use those doctor's brains of yours for something else, whatever it might be.	Has not told Dana what to do, but by reflecting the surface feelings at the beginning, and the perceived underlying feelings along the way, makes it easy for Dana to talk about the "real" issues.
That's a lot to think about. Good stuff. Maybe I'll go over to school tomorrow and talk to that counselor again.	That seems real smart to me. Could we meet over at Burger World for a bite, say 3:30 tomorrow?	Affirms Dana's plan. Request to get together the next day shows continuing interest and provides a low key measure of accountability for Dana to go talk with the counselor.

IDIOSYNCRATIC CREDIT

One of the fundamental precepts of this communication model is that it helps establish a base relationship through facilitative communication before implementing action dimensions. An exception to this rule, however, involves helpers who have what we call "idiosyncratic credit" with the helpee.

Idiosyncratic credit means that the helpee grants privileges to a helper because of who or what the helper is. This is desirable in that one may be able to give advice more quickly, but on the other hand, if the client is not ready to move quickly, idiosyncratic credit may lead to problems. This is partly why many helpees do not adhere to treatments.

There are four major reasons why idiosyncratic credit may be given to a particular helper:

1. *Degrees, title, vocation.* Consider "labels" such as doctor, president, judge, minister, attorney, coach, teacher-of-the-year, champion, palm reader. Often, whether or not the persons who carry these labels have the expertise they are credited with, they are respected by different individuals to a greater or lesser degree. Therefore, they are able to influence, to become "action-oriented" with the individual whose respect they have.
2. *Common experience.* That one gives credibility to and acts upon the suggestions of persons whose background is similar to one's own is well established and partially accounts for the success of self-help groups such as Alcoholics Anonymous and Synanon.
3. *Association.* You get more respect as an individual if you are a member of a team or organization that is respected. As a member of the education profession you get "credit" for extensive expertise—you are granted privileges that a person outside the profession does not have.
4. *Reputation.* Some individuals, because of their perceptual skills and good sense, become known as persons whose advice is worth taking. They discover, perhaps to their own surprise, that others seek them out for their opinions. Some popular newspaper columnists, because of their acceptance by a wide readership, are often successful in giving advice abruptly and pointedly. If you were able to give the same advice in a similar situation, your credibility might be questioned. Thus, a response which would be level 2.0 from one person can have a level 4.0 impact on a helpee when given by a person whose advice is deemed reputable. Idiosyncratic credits often mean the difference between a level 2.0 response and a level 4.0 response.

Even though the base relationship may be acknowledged initially, ultimately, it must be *earned*. For example, a patient might visit the office of Alice Johnson on the strength of her DMD degree. The patient will grant Dr. Johnson the authority *once* to apply her professional expertise—to drill or extract at her judgment—as a result of her idiosyncratic credit. But the patient will not likely return to Dr. Johnson unless the services are satisfactory. Dr. Johnson must *earn* future opportunities to help.

EXERCISE 15-1 Responding with Facilitation

Behavioral objective: The trainee will be able to write facilitative helper responses in a natural style at level 3.0 or above on the Global Scale.

Write facilitative responses to the helpee's statements in the following stimulus situations. Remember that not only the content but also the affect of the helpee's statement must be included in the response.

Helpee Situation 1

Student to teacher: "Everybody in my crowd is applying to business schools for next year, but I don't know if I'm smart enough to make it in business."

HELPER RESPONSE _____

_____

Helpee Situation 2

Student to teacher: "I've got a term paper to do in English, but things are so noisy around my house I'm having trouble concentrating."

HELPER RESPONSE _____

_____

Helpee Situation 3

Teacher to teacher: "With all the pressure on us to raise SAT scores, coupled with unmotivated students and gobs of paperwork, I'm ready to give it up."

HELPER RESPONSE _____

_____

Helpee Situation 4

Parent to teacher: "I know that I should give Judy more help with her homework, but after working all day and fixing dinner I just don't have the energy. It is really difficult being a single parent."

HELPER RESPONSE _____

_____

Helpee Situation 5

Eighth grader to teacher: "My mom and all my relatives say it's better to have a baby than to get an abortion. Ever since I decided to have my baby, everybody at school is prejudiced against me."

HELPER RESPONSE _____

_____

EXERCISE 15-1 *Continued*

Helpee Situation 6

Student to student: "I really want to be a teacher, but I'm afraid to tell my parents because they both plan for me to be an engineer like them."
HELPER RESPONSE _____

_____

Helpee situation 7

Twelfth grader to teacher: "I'm so excited! I met this great 'hunk' this weekend and I think he really likes me."
HELPER RESPONSE _____

_____

Helpee Situation 8

Tenth grader to teacher: "It seems like everyone who has his own car is popular with the girls. My parents say I can't get a car until I'm a senior."
HELPER RESPONSE _____

_____

THE USE OF QUESTIONS IN THE HELPING RELATIONSHIP

One of the most prevalent forms of communication is the question. We include this section so that educators can evaluate themselves on their use of questions and can learn more appropriate ways to communicate when indicated. First, let us consider when the use of questions is indicated in interpersonal communication.

Appropriate Use of Questions

To Obtain Identification Data or Objective Information
Data about the helpee may involve information required by the board of education or the school. General information forms are frequently completed on all helpees who seek agency assistance. Even though the information may appear to be rather straightforward, some of it might be embarrassing to the helpee. For this reason the suggested method is to have the helpee complete the form as fully as possible before the helper checks it for completeness and accuracy. In many instances open-ended questions that elicit spontaneous helpee self-disclosure may be preferred over direct questions. The latter al-

low helpees time to weigh how they want to answer the question—regardless of accuracy or authenticity—to please the helper.

To Clarify
When the helpee is being vague or evasive, a well placed question may be useful for clarification. For instance, if a helpee is having difficulty describing a feeling, the educator maybe able to suggest the right word. In this way helpers can often test any hypotheses they may have about situations.

To Pinpoint
There are occasions when educators need specific information from the helpee. For example, when teachers are faced with a first aid situation, they need to be very specific in the interaction. Direct questions are usually the best means for obtaining specificity of feedback in this case. Specificity is especially important in defining a problem and in describing a plan of action or steps to be taken in problem solving. (Perceiving and responding with concreteness is discussed in the following chapter.)

Inappropriate Use of Questions

Perhaps the greatest misuse of direct questions is the tendency to rely on them to carry on a conversation. The use of direct questions may have the following deleterious effects on the relationship between a helper and a helpee.

Creating a Dependency Relationship
The use of direct questions by the helper places the helpee in a dependent relationship. The helpee who answers the question depends on the helper for the solution and therefore begins to expect more from the helper and less of himself or herself. This is especially true when the helper gives good advice, because it places the helpee in the position of seeking out other helpers (or returning to the same one) when new problems develop.

Placing the Responsibility for Problem Solving on the Helper
When the helper asks a direct question related to the helpee's problem, the message is that the helper is the expert and will offer a solution once the question is answered. The helper may make the same assumption and may respond to this unspoken agreement even when it is not in the best interest of the helpee—in the sense that it is the helper's solution and the helpee may or may not be able to apply it to the problem.

Reducing Active Involvement of the Helpee
in the Solution of the Problem
Often the greatest harm that occurs from the use of direct questions is the tendency of the helpee to place with the helper the responsibility for the

helpee's behavior resulting from the proffered solution. If the attempt at problem solving is successful, the helpee does not accept credit, and likewise if it is unsuccessful the helpee does not accept "blame." The success of a democratic society depends on people who will assume responsibility for their behavior. The tendency to rely on the expert (to "blame" the expert for the helpee's behavior) is ultimately self-defeating.

Reducing Helpee Self-Exploration
Frequent use of direct questions tends to interfere with in-depth self-exploration by the helpee because the helper has unwittingly accepted this task. When the helper controls the direction of the problem-solving attempt, especially early in the process, the helpee becomes discouraged from volunteering what the helpee thinks is relevant. After a few relevant questions are asked, the helper's questions frequently become hit-or-miss, whereas the helpee's voluntary self-disclosure, if it is not hindered by frequent direct questions, is more likely to be related to the issues the helpee perceives to be important. Once the response set—helper question followed by helpee answer—is established, it becomes difficult to turn over the initiative to the helpee.

Producing Invalid Information
Many direct questions have within them what the questioner wants to hear—preferred answers. Since most helpees want to be liked and respected by their helpers, they try to oblige by "listening between the lines" for what the helper wants to hear. When they give responses in accord with what they think the helper wants to hear, they may communicate information that is not entirely accurate. The helper thus is in a position to make diagnoses based on inaccurate information.

Producing Unrealistic Helpee Expectations
It is important for helpees to have confidence in their helpers, but it is even more important for helpees to develop confidence in themselves. The helper's use of direct questions inadvertently communicates to the helpee that all the helpee has to do to solve the problem is to answer the questions and a solution will follow. By becoming a reactive helpee during the interview phase of problem solving, the helpee does not learn how to assume the proactive role that is necessary if the helpee is to follow through with a program of problem resolution.

Producing Helpee Resentment
Many questions are asked by "helpers" out of curiosity rather than because they have direct bearing on the situation. These probes generally create resentment within the helpees. It is difficult to build an interaction around questions, because it is rare when a helper can ask more than a dozen relevant

questions; therefore the longer the interaction, the more likely that the questions will become progressively more irrelevant.

Facilitative responses give something (empathy, respect, and warmth) to helpees. They provide an atmosphere in which helpees are comfortable being themselves. In contrast, questions demand something from helpees, and therefore may be threatening to them. The helpees may fear that they will be pushed into areas they are not ready to deal with, and respond only superficially or seek to shift the conversation to another topic.

Creating a "Lazy," Inattentive Helper

When helpers feel that they can always ask helpees for clarification of a statement or feeling, they often pay less attention to the helpees and thus miss many cues. In other words, they do not attend fully to the helpees and rely on the helpees to "help them out," thus placing themselves in the role of helpees whom they are supposed to be helping. The extent to which the helper has to ask questions of the helpee is a benchmark of the degree to which the helper is in tune with the helpee or is capable of helping the helpee—the greater the number of questions, the less likelihood that the helper can assist the helpee.

Remember, these nine outcomes are the result of *direct* questions used by the helper. Open-ended questions, on the other hand, usually do not have the same effect because they encourage helpee involvement and self-exploration. Therefore, the potential helper should develop expertise in the use of open-ended questions and statements. Some examples of open-ended questions and statements are the following:

"What kinds of things have you tried?"

"Could you describe some things you have considered doing?"

"I assume you have considered a number of things you could do."

"I assume you have some ideas about the reaction if you tried _____."

"What would you predict would happen if you tried _____?"

"In what other kinds of situations do you find yourself feeling _____?"

"Other teachers must have similar reactions if _____ is so inconsiderate."

▶ 16

Perceiving and Responding with Concreteness

In this chapter you will learn how to use the scale for rating helper statements on the dimension of concreteness described in Chapter 1. As with previous scales, you will learn to discriminate between Harmful/Not Helpful, Helpful, and Very Helpful styles of responding (see Table 16-1).

Concreteness, or specificity of expression, involves the direct and thorough communication of specific feelings and experiences, regardless of their emotional content, by both helper and helpee. During the early stages of helping, concreteness enriches empathy. It also encourages the helpee to attend specifically to problem areas and emotional conflicts. The effective helper focuses attention on helpee statements that are rich in clearcut or specific data. The productive helper responds to these data with clear, concise, detailed statements, thus modeling concreteness. These actions demonstrate to the helpee that the helper is willing and able to discuss feelings and problems in detail. Consequently, the helper's selective attention to specific data, and modeling of specificity in communication, serves to encourage the helpee to clarify his or her own feelings and experiences. These initial steps—to reinforce self-exploration and problem exploration—are critical steps in the helping process.

After a problem has been explored concretely, the helper begins to reinforce the helpee for generalizing about his or her situation or putting it in perspective on a larger scale (lower levels of helpee concreteness). This encourages the helpee to explore more freely and broadly his or her "self" and his or her problems. To understand more fully, the helpee must relate specific concerns to other conscious and heretofore unconscious aspects of his or her life.

The effective helper also obtains additional information from the helpee through the appropriate use of questions.

TABLE 16-1   Concreteness Scale

Harmful/Not Helpful	Minimally Helpful	Very Helpful
Is specific but inaccurate, or premature and hurtful. Leads or allows helpee to deal only with abstract or vague generalities. Uses general/intellectual terms which fail to focus on specific manifestations of helpee concerns. Asks helpee to be more specific without modeling specificity.	Responds to some of helpee's personally relevant material in specific terms. Helper models specificity but accepts abstractions on part of helpee.	Responds to all of helpee's personally relevant feelings and experiences in a specific and thorough manner and actively encourages helpee to clarify vague statements. Assists helpee in identifying additional conflicts, specific options, plans for problem solving or summarizing newly acquired self-knowledge.

OPEN-ENDED AND CLOSE-ENDED QUESTIONS

As we have noted, skilled helpers not only model specificity, but they also solicit it from helpees. A common form of solicitation is asking questions. Questions can be quite productive, particularly when used judiciously and posed with empathy and respect.

Helping professionals often categorize questions as being of an open- or close-ended nature. *Close-ended questions* delimit a topic, ask for specific information, and do not allow the helpee many options in answering. The helpee is usually constrained to respond with a "yes" or "no," or a few words. Such questions are nevertheless quite useful and appropriate in many circumstances. Close-ended questions are a quick and direct way of obtaining information about the helpee. Some examples of close-ended questions are:

"What is your name?"
"Do you need any help with your assignment?"
"Do you have enough textbooks for your students?"
"Are you feeling ill?"

Open-ended questions invite helpees to give their views on topics in a free and unrestricted way. Such questions encourage helpees to speak as much as they would like, using their own words. Open-ended questions encourage self-exploration as well as self-understanding. Some words that are commonly used with these kinds of questions are, "what," "how," and "in what way." A few illustrations of open-ended questions are:

"What would you say are the advantages and disadvantages of dropping out of school?"

"How do you feel about that?"

"In what way do you find me being disrespectful to you?"

"What do you like most about your new friends?"

Perhaps we would do well to also briefly discuss "why" questions. "Why" questions may be useful in gathering information but effective helpers are careful not to overuse them. "Why" questions are practical when you anticipate that the helpee knows the answers and will not be uncomfortable sharing these answers.

For example:

"Why is it best not to drink and drive?"

"Why is basketball your favorite sport?"

However, an over-reliance on such questions can lead the helpee to feel that he or she is being interrogated. "Why" questions often tend to put the helpee on the spot to explain his or her motives, reasons, or goals—when the helpee is unaware of such information, he or she may easily become self-conscious, embarrassed, confused, or ashamed. "Why" questions can also be problematic if the helpee's motives are socially undesirable. In such cases the helper is likely to inadvertently foster lying and deceit on the part of the helpee. The appropriate use of questions is addressed in greater detail in Chapter 15, Facilitative Responding.

The example below is designed to illustrate the foregoing principles.

Mary is an administrator who has been told by several colleagues that she is racially prejudiced. A skilled helper might facilitate her coming to understand the origin of her prejudice and the types of situations where she is likely to act it out. As she explores her biases, she might begin to gain a better perspective. Mary may come to realize that her parents have subtly passed on their prejudices to her. She may also come to see that she has not extended herself openly to people from culturally diverse backgrounds because of her fears of being socially ostracized by her prejudiced friends.

During later stages of helping (action), helpers move back to high levels of concreteness. Helpees are now trying to choose specific alternatives so that they can take corrective action. Helpers assist them in formulating specific goals and means to achieve these goals. As helpers respond with specific alternatives they also reinforce concrete suggestions of helpees. For example, the helper may wish to use Rational-Emotive Therapy concepts (Dryden and Ellis 1988; Ellis and Harper 1975) first to help Mary realize how she continues to make herself anxious by subscribing to the irrational attitude that she desperately needs the absolute approval of her prejudiced friends. Once she is helped to challenge her attitude, she may realize that she had been exaggerating the importance of their *complete* approval. She may then learn to view their disapproval as unfortunate but hardly catastrophic. This type of attitude adjustment would help her become more rational, allow her greater personal autonomy, and expand her freedom of choice. Using role-playing techniques, the helper might then have Mary practice how to be thoughtfully assertive with friends when they make prejudicial remarks. Once she felt minimally confident with her assertive skills, she might be given a homework assignment to assert herself with the prejudiced friend by whom she felt least threatened. She would then be encouraged to continue standing up for her beliefs with persons who might offer greater degrees of disapproval. Hopefully, Mary would learn to represent her views in a respectful yet courageous manner. She might also be encouraged to make more personal contacts with people from culturally diverse backgrounds in her school and community, expecting that as she increased her database of unique individuals she would be less inclined to make unreasonable judgments about populations as a whole.

HELPEE CONCRETENESS

It is also important for the helper to be aware of the concreteness of helpee statements. Communicating with helpees who are vague, abstract, or whose speech is disorganized is difficult. When the helpee shows low levels of specificity, it is especially important for the helper to display high levels of concreteness in order to encourage the helpee to focus on specifics.

ILLUSTRATION OF THE CONCRETENESS SCALE

The helpee situation below illustrates the three levels of the Concreteness Scale. Ratings are based on the criteria of the Concreteness Scale alone. The responses might be rated differently on other dimensions.

In his book, *Black and White Styles in Conflict*, Kochman (1981) points out that blacks and whites use different conceptual frameworks to answer the question, "When does a fight begin?" The helpee situation below deals with this theme. The three levels of the Concreteness Scale are illustrated and discussed.

Amy is a white, female, beginning physical education teacher in a predominantly black, inner city junior high school. Two black male students on opposite softball teams begin to argue loudly over a close play at second base. They are both puffing out their chests, glaring at one another, and making numerous energetic gestures with their hands and arms. No physical contact was made. Amy escorted the two young men to the principal's office. She informed the principal (a black male), that they were "fighting" on the softball diamond and that the "fight" had already begun when the two youths began to get vulgar, loud, and angry. Both students appeared to be surprised and angered by her accusation. They told the principal that they were just "arguing."

Later, while alone with the principal, Amy says, "I don't understand what is happening here. I know what I saw. They were fighting. But, they really seemed surprised when I told you what happened."

Helper Responses

HARMFUL: "You don't seem to know much about black culture."

> The principal's message is certainly specific, but it is also premature and hurtful. The principal knows that new teachers are likely to be anxious and unsure of themselves in some ways. Yet, he doesn't appear to be the least bit concerned about supporting Amy or helping her learn something constructive from this incident. Amy may well learn to be fearful of this authority figure.

NOT HELPFUL: "Adolescence is a period of turmoil and conflict—a search for identity and meaning."

> This response is general and very intellectual. It does not deal with Amy's specific concerns. She will likely see this reply as useless.

NOT HELPFUL: "How do you account for their reaction to what you said?"

> The principal asks an interesting question, soliciting Amy to be more specific. But note that he has not yet responded concretely himself to the personally relevant information she has already given him. She may not feel encouraged to give him *more* data, considering that he didn't seem to process the information already shared.

HELPFUL: "You're confident that you saw a fight so you're puzzled by their reaction to what you said to me."

The principal succinctly states what he views as Amy's primary concerns. His response is relevant and specific. This reply illustrates how high levels of concreteness may serve to sharpen empathic communications.

VERY HELPFUL: "You noticed the young men's behavior and thought they were having a problem with each other. You called it a "fight" and they called it an "argument." Do you think it would help if we define these terms from a cross-cultural point of view?"

The principal's communication is concrete and thorough. It focuses Amy's attention on a topic that he believes will be fruitful. His question invites her to engage in constructive dialogue regarding cultural differences.

VERY HELPFUL: "You did what you thought was right because you felt that the students were out of control. I'm glad you came to me. If we put our heads together I think we'll be able to understand the situation from their perspective. Perhaps we can explore this further. What time would be convenient for you?"

The principal empathizes with Amy in a way that is quite supportive. His communication is very specific, and he assumes a leadership function as he respectfully tries to make plans to solve this problem with her. When they get together, the principal will use high levels of concreteness to help Amy appreciate the different conceptual frameworks that blacks and whites frequently use in defining when a fight begins. He will share with her that whites generally consider "fighting" to have started when violence is imminent (*before* it has actually occurred). The intensity of the anger, the tense gesturing and the verbal insults are signs to whites that a fight has begun and that the situation is out of hand. He will then advise her that blacks usually establish a clear boundary between words and actions. Although blacks would see the above signs as a *possible* prelude to fighting, they would conclude that the students had just been "arguing" up to that point. It is important to understand differences in the two cultures regarding verbal assertion and expression.

EXERCISE 16-1 Perceiving Concreteness

Behavioral objective: The trainee will be able to rate responses on the Concreteness Scale with an average discrepancy of 0.5 or less.

Rate each of the helper responses on the Concreteness Scale using the key below. Place the number (1, 2, or 3) in the blank to the left of the helper response.

Harmful/Not Helpful	Helpful	Very Helpful
1	2	3

Helpee Situation 1

A college freshman at a state university is speaking with her roommate of one semester. The young women have disclosed quite a few intimacies and get along fairly well.

"I'm in a bind. On the one hand, I told my parents that they needn't worry about me getting involved with drugs or alcohol. On the other hand, I made that statement before I'd been here and seen how many kids drink or smoke a little pot. It seems to take the edge off. I've been pretty stressed out lately and it really seems to work for me."

Helper Responses

_____ 1. "When was the last time you spoke with your parents about this?"

_____ 2. "Aren't you a little old to be hung up on what your parents think?"

_____ 3. "You're in a jam. You promised them one thing but you're doing another."

_____ 4. "Conflicts between parents and their offspring are inevitable."

_____ 5. "You don't want to lie to your parents or give them cause to worry, but you want some relief from tension. Tennis, swimming, and reading work pretty well for me. Besides alcohol or pot, what else do you think might work for you?"

Check the Answer Key at the end of the chapter for the correct ratings, and calculate your average discrepancy score by dividing the sum of the individual discrepancy scores by five. Review the ones you missed to learn why they are rated as they are, then proceed to Helpee Situation 2.

Helpee Situation 2

Acculturation has been widely discussed as a unidimensional process, viewing immigrants as adopting host-culture values and behavior

Continued

EXERCISE 16-1 *Continued*

while simultaneously discarding most attributes of their culture of origin (Szapocznik, Kurtines, and Fernandez 1980). However, Rapee (1989) points out that "cultural pluralism" is becoming ever more acceptable, where the healthy norm is defined as one in which immigrants participate in both communities. Szapocznik and his colleagues also note that this is particularly true for second generation youths who directly experience the contrast between familial and educational institutions, where the former transmits the culture-of-origin norms and the latter introduces the host cultural norms. Szapocznik, Scopetta, Kurtines, and Arnalde (1978) also report that immigrants who acculturate unidimensionally experience a higher rate of psychosocial maladjustment. The helpee situation below deals with biculturalism.

You are a sixth grade teacher in Miami, Florida. Carlos, one of your students, was born in Colombia and came to the United States two years ago. You have noticed that whenever others ask him where he is from he gets uncomfortable and replies, "Cuba." One day after school you bring this observation to his attention. After talking for a while, he confides in you, "My grandparents are always telling me to be proud of my roots. They're the ones who make me speak Spanish. But I tell people I'm Cuban because everybody in the United States thinks that if you're from Colombia you and your family must be dealing drugs."

Helper Responses

_____ 6. "Sounds like you're afraid to tell people where you were born because you fear they will hold it against you."

_____ 7. "If you had any courage you'd stand up to others and show them that you're proud of your heritage regardless of what they think."

_____ 8. "What do your parents do for a living?"

_____ 9. "You hide the truth from others because you're afraid of their disapproval. That must be very uncomfortable for you. If you knew a lot of good things about Colombia, would that help you relate to others, and perhaps even your grandparents, better?"

_____ 10. "You know that the Cubans are pretty well accepted around here so you identify yourself with them. You're pretty sure people would put you and your family down if they knew the truth. Could this kind of deception cause you any problems?"

Check the Answer Key at the end of the chapter for the correct ratings, and calculate your average discrepancy score by dividing the sum

EXERCISE 16-1 *Continued*

of the individual discrepancy scores by five. Review the ones you missed to learn why they are rated as they are, then proceed to Helpee Situation 3.

Helpee Situation 3

Dr. Porter is an experienced high school principal. He is speaking with his new assistant principal about one of his teachers, Mrs. Blake. Mrs. Blake did her student teaching in this same school and has been there ever since. For sixteen years she has managed to keep her job despite her gross incompetencies. Dr. Porter says: "For the last three years I've been focusing on the issue of teacher competency. Overall, I think the future is bright for our staff. Unfortunately, there remains one glaring example of my impotency as an administrator—Mrs. Irene Blake. Her methods of discipline are cruel, her lesson plans sketchy, her writing skills are poor, she abuses her sick leave, she is largely uncooperative with her peers, and her rapport with the students and their parents is pathetic. She has shown no willingness to accept help or direction from others and becomes highly defensive when confronted with these problems. I have documented all of my criticisms to the point where her folder is several inches thick. The school board has shut their eyes to my complaints because they're afraid of the union. I'd sleep better if she'd retire, but at this point I'd settle for her being transferred. The union rep assured her, in front of me, that her position on my staff is secure—it looks as though he may be right."

Helper Responses

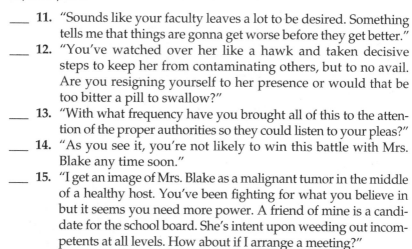

____ 11. "Sounds like your faculty leaves a lot to be desired. Something tells me that things are gonna get worse before they get better."

____ 12. "You've watched over her like a hawk and taken decisive steps to keep her from contaminating others, but to no avail. Are you resigning yourself to her presence or would that be too bitter a pill to swallow?"

____ 13. "With what frequency have you brought all of this to the attention of the proper authorities so they could listen to your pleas?"

____ 14. "As you see it, you're not likely to win this battle with Mrs. Blake any time soon."

____ 15. "I get an image of Mrs. Blake as a malignant tumor in the middle of a healthy host. You've been fighting for what you believe in but it seems you need more power. A friend of mine is a candidate for the school board. She's intent upon weeding out incompetents at all levels. How about if I arrange a meeting?"

Continued

EXERCISE 16-1   *Continued*

Check the Answer Key at the end of the chapter for the correct ratings, and calculate your average discrepancy score by dividing the sum of the individual discrepancy scores by five. Review the ones you missed to learn why they are rated as they are.

EXERCISE 16-2   Responding with Concreteness

Behavioral objective: The trainee will be able to write helper responses in a natural style that is rated as Helpful or Very Helpful on the Concreteness Scale.

Read each helpee situation and try to pinpoint specific and personal concerns in the statements. Formulate your response and write it down as quickly as possible to retain the conversational style. If you have trouble identifying helpee feelings or wording your responses, consult Appendix B, Vocabulary of Affective Adjectives, and Appendix C, Speaking the Helpee's Language with Empathic Leads. Check your response against the criteria of a helpful response on the Concreteness Scale. If your response is not Helpful or Very Helpful, rework it to meet at least the Helpful criteria.

Helpee Situation 1

Don, a college sophomore, is shy and retiring. He is majoring in elementary education and is taking his first field experience with you, a veteran classroom teacher. He says: "If . . . if you're not too busy . . . uhm . . . I'd like a word with you. I don't know what I'm supposed to do. I don't know how this is gonna sound, but I don't . . . I just don't know if I belong here. They tell me that elementary ed is nowhere. My father is a big banker and he's always explaining to me how I can, well, make a lot of money if I switch . . . but this idea keeps rattling around in my brain—kids *like* me, and I like them. I just don't know . . . ."

HELPER RESPONSE _____

_____

Helpee Situation 2

Colin is a young black Jamaican-born male majoring in elementary education. He is speaking with a middle-aged male teacher who supervises him in his field experience. "You know, I love being in America. However, I have trouble understanding the racial prejudice in this country.

EXERCISE 16-2 *Continued*

There is so much prejudice here based on race and skin color. It's difficult to adjust to."

HELPER RESPONSE _____

_____

Helpee Situation 3

You are an elementary school teacher. You have become friends with the school counselor. Both of you genuinely enjoy children and are loyal supporters of children's rights. The counselor says: "Some of these teachers really drive me up a wall. They complain about their 'problem' students to no end, but when we sponsor a workshop on behavior mod or conflict resolution, these same teachers rarely show up."

HELPER RESPONSE _____

_____

Helpee Situation 4

Sharon is a sensitive, bright, and compassionate twenty-year-old college junior majoring in secondary education. She is speaking with her faculty advisor: "I've just received my assignment for student teaching and I can feel my stomach all twisted up in knots already. They've paired me up with Mr. Gumblinski. I had to work with him for field experience and it made me really uptight. He's very authoritarian in his methods and seems to have a rough time motivating the students. They resented his heavy-handed methods and so did I."

HELPER RESPONSE _____

_____

Answer Key for Exercise 16-1

Helpee Situation 1

1. 1 (solicits specificity without modeling it)
2. 1 (specific but premature, hurtful)
3. 2 (specific, relevant)
4. 1 (abstract, overly intellectual)
5. 3 (models and actively solicits specificity, invites her to enumerate possible options)

Continued

Answer Key *Continued*

Helpee Situation 2

6. 2 (specific response to some of the helpee's personally relevant material)
7. 1 (premature and hurtful)
8. 1 (general, fails to focus on helpee's concerns; solicits specificity)
9. 3 (concrete and thorough; tactfully suggests an appropriate action for helpee to consider)
10. 3 (responds to all of the helpee's concerns in a specific and thorough manner; encourages helpee to explore the self-defeating nature of his behavior)

Helpee Situation 3

11. 1 (specific but inaccurate)
12. 3 (models and actively solicits specificity, examination of values)
13. 1 (solicits specificity without modeling it)
14. 2 (clearcut specific)
15. 3 (models and actively solicits specificity, suggests a plan of action)

REFERENCES

Dryden, W., and A. Ellis. 1988. "Rational-emotive therapy." In K.S. Dobson (Ed.), *Handbook of Cognitive-Behavioral Therapies* (pp. 214–272). New York: Guilford Press.

Ellis, A., and R. Harper. 1975. *A New Guide to Rational Living* (Rev. ed.). Hollywood, CA: Wilshire Books.

Kochman, T. 1981. *Black and White Styles in Conflict.* Chicago: The University of Chicago.

Rapee, S. 1989. "A descriptive study of cognitive inaccuracies and acculturation difficulties among Soviet Immigrant Jews." Unpublished doctoral dissertation; Miami Institute of Psychology, Miami, Florida.

Szapocznik, J., W. Kurtines, and T. Fernandez. 1980. "Bicultural involvement and adjustment in Hispanic-American youths." *International Journal of Intercultural Relations, 4,* 353–365.

Szapocznik, J., M. Scopetta, W. Kurtines, and M. Arnalde. 1978. "Theory and measurement of acculturation." *Journal of Psychology 12,* 113–130.

▶ 17

Perceiving and Responding with Genuineness

In this chapter you will find out how to use the scale for rating helper statements on the dimension of genuineness, described in Chapter 1. As with previous scales, you will learn to discriminate between Harmful/Not Helpful, Helpful, and Very Helpful styles of responding.

HELPER GENUINENESS

When you "have it all together" you are unified, integrated, or congruent, that is, genuine. When you are genuine you are being the person you are from moment to moment. More specifically, genuineness refers to the extent to which you are consciously aware of and acceptant of your visceral feelings and accurately match appropriate verbal and nonverbal communications to them. The "appropriate" in the preceding sentence refers to the fact that in this model we are concerned with what might be more accurately labeled as *constructive genuineness*. Thus, people who are integrated mean what they say and, at the deepest levels, say exactly what they feel, keeping in mind that they are trying to be helpful to the helpee.

Rogers and Truax (1967, p. 101) describe this dimension as follows: "Genuineness means that the helper is operating without a front or facade, openly being with the feelings and attitudes that are presently in him. This, of course, requires self-awareness and the ability to communicate such experiences if appropriate. It also means that the helper meets the helpee on a person-to-person basis, as he is being himself and not denying himself."

Egan (1986) elaborates on a number of other characteristics of genuineness. He writes that genuine helpers do not take refuge in their professional roles

because helping is part of their lifestyle. This writer also emphasizes the importance of being spontaneous yet not unrestrained. He notes that effective helpers
are tactful but they do not continually weigh what they are about to say to
helpees. Finally, he discusses the importance of assertiveness, consistency, and
remaining nondefensive when negative feelings are directed at you.

Although genuineness is a complicated concept, we all tend to recognize
it in an intuitive or common sense manner. For example, each of us can
quickly sense from the tone of voice, gestures, or mannerisms of some of the
actors used in TV commercials that they are "playing a role." They are "putting on a facade" in saying things they don't feel. You do not experience the
person; you experience the role.

Whenever we communicate from a state of incongruence between our
feelings and our awareness of these feelings, we tend to send discrepant or
contradictory messages. When the discrepancy is between awareness and
communication we may think in terms of falseness and deceit. When the
incongruence is between visceral experience and awareness we may think in
terms of defensiveness or denial of awareness. In either case, it will be harder
for others to know where they stand with us. Eventually, we may be perceived as being untrustworthy. When we are genuine, we use no facade to
disguise how we feel, and there is no question as to whether or not we are
aware of how we truly feel. We are dependably real.

HELPEE GENUINENESS

It is important for the helper to assess the helpee's level of genuineness. The
helpee who protects himself or herself with facades and hides behind elaborate
roles is difficult to assist. However, the helper who, over a period of time,
consistently offers high levels of the conditions of human nourishment is likely
to increase the genuineness of the helpee. But, when the helper and helpee
retreat to the safety and barrenness of their roles, very little of value can occur.

ILLUSTRATION OF THE GENUINENESS SCALE

The helpee situation below illustrates the three levels of the Genuineness
Scale. Ratings are based on the Genuineness Scale alone. The responses might
be rated differently on other dimensions.

Helpee Situation

Gene is a husky ninth-grader, the oldest of six children. He and his family are
poor and hard-working farmers. Gene attends school in a middle-class neighborhood quite a distance from the farm. Several of the school bullies fre-

TABLE 17-1   Genuineness Scale

Harmful/Not Helpful	Minimally Helpful	Very Helpful
Uses feelings to punish helpee. Significant incongruence between response and true feelings. Helper is deceitful or defensive. Some incongruence between helper's feelings and verbal/nonverbal expressions; response is role played.	No incongruence between expressions and feelings; expression is controlled.	Full congruence between response and true feelings. Spontaneous and dependably real. Uses positive and negative feelings constructively.

quently taunt him and physically provoke him in regard to his background. Gene is basically a responsible adolescent. His parents have asked him to avoid these bullies whenever possible but they support him for standing up for his rights. Gene has had two fist fights in the past two months. His teacher, Mrs. Webb, is emotionally inhibited and quite uncomfortable with the open expression of anger. She has written several letters to Gene's parents requesting that they teach him to keep his hands to himself. Gene's father finally decides that he's had enough of her "cheap advice" and phones the principal. Mr. Scott, the newly assigned principal, has heard from reliable sources that the school has a few bullies, but he is not familiar with what has happened to Gene. He hears Gene's father say: "This here is Jim Beecher and I'm callin' to get one thing straight with you, mister. I'm sick and tired of you people tryin' to tell me how to raise my boy! Gene's a good boy and he don't look for no trouble, but he ain't gonna act like no sissy when those bullies try to push him around."

Helper Responses

HARMFUL: "Well, I'm certainly most interested in hearing more about this" (as the principal holds the telephone receiver away from his ear, positions it so his assistant can hear, smiles sarcastically, and begins to make faces).

> Clearly the principal has little real concern for Mr. Beecher; he is making light of his problem and withdrawing from it. Mr. Beecher is deprived of vital nonverbal cues relating to the principal's true feelings, subsequently, he may be duped by his deceitful response. If Mr. Scott continues to perpetuate the fraud, Mr. Beecher will probably not be fooled for long.

HARMFUL: "Now hold on a minute, pal! You can't talk to me like that! I've been on this job for just two weeks and I can't be held responsible for anything that happened before my arrival. Let's get that straight!"

The principal begins by refusing to accept the parent's manner of presentation; he tries to "put him in his place," thus using his feelings to punish the caller. Then he defensively tries to absolve himself from any present responsibilities to Mr. Beecher and his son by pointing out that he is a new arrival and has no obligations to them for the past. Mr. Beecher is quite embittered to begin with. But after hearing aggressive and defensive responses like these from the principal, his frustration is likely to increase.

NOT HELPFUL: "As the principal of this school I assure you that I'll do all I can to help you."

The new principal feels unprepared for this confrontation. He is taken aback but speaks in a firm voice and pretends to be in control. The principal cannot be faulted too much. After all, what he says is quite socially acceptable, and he appears to be "reading his lines" from the standard principal's "script." A closer examination, however, may reveal signs of incongruence between what he is feeling (anxious) and how he speaks (firm and at ease). By retreating to the apparent safety of a fixed role, Mr. Scott may further alienate Mr. Beecher over a period of time.

HELPFUL: "You're obviously fed up with people interfering with your family affairs. I find myself in an awkward spot, though. I've only been in this school two weeks and I'm not familiar with your son's situation other than what you've just told me."

The principal shows congruence between his expression and his feelings. He is, however, hesitant to fully express how he is feeling in response to Mr. Beecher. In addition, although Mr. Scott may be favorably disposed toward helping students, he makes no reference to his future intentions toward Gene. Helpers who respond to helpees with such controlled expressions are seen as real and trustworthy. Though helpees may sense that you are withholding some of your deeper feelings, they know that they can trust what you have communicated thus far. Helpees are inclined to gradually lay aside their defenses as such helpers continue to show that their intentions are constructive and that they themselves are not afraid to relate openly.

VERY HELPFUL: "You very much resent school officials who try to tell you how you should be bringing up your son. I respect your right as a parent to feel that way, but frankly, I'm a little uncomfortable. I'm new at this school and I don't even know who your son is. I'll do what I can to help Gene maintain his strength of character. And it looks as though there are some aggressive students that need to learn more about tolerance and self-control. I'll start looking into this matter. Could we meet together sometime next week?"

Mr. Scott withholds nothing from Mr. Beecher. He is fully congruent, spontaneous, and dependably real, as he says exactly what he is thinking and feeling. As Mr. Beecher does not appear to like "beating around the bush," he will no doubt appreciate Mr. Scott's directness and authenticity. Both men will probably waste little time in getting to the root of Gene's problem with his offensive classmates.

Helpers who strive to be deeply and constructively genuine work toward a fully sharing relationship. They well understand the self-destructive behaviors of themselves and others and work toward the reduction or elimination of such patterns. Such helpers are maximally effective in their efforts to promote helpee growth and/or problem resolution. Their credibility simply makes their impact more potent.

EXERCISE 17-1   Perceiving Genuineness

Behavioral objective: The trainee will be able to rate helper responses with an average discrepancy score of 0.5 or less.

Rate each of the helper responses on the Genuineness Scale, using the key below. Place the number (1, 2 or 3) in the blank to the left of the helper response.

Harmful/Not Helpful	Helpful	Very Helpful
1	2	3

Helpee Situation 1

Diane Hill is a 22-year-old fifth grade teacher. She knows her subject matter well but realizes that she has a lot to learn about classroom management. The assistant principal and several other teachers have been working with her when they can. She is in her classroom awaiting the arrival of a group of parents who are coming to observe her classroom during National Education Week. She alternates between smoothing out her skirt, glancing at the doorway, rearranging the bulletin board,

Continued

EXERCISE 17-1 *Continued*

and reminding the students to be well-behaved. A student says to her: "Mrs. Hill, aren't you nervous with all the parents coming to watch our class this morning?"

Helper Responses

_____ 1. "I'm only nervous because I can't trust you to behave like human beings. If you embarrass me in front of your parents, you'll be sorry."

_____ 2. "Teachers get used to things like this. It goes with the territory."

_____ 3. "I'm so nervous my knees are shaking. It would mean a lot to me if you all pull together and give me a hand."

_____ 4. "Yes, I feel a little shaky."

_____ 5. "Yes, I'm tense. You kids haven't exactly been angels with me and I've been rough on you. I'm trying hard now to see that we all get along better, and I know I need your cooperation to make a good impression on your parents."

_____ 6. "I should hope not. After all, your parents are just ordinary people."

Check the Answer Key at the end of the chapter for the correct ratings and calculate your average discrepancy score by dividing the sum of the individual discrepancy scores by six. Review the ones you missed to learn why they are rated as they are, then proceed to Helpee Situation 2.

Helpee Situation 2

You are the principal of a large metropolitan high school. The crime wave in your community is rising at an alarming rate. Dozens of your students already have police records. During the past three months a number of assaults with weapons have occurred on campus; in one of these incidences, the victim was a teacher. The school now has two full-time police officers but the situation is still making everyone ill-at-ease. You decide that it is time for the school and community to band together. You help form a multidisciplinary committee and plan what you believe will be a stimulating program of dialogue. Your program includes presentations by students, faculty, police, psychologists, local business people, ministers, and community leaders. It is the night of the program. Due to your extensive advertising you were expecting a minimum of 200 guests—only about 30 people show up. You are usually quite energetic and optimistic, but tonight you are quiet and obviously discouraged. Midway through the program a parent says to you, "How do you feel about the small turnout tonight?"

EXERCISE 17-1 *Continued*

Helper Responses

_____ 7. (Speaking hurriedly) "Why should I feel bad about it?"
_____ 8. "Pretty bad."
_____ 9. (Changing facial expression to appear undaunted) "In my line of work you learn to take such things in stride. You just can't let problems like this really get to you."
_____ 10. "I don't think anyone here has a right to make any snap judgments about those not in attendance."
_____ 11. "I'm happy you're here (smiles warmly) but, frankly (face and voice become serious), I'm deeply disappointed. If more of us don't pull together, then the criminal element of this community is going to become more powerful."
_____ 12. (Speaking slowly and in a low voice) "I'm sad. I was really looking forward to a big turnout. I keep looking around and wondering what we can do next to try and get the people involved. I must admit, though, I don't feel too optimistic right now."

Check the Answer Key at the end of the chapter for the correct ratings and calculate your average discrepancy score by dividing the sum of the individual discrepancy scores by six. Review the ones you missed to learn why they are rated as they are, then proceed to Helpee Situation 3.

Helpee Situation 3

You are a dedicated and hard-working sixth grade teacher. When you are not teaching, you are planning, grading papers, or attending in-service workshops. You have come to treasure your half-hour lunch breaks—the one time you have each day to be by yourself and get some rest. The assistant principal at your school is authoritarian and aggressive. He is used to getting his own way by manipulating other people. For the past six months you have patiently tried to overlook his rudeness and have gone overboard to cooperate with him. You are alone in your classroom eating a sandwich when he walks in and says, "I hate to break in on you, but the art teacher needs to pick up some materials down the street for her classes this afternoon. Her car won't start. I'm sure you won't mind giving her a lift." You do mind, quite a bit.

Helper Responses

_____ 13. "You're saying she needs a ride pretty badly. No problem. I'll go help her pick up the supplies."
_____ 14. "I was really planning to put my head down for a little while—I'm really bushed. I do like Sally, though, so if she'd like to use my car, tell her I wouldn't mind."

Continued

EXERCISE 17-1   *Continued*

___ **15.** "We teachers are sick and tired of being exploited by you! You are a manipulative bully and a selfish man. It's about time somebody set you straight!"

___ **16.** (Speaking calmly and firmly) "I'd really prefer that you get someone else to help her. I'm sure you'd agree that I've done more than my share to lend a hand around here."

___ **17.** (Smiling broadly and rising quickly to her feet) "I'd be happy to help you—I wasn't doing anything important."

___ **18.** (Speaking calmly and firmly) "I'd rather not give up my break."

___ **19.** "I work really hard around here. I've gone along with your program for some time now. At this point I deserve a break. Perhaps some of the other teachers or staff would be willing to lend you a hand."

Check the Answer Key at the end of the chapter for the correct rating and calculate your average discrepancy score by dividing the sum of the individual discrepancy scores by seven. Review the ones you missed to learn why they are rated as they are.

EXERCISE 17-2   Responding with Genuineness

Behavioral objective: The trainee will be able to write helper responses in a natural style that are rated as Helpful or Very Helpful.

Read the helpee situation and formulate your response as though you were speaking to the helpee. Write it down as quickly as possible to retain the conversational style. If you have trouble identifying helpee feelings or wording your responses, consult Appendix B, Vocabulary of Affective Adjectives, and Appendix C, Speaking the Helpee's Language with Empathic Leads. Check your responses against the criteria of helpful responses on the Genuineness Scale. If your response is not Helpful or Very Helpful, rework it to meet the appropriate criteria.

Helpee Situation 1

You are a college student living in a sorority house. Your roommate has recently gotten engaged to a young lawyer. You have met him on several occasions but do not know him well. You and your date have just finished dining at a cozy restaurant far from the campus. As you are leaving, you see your roommate's fiance with another woman. They are

EXERCISE 17-2   *Continued*

staring lovingly at each other and drinking a toast. From where he has his other hand, you know she is not his sister. When you get back to the house, your roommate says, "Barry just called me from the office. Poor thing has been working all night on a brief. He's trying to make a good impression on the firm so that maybe he'll be a partner by the time we're ready to get married. Aren't I lucky to have such a dedicated fiance?"

HELPER RESPONSE _____

_____

_____

Helpee Situation 2

You are a very young, very attractive, and socially popular teacher intern. You became socially active in middle school and in high school you were elected queen of the senior prom. Janice strikes you as a very lonely as well as homely senior. She is self-conscious, withdrawn, and socially awkward. She says to you: "The senior prom is just two weeks away. It doesn't look like there's a boy on earth that is interested in taking me. I guess I should have known this was gonna happen. (Showing interest in you) Did you go to your senior prom?"

HELPER RESPONSE _____

_____

_____

Helpee Situation 3

Sam, an eleventh grader, has been in two of your classes during his high school career. You know him well and he respects you a great deal. For the past year he has talked a lot about going to an Ivy League college. Sam is a below average high school student, and you don't think he would stand a chance of being accepted by an Ivy League school. Finally, he asks you the big question: "I'd like to go to Princeton. Would you write a letter of recommendation for me?"

HELPER RESPONSE _____

_____

_____

Helpee Situation 4

You are a high school teacher. One of your students, Lisa, is known to be sexually promiscuous. Lisa does poorly in her academic work; her other teachers describe her as defiant and disruptive. Though she is inatten-

Continued

EXERCISE 17-2 *Continued*

tive in your class, she is not a behavior problem. She seems to respect you for the support you have given her. One day after school, Lisa drops by to speak to you. She says: "This is the pits. You know . . . I can't talk to my parents—they don't understand me and never will. But . . . I don't know who I can talk to (she becomes tearful). I took one of those home pregnancy tests and it came out positive."

HELPER RESPONSE _____

_____

_____

Helpee Situation 5

You were born and raised in Haiti. You obtained your graduate degree in social work at an American university. You have been in this country for many years and are well acculturated. You are sent to investigate a charge of child abuse that a school teacher submitted to your agency. You drive to the child's home address, knock on the door, and are greeted by the child's Haitian grandmother. After introducing yourself, you advise her that you are there to investigate a complaint of physical abuse against her grandson. The lady appears to be taken aback with your remark. The following dialogue (translated to English), takes place in Creole.

>   GRANDMOTHER: "That is a Haitian accent I detect, is it not?"
>   SOCIAL WORKER: "Yes, ma'am."
>   GRANDMOTHER: "And that is your own new automobile in my driveway?"
>   SOCIAL WORKER: "Yes, it is."
>   GRANDMOTHER: "Well, you appear to be an educated young lady. I imagine that you attended college and earned a degree. Would you say that you turned out to be a responsible adult?"
>   SOCIAL WORKER: "I believe so."
>   GRANDMOTHER: "Then, let me ask you one more question young lady. Did your parent use corporal punishment in raising you?"
>   SOCIAL WORKER: "Yes, they did, but that's not the point."
>   GRANDMOTHER: "I believe I've made my point, thank you."

HELPER RESPONSE _____

_____

_____

Answer Key for Exercise 17-1

Helpee Situation 1

1. 1 (punitive, degrading, threatening)
2. 1 (role played, some incongruence)
3. 3 (fully congruent; spontaneous; dependably real)
4. 2 (controlled expression)
5. 3 (spontaneous, fully congruent, constructive use of negative feelings)
6. 1 (defensive or deceitful)

Helpee Situation 2

7. 1 (defensive)
8. 2 (controlled expression)
9. 1 (some incongruence, role played)
10. 1 (punitive, defensive)
11. 3 (spontaneous; fully congruent; highly credible)
12. 3 (spontaneous, fully congruent; uses negative feelings constructively)

Helpee Situation 3

13. 1 (significant incongruence; deceitful or phony)
14. 3 (spontaneous, fully congruent, thoughtfully assertive)
15. 1 (punitive, devalues person)
16. 3 (fully congruent; dependably real; constructively assertive)
17. 1 (significant incongruence; phony; emotionally dishonest; acquiescent)
18. 2 (congruent; controlled expression; assertive)
19. 3 (fully congruent; spontaneous; dependably real; uses negative feelings constructively; thoughtfully assertive)

REFERENCES

Egan, G. 1986. *The Skilled Helper: A Systematic Approach to Effective Helping.* Pacific Grove, CA: Brooks/Cole Publishing Company.

Rogers, C.R., and C.B. Truax. 1967. "The therapeutic conditions antecedent to change: A theoretical view." In C.R. Rogers (Ed.), *The Therapeutic Relationship and Its Impact.* Madison, WI: The University of Wisconsin Press.

▶ 18

Perceiving and Responding with Self-Disclosure

In this chapter you will become familiar with a scale for rating helper statements on the dimension of self-disclosure as described in Chapter 1. As with preceding scales, you will learn to discriminate between Harmful/Not Helpful, Helpful, and Very Helpful ways of communicating.

HELPER SELF-DISCLOSURE

As has been pointed out previously, helpers will usually be most effective if they use self-disclosure sparingly in the early stages of a helping relationship. As the relationship progresses, however, helpees typically become more curious about their helpers and indicate an interest in getting to know them better as unique individuals. That is, helpees seek to personalize the relationship and learn just whom they are relating to. Particularly after helpers have established a good basic relationship with helpees is it appropriate for them to reveal themselves in a more personal manner. High-level helpers will genuinely and concretely disclose themselves in a number of ways.

They may share experiences from the past, explaining where they have been, what they have been through, and how they got through it. They may discuss changes that they have made in their attitudes, feelings, or actions. Helpers may even choose to talk about some of their own self-doubts, hang-ups, or limitations. However, we would all do well to realize that some common sense must prevail when using self-disclosure. In cases where what you are about to reveal is honest but likely to overwhelm the helpee, the material would best be kept to yourself. This point can be perhaps humorously illustrated by the following dialogue. The patient lying on the operating table says,

"Doctor, I'm really nervous. This is my first operation." The surgeon replies, "I know how you feel. This is my first operation, too." The important thing to remember about self-disclosure is that, used appropriately, it does not distract the helpee from doing his work. It facilitates the development of the helping relationship. Effective helpers do not meet their helpees wearing a mask; they are willing to be known as unique human beings and are easy to get to know.

ILLUSTRATION OF THE SELF-DISCLOSURE SCALE

The helpee situation below illustrates the three levels of the Self-Disclosure Scale (Table 18-1). Ratings are based on the Self-Disclosure Scale alone. They might be rated differently on other dimensions or on the Global Scale.

Finkelhor, Avaji, Baron, Browne, Peters, and Wyatt (1986) conducted a review of the current research on the sexual abuse of children. These writers concluded that the perpetrators were as follows:

Friends	32–60 percent
Uncles/older siblings	16–42 percent
Father/stepfather	7–8 percent
Strangers	1 percent

Although the victims ranged from infants to late adolescents, the most common age range for victimization was 9–12 years.

Kaplan and Sadock (1991) estimate that currently there are between 150,000 to 200,000 new cases of child abuse each year. They write:

Children who are stimulated sexually by an adult feel anxiety and overexcitement, lose confidence in themselves, and become mistrust-

TABLE 18-1 Self-Disclosure Scale

Harmful/Not Helpful	Minimally Helpful	Very Helpful
Discloses personal information exclusively to meet own selfish needs; disillusions or overwhelms helpee, inviting a role-reversal. Remains detached; reveals nothing personal. May answer direct questions hesitantly and briefly.	Volunteers, in a general fashion, personal information relevant to helpee's concerns.	Spontaneously volunteers detailed personal information relevant to the helpee's concerns; disclosure may be of an intimate nature and involve a degree of risk.

ful of adults. Seduction, incest, and rape are important predisposing factors to later symptom formations, such as phobias, anxiety, and depression. The abused children tend to be hyperalert to external aggression, as shown by an inability to deal with their own aggressive impulses towards others or with others' hostility directed toward them. (p.785)

Helpee Situation

For the first six months that nine-year-old Linda has been in school she has been an outgoing, friendly, and popular high achiever. For the past several weeks, though, she has been quiet, withdrawn, regressed, and performing poorly in academics. Whenever the teacher has tried to speak to her about these drastic behavioral changes, she has reacted with fear and distrust. The teacher has referred Linda to Dr. Mann, the school district's chief psychologist. After several play therapy sessions in which Linda has spontaneously postured dolls demonstrating various sexual acts and using explicit sexual language, she says to Dr. Mann, "Suppose they keep touching you where they shouldn't and tell you it's a secret. And if you tell the secret, they'll go to jail and it would be all your fault. What would you do?"

Helper Responses

HARMFUL "I'd show that stupid jerk that I wasn't afraid of him or anybody else and that he couldn't make me do anything I didn't want to do! That's what you need to do!"

The helper dominates the interaction by focusing on his own prowess exclusively. Seemingly unaware of the helplessness, fear, guilt, and confusion that sexually abused children experience, he offers a "solution" that is clearly absurd for a nine-year-old victim. In addition, the helper would do well to remember that the vast majority of offenders are persons known to the child. This might be the parent, stepparent, mother's boyfriend, sibling, other relative, neighbor, doctor, teacher, or preacher.

Thus, by referring to the offender as a "stupid jerk," Dr. Mann may actually trigger a defensive response from Linda. She is likely to feel overwhelmed by this type of self-disclosure and become disillusioned with the helper's ability to assist her.

NOT HELPFUL "Linda, honey, we're here to talk about you and your experiences. What I might do in a case like this is really not very important, is it?"

Dr. Mann actively remains detached from Linda as he refuses to reveal any personal information about himself relevant to her serious conflict. Linda is anxiously seeking some guidance from an authority figure at a time when other authority figures may well be destroying their bonds of trust with her. Linda will probably be disillusioned with Dr. Mann's ability to help her. Her intrinsic sense of childhood helplessness will no doubt be increased.

NOT HELPFUL "Well, ah, I don't really know what I'd do, Linda."

The helper answers the helpee's question with a brief response, but volunteers no personal information. Linda has no idea what the helper's personal reaction to such a situation might be, nor does she know whether the helper has ever experienced a similar situation.

HELPFUL "First of all, if I were your age, I'd be very scared and confused. Yet, I'd hope that I would have the courage like you to talk to somebody. Something like that happened to me once, but I was a little older than you and I was more angry than afraid."

The helper volunteers personal information in general terms. The material shared is relevant to the helpee's problem and keeps the focus of the interaction on the helpee. Linda learns a little more about Dr. Mann as a person and is in a better position to identify with him more closely. This should strengthen the therapeutic alliance.

VERY HELPFUL "The first time my uncle touched me like that was when we were wrestling. He loved me a lot and he lived in the house with us. He was always my favorite uncle and he told me that my parents would never let me see him again if I said anything. I didn't know what to do—I just acted like it didn't happen. It went on for months. I was 12. One day I just got tired of being angry and scared. I told the truth to my parents. They were shocked but real nice to me. They made him leave right away. They taught me that I have a right to say 'No' to anybody who tries to touch me like that."

Dr. Mann freely and spontaneously discloses intimate personal information relevant to Linda's conflict. The material that he shares involves a high degree of risk taking. This type of self-disclosure will often elicit feelings of universality between people, that is, the perception that "You are not alone. We're all in the same boat." Such feelings decrease the helpee's sense of isolation and loneliness and increase feelings of self-acceptance. This type of high-risk self-disclosure, when properly timed, will usually be interpreted by the helpee as a sign of the trust you are placing in him or her. Subsequently, the helpee often will go on to imitate the helper's lead and place more trust in him or her. Self-disclosure tends to beget self-disclosure.

EXERCISE 18-1   Perceiving Self-Disclosure

Behavioral objective: The trainee will be able to rate helper responses on the Self-Disclosure Scale with an average discrepancy score of 0.5 or less.

Rate each of the helper responses on the Self-Disclosure Scale, using the key below. Place the number (1, 2, or 3) in the blank to the left of the helper response.

Harmful/Not Helpful	Helpful	Very Helpful
1	2	3

Helpee Situation 1

Maria is a reading consultant for a publishing company. She is speaking to Ron, who is a counselor in the school where she has come to offer a workshop. "All week long the principal has been telling the teachers that I'd be here today for the in-service workshop. Only two teachers showed up, and this school is one of the weakest in reading in the county. I don't understand it. After all, it is a planning day and my workshop was only an hour in length. What went wrong?"

Helper Responses

_____ 1. "I don't know, Maria, but I can understand how frustrating it is for you."

_____ 2. "I don't prefer to conjecture about the actions of my colleagues."

_____ 3. "I can identify with your frustration. I've put on several workshops for the teachers and they've also been poorly attended."

_____ 4. "Frankly, something tells me that it's not us, but them. Many of the teachers here are incompetent, uncaring, and apathetic. The kids are the ones you and I probably feel most sorry for. Without adequate reading skills they'll be severely handicapped."

_____ 5. "I've been in this school for three years and I'm about ready to put in for a transfer. The principal knows nothing about counseling. He thinks I should be his assistant disciplinarian and that's it! If I try to organize a counseling group for the troubled kids, he finds ways to disrupt it. Normally, I'm a pretty patient man, but everyone has a breaking point. What do you think I should do?"

_____ 6. "I'm sorry you didn't have a better showing. I've had similar results in this school. I think teacher burnout is part of the problem."

EXERCISE 18-1   *Continued*

Check the Answer Key at the end of the chapter for the correct rating and calculate your average discrepancy score by dividing the sum of the individual discrepancy scores by six. Review the ones you missed to learn why they are rated as they are, then proceed to Helpee Situation 2.

Helpee Situation 2

Denise has been married to Eric for three years. She is having lunch with the assistant principal and says to her, "I love to teach, but I'd also like to be a mother. What a mess! Eric and I both want children, but we agree that without my salary we couldn't manage. I don't want to just bear children and then watch someone else raise them. I think I should be with them full-time for at least the first several years. I'm thirty-one years old now, and I can't picture myself waiting much longer if we're going to start a family. Did you work when your kids were young?"

Helper Responses

_____ 7. "My husband and I agreed that I would stay home until the youngest child started school."

_____ 8. "Denise, I know you mean well, but I never mix my personal with my professional life."

_____ 9. "Like you, I felt some time pressure since I was in my thirties when we decided to have children. During that period, John's business was not doing well, so this is what we worked out. My mother babysat for two days a week while I did substitute teaching. John made some extra money by doing landscaping on the weekends. We had to watch our budget closely, but it brought us together. Would anything like that work for you?"

_____ 10. "I wish I had worked when they were young—just to get a break from them. Kids can be very draining, let me tell you. Both of mine were colicky babies and hyperactive toddlers. Those early years weren't much fun and let me tell you, the older they get the worse they are."

_____ 11. "No."

_____ 12. "You want kids pretty badly but you're not sure if you can afford them. Fortunately, Denise, the economy wasn't so bad in my day. We were able to get by on John's salary, so I took a couple of years off. But I still felt somewhat guilty when I returned to teaching. Does guilt play much of a role in your conflict?"

Check the Answer Key at the end of the chapter for the correct ratings and calculate your average discrepancy score by dividing the sum

Continued

EXERCISE 18-1   *Continued*

of the individual discrepancy scores by six. Review the ones you missed to learn why they are rated as they are.

Helpee Situation 3

You earned your education degree after your own children were adults. You are in your first year of teaching. Henry Toon has been in your kindergarten class for three weeks. You have noticed that he fails to articulate certain speech sounds, such as *sh*, *ch*, and *th*. However, his speech is completely intelligible. You have observed Henry carefully and you have not noticed any general impairment in his intellectual functioning.[1] You telephone Henry's mother, inform her of your observations, and ask her if she has noticed this problem. Mrs. Toon replies, "You damn teachers don't have anything better to do than call me up to tell me my kid is retarded! I'm a single parent trying to make it with three kids! Do you have any idea what that's like?"

Helper Responses

____ **13.** "Well, my husband and I did raise a son."
____ **14.** "Listen! My first two husbands were drunks. They both abused me and then just disappeared. I don't particularly like teaching but I need to support myself."
____ **15.** "I had to raise three children on my own after their father got killed in Vietnam. I think I can identify somewhat with your struggle. But, I don't think Henry is retarded, I do think he may have a developmental speech disorder. I had a problem like this with my oldest daughter. Speech therapy worked wonders for her. I hope Henry's situation turns out to be nothing serious."
____ **16.** "I've been through some hell in my own family. My son has muscular dystrophy so I think I know what it's like to be stressed out. Henry shows no signs of being retarded—hopefully it's just a correctable speech problem. I'd like to have him seen by our speech therapist if that's all right with you."
____ **17.** "I'm a single parent, too. I know how difficult it can be."

Check the Answer Key at the end of the chapter for the correct rating and calculate your average discrepancy score by dividing the sum of the individual discrepancy scores by five. Review the ones you missed to learn why they are rated as they are.

---

[1]These symptoms are consistent with a possible Developmental Articulation Disorder. *American Psychiatric Association: Diagnostic and Statistical Manual of Mental Disorders, Third Edition, Revised.* 1987. Washington, DC: American Psychiatric Association (pp. 44–45).

EXERCISE 18-2   Responding with Self-Disclosure

Behavioral objective: The trainee will be able to write helper responses in a natural style that are rated as helpful or very helpful on the Self-Disclosure Scale.

Read each helpee situation and formulate your response as though you were speaking to the helpee. Write it down as quickly as possible to retain the conversational style. If you have trouble identifying helpee feelings or wording your responses, consult Appendix B, Vocabulary of Affective Adjectives, and Appendix C, Speaking the Helpee's Language with Empathic Leads. Check your response against the criteria of helpful responses on the Self-Disclosure Scale. If your reply is not Helpful or better, rework it to meet the appropriate criteria.

Helpee Situation 1

Art is a sophomore at a state university. He lives in a residence hall on campus but has come home for the weekend. He is speaking with his father. "You know, Dad, I got an F in chemistry last week, but I just can't make myself study. I piddle the time away in my dorm, wax the car, or just read magazines, even though I've got another test coming up. I want to do well, but I just can't seem to get disciplined."

HELPER RESPONSE: _____

_____

_____

_____

Helpee Situation 2

A college junior who is a newlywed relates her feelings to a married female friend. "I'd really like to quit school and have more time with my husband. He's in his last year of medical school and says he can study better when I'm around. I could always finish school later. My folks, on the other hand, keep pressuring me. They've sacrificed a lot to put me through college. I'd hate to disappoint them after all they've done for me."

HELPER RESPONSE: _____

_____

_____

_____

Helpee Situation 3

You are 22 years old and teaching at the high school level. You yourself have a few acne scars left over from some serious skin problems in your

Continued

EXERCISE 18-2   *Continued*

recent past. Steve is in one of your classes. His acne condition is extensive. His face is inflamed and full of pimples. He says to you, "You're a young guy and you seem to be pretty popular with the young female teachers in school here. Did you ever have problems with your skin that made you want to crawl under a rock?"

HELPER RESPONSE: _____

_____

_____

Helpee Situation 4

You are a third generation Latina and you work as a school counselor. One of the kitchen workers in the school has recently moved to the United States from Puerto Rico. She and her husband grew up in a poor neighborhood. Neither graduated from high school, and their English skills are barely adequate. She confides in you that she suspects that he is seeing another woman. She explains that she already has three children and is fearful of becoming pregnant or catching a sexually transmissible disease from him. She asks you for your advice. You know that encouraging rather unacculturated Hispanic women to be assertive with their husbands is unwise. Such behavior, being contrary to subcultural norms, often triggers a violent reaction.[2]

HELPER RESPONSE: _____

_____

_____

_____

Answer Key for Exercise 18-1

Helpee Situation 1

1. 1 (even though the helper offers some helpful empathy, he answers her direct question briefly but does not volunteer information)
2. 1 (actively remains detached and refuses to self-disclose)
3. 2 (volunteers personal information in a general manner)
4. 3 (spontaneously volunteers specific critical observations and takes a risk)

[2]Hepworth, D.H., and J.A. Larsen. 1993. *Direct Social Work Practice*. Pacific Grove, CA: Brooks/ Cole Publishing Company (p.260).

Answer Key *Continued*

5. 1 (selfish disclosure; overwhelming role reversal)
6. 2 (volunteers general information)

Helpee Situation 2

7. 2 (volunteers relevant personal information in a general way)
8. 1 (actively remains detached and refuses to self-disclose)
9. 3 (spontaneously volunteers specific experiences and feelings in depth while keeping the focus on the helpee's concerns)
10. 1 (changes focus to herself; overwhelming role reversal)
11. 1 (answers direct question briefly)
12. 3 (spontaneously volunteers detailed personal information)

Helpee Situation 3

13. 1 (answers direct question but hesitantly and briefly)
14. 1 (discloses personal information exclusively to meet own selfish needs; disillusions and overwhelms helpee)
15. 3 (freely volunteers detailed personal information relevant to the helpee's problems; response also instills hope)
16. 3 (spontaneously volunteers intimate personal information, then moves on to problem solving)
17. 2 (volunteers, in a general fashion, personal information)

REFERENCES

Finkelhor, D., S. Avaji, L. Baron, A. Browne, S.D. Peters, and G.E. Wyatt, 1986. *A Sourcebook on Child Sexual Abuse.* Newbury Park, CA: Sage Publications.

Kaplan, H.I., and B.J. Sadock. 1991. *Synopsis of Psychiatry: Behavioral Sciences/Clinical Psychiatry.* (6th Ed.). Baltimore, MD: Williams & Wilkins.

▶ 19

Perceiving and Responding with Confrontation

In the next two chapters you will incorporate into your repertoire of skills two additional dimensions that involve being evaluative: confrontation and immediacy of relationship. These dimensions are referred to as action dimensions because it is through their implementation that the helpee's action toward problem resolution frequently is generated. Table 1-1 in Chapter 1 illustrates this process. In studying this chapter you will learn to use the action dimension of confrontation. In the next chapter you will study the dimension of immediacy of relationship.

In earlier chapters you were introduced to the transition dimensions of concreteness, genuineness, and self-disclosure. You learned that when you moved to additive levels on these dimensions, that is, included elements in your response that had not been part of the helpee's statement, you had to draw upon your own experiences. In doing this you did not remain entirely nonevaluative or unconditional with the helpee. The helper can risk being evaluative (judgmental or conditional), but it is generally best to do so only after building a strong relationship with the helpee. The repeated use of the facilitative dimensions of empathy, respect, and warmth, and of the facilitation/action dimensions of concreteness, self-disclosure, and genuineness, will help establish the kind of relationship wherein confrontation may prove highly constructive.

It is important to note that the word "confrontation" is often associated with the stripping away of a person's defenses and brutally exposing his or her weaknesses or inadequacies. However, the type of constructive confrontation that we advocate with this model is of a different nature. It is not punitive and it is not cruel. High-level confrontations are invitations to the helpee to examine the inconsistencies in his or her life or to make better use of personal strengths and resources. Confrontation is strong medicine, and in the hands of a skillful helper, it can be very constructive.

We have previously (see Chapter 1) defined one form of confrontation as helpers informing helpees of a discrepancy between things that they have been saying about themselves and things they have been doing. Most broadly speaking, confrontation may be viewed as the act of pointing out the differences between two behaviors, two statements, or between a behavior and a statement. The value of confrontation is that it provides the helpee with another point of view to consider in the process of self-examination. If the helper is competent, his or her perception of the helpee will often be more accurate than the helpee's perception of himself or herself, particularly when the helpee is caught up in a conflict situation and strong emotions are involved (powerful emotions work to narrow perceptions). Thus, helpees who remain open to such confrontations are in a position to learn to reduce "blind spots" in their personalities and learn to perceive themselves more accurately.

Again, there is a scale to use (see Table 19-1) in rating helper statements on the dimension of confrontation. At this point it is important that we draw your attention to an important procedural item. In Chapter 1 you learned how the various dimensions are progressively applied in the helping relationship. Facilitative confrontation presupposes high levels of the other dimensions described in this manual. Confrontation without a base relationship created through the communication of empathy, respect, warmth, genuineness, concreteness, and self-disclosure is rarely helpful. You also learned that confrontation and immediacy were the most potentially threatening of the core dimensions of a helping relationship. Because of the potential for harm, if applied prematurely, the action dimensions of confrontation and immediacy are generally not applied at the rated Helpful or Very Helpful levels until a secure base is built. As we pointed out in Chapter 1, we believe that the constructive helper takes the time to develop a base relationship so that he or she "earns the right" to become conditional and confrontive.

TABLE 19-1   Confrontation Scale

Harmful/Not Helpful	Minimally Helpful	Very Helpful
Contradicts, ignores or accepts helpee discrepancies. Gives advice or direction prematurely. Reflects helpee's feelings about discrepancies or remains silent about them.	Tentatively points out discrepancies in helpee's behavior, but not the directions in which these lead.	Clearly points out discrepancies in helpee's behavior and the specific directions in which these lead.

Confrontation is wasted unless the helpee can use what has been said. Confrontation can be very damaging and is often threatening to the helpee if it triggers disabling levels of helpee anxiety. However, a certain amount of anxiety on the part of the helpee will actually increase the chances of a confrontation's being useful. Some general guidelines about the conditions that regulate the intensity of confrontation appear below.

REGULATING THE INTENSITY OF CONFRONTATION

These things make confrontation less intense and less threatening:

1. Establish a good base relationship of mutual trust and caring.
2. Precede the confrontation with responses rated at level 3.0 on the Global Scale.
3. Generalize. Talk about people in general instead of the helpee in specific. This allows the helpee to perhaps get the message in an indirect and less threatening manner. For example, "Many people find that when they are rude to students, the students are much more likely to be rude to them."
4. Build in some "wiggle room" for the helpee's ego by phrasing your confrontations in a tentative rather than a definite manner. Use words such as *sometimes, every once in a while, perhaps,* or *maybe.* For example, "Every now and then most students will think about ways to get out of doing classroom work—that's only natural." This type of communication style makes it easier on the helpee because it is not accusatory in nature.
5. Use humor. This is a particularly good general rule to follow. However, a note of caution is warranted. Whenever confrontation is being used in a disciplinary or enforcement situation, humor should probably be used sparingly. Otherwise, the warmth that is generally communicated in humor may inadvertently weaken the strength or seriousness of your confrontation.
6. Consider the spirit in which confrontation is given. There is no justification for being punitive, vengeful, or hurtful when you are functioning as a professional helper.
7. Improve the attractiveness of your own life. If you are living your life in a way that other people would like to imitate, it is easier for them to accept help from you.

These things make confrontation more intense and threatening:

1. Personalize. Make it clear to the helpee that you are talking about her or him.

2. Specify events. A high level of concreteness forces the helpee to either accept or reject the accuracy of what you say.
3. Deal with issues close in time. There is more threat involved in dealing with behavior that is close in time than with something that happened a long time ago.
4. Deal with actions instead of just words. If you are talking about something the other person said, it is easy for that person to say, "That is not what I meant." It is more difficult to rationalize behavior than it is to explain away words.
5. Use what the helpee has said or done earlier to contradict what the helpee is saying or doing now.

The intensity of confrontation must be strong enough for the confrontation to have an effect, but not so strong that it causes the helpee to feel inadequate or unable to act constructively. Regulating the intensity requires the helper's best judgment. It is desirable to begin with gentle confrontation and raise the intensity gradually, being guided by the helpee's reaction to the confrontation.

If confrontation is too strong, several undesirable outcomes may occur:

1. The helpee uses defense mechanisms to build a wall between the two of you, thus reducing constructive communication.
2. The helpee is driven away.
3. The helpee is angry and goes on the attack, which is likely to ruin your chances of helping.
4. The helpee pretends to accept the confrontation but actually ignores it.
5. The helpee feels helpless and seeks to become inappropriately dependent on the helper.

If the confrontation is too weak, the outcome can also be undesirable:

1. The helpee loses respect for you, and may assume that you don't really believe in what you are talking about or that you do not have the courage to speak up on behalf of your own beliefs.
2. There is no effect. The helpee does not notice the purpose of your confrontation so it "goes in one ear and out the other."
3. Your confrontation is so feeble that it actually reinforces the discrepant behavior. The confrontation is interpreted as if you had said, "I think that this discrepancy is really okay, but I was obligated to say something to you about it as a mere formality."

If any of the effects listed under a "too strong" or "too weak" confrontation occur, the likelihood of the confrontation being useful is reduced. Above all, the helpee must sense that the helper is being real, not "playing games" or being phony in his or her confrontation. As a general rule, it is wise not to confront unless you have established a base relationship and plan to stay involved with the person. On the other hand, confrontation is an essential element in enforcement and disciplinary situations. In such cases the establishment of a helping relationship may be secondary to the need for regulation and control.

TWO TYPES OF CONFRONTATION

Experiential

An experiential confrontation points out discrepancies the helper has noticed in his or her own personal experiencing of the helpee: (1) the helpee may be contradicting something he or she has previously stated, (2) the helpee's behavior may contradict verbal expression, or (3) the helpee's experiencing of himself or herself may be different from the helper's experiencing of the helpee.

An experiential confrontation may refer to limitations (confrontation of weakness) or to resources (confrontation of strength).

Didactic

In didactic confrontation the helper provides the helpee with additional information concerning problems. The helper may point out helpee behaviors that are socially undesirable or fill in gaps in the helpee's information about social reality. Another type of didactic confrontation is when the helper enforces a regulation, or exercises some kind of social control over the helpee. Some didactic confrontations deal with inappropriate helpee behavior, and that particular situation is discussed in Chapter 22, Responding to Inappropriate Communication. An example of a confrontation about social reality would be to say to the helpee, "Perhaps you are not aware of this, but when you are in a small group you tend to interrupt others quite a bit. I've noticed their looks of displeasure and annoyance. Even though what you have to say may be of interest to them, their negative feelings may keep them from truly listening to you."

ILLUSTRATION OF THE CONFRONTATION SCALE

The helpee situation below illustrates the three levels of the Confrontation Scale. Ratings are based on the criteria of the Confrontation Scale alone. The responses might be rated differently on other dimensions.

Helpee Situation

You are a high school Spanish teacher. Larry, one of your students, comes to class 30 minutes late. Avoiding eye contact, he hands you a pass that is barely legible. The signature looks forged. You say nothing to him. After school you check with Mr. Sledge, the teacher whose name appeared on the pass. He assures you that it was counterfeit. This is the first time Larry has given you any problems. The next day you ask him to meet you after class. When he does, you silently hand him back his pass, your face is neutral. He snaps back, "I didn't do anything wrong!"

HARMFUL (Caustically): "Larry, next time I'd suggest that you practice more on your forgeries before you hand them in—you're a little deviate and I'm no fool!"

Such sarcastic and premature advice coupled with a negative label, and delivered so bluntly, is almost sure to be followed by a defensive response from the helpee.

NOT HELPFUL: "I . . . uhm . . . well, I just wanted to . . . to compliment you on the report you handed in today."

Though the helper started to deal with the issue (by handing Larry the pass), the helper then backs down and ignores the discrepancies. Helpers sometimes nervously inhibit the expression of their true feelings for fear of hurting others or being hurt by them. But such a passive stance, with its accompanying emotional dishonesty, helps neither the helper nor the helpee.

NOT HELPFUL: "You're angry with me for bringing up the subject of the pass."

The helper does not refer to any of the discrepancies expressed by the helpee, but simply reflects the helpee's current obvious feelings about the situation.

HELPFUL: "Sometimes, when we do things against our conscience, we get nervous, then instead of showing the nervousness, we hide it behind our anger."

In this tentative expression of a discrepancy, the helper minimizes the threat of the confrontation by using the tentative word, "sometimes," and by generalizing (using "we" instead of "you").

HELPFUL: "I showed the pass to Mr. Sledge yesterday; I think you can guess what he told me."

> In this didactic confrontation the helper brings up a discrepancy in the form of additional information. The helper then tactfully, and indirectly, invites the helpee to respond and explore the problem further.

HELPFUL: "Larry, yesterday you didn't look me in the eye when you handed me the pass. I got to wondering why, and when I looked at the signature, I knew something was wrong. Mr. Sledge told me he knows his handwriting is bad, but not *that* bad."

> The helper uses an experiential confrontation, pointing out discrepancies the helper has noticed. Although it uses a past timeframe, it is personalized and specific, and thus more intense. The helper then uses humor to cautiously reveal that the evidence has been properly examined by the supposed author and found to be counterfeit. The use of humor which lightens the impact of the confrontation, is not contraindicated given that this is the student's "first offense" with this teacher.

VERY HELPFUL: "Larry, it's not like you to break the rules, so I figure that maybe you had a good reason for coming to class late and trying to cover it up. Mr. Sledge looked at your pass and assured me that that was not his signature. I don't want this one incident to damage my trust in you. Can we talk?"

> The helper clearly points out some discrepancies (no history of rule breaking, counterfeit pass) to Larry and the specific direction in which these lead (possible damage to bonds of trust). This low-keyed and acceptant style will likely encourage Larry to review his conduct and learn to be more honest with his teacher.

EXERCISE 19-1   Perceiving Confrontation

Behavioral objective: The trainee will be able to rate helper responses on the Confrontation Scale with an average discrepancy score of 0.5 or less.

Rate each of the helper responses on the Confrontation Scale using the key below. Place the number (1, 2, or 3) in the blank to the left of the helper response.

Harmful/Not Helpful	Helpful	Very Helpful
1	2	3

EXERCISE 19-1 *Continued*

In the next four situations you may assume that the helper and the helpee have developed a strong base. It is difficult to rate high levels of confrontation without further samples of the interaction, but do your best. You may later wish to discuss your rating with the trainer and/or other members of your class.

Helpee Situation 1

Betty and Jack have been working together in a racially mixed middle school for nearly one year as principal and assistant principal respectively. Yesterday, Jack chaired a faculty meeting to discuss the issue of sex education classes for the students. Shortly after the topics of AIDS, condoms, homosexuality, and abortions were introduced, the discussion turned into a heated debate. The majority of the black teachers were loud, animated, and hotly argumentative, while most of the whites were (like Jack) rather calm, rational, and reserved. After a while, Jack appeared to become quite uncomfortable and said to the group, "Getting loud and emotional and losing self-control is not the way that any of us should be dealing with this subject." Betty has heard similar remarks from her assistant in the past. She decides that it is time to confront him. She is alone with Jack in his office. He says, "I felt that I chaired that meeting pretty well yesterday. Don't you think so?"

Helper Responses

_____ 1. "You're pretty satisfied with your performance, Jack."

_____ 2. "Jack, I don't know if you're aware of it, but yesterday I heard you repeat a pattern that I've noticed a number of times in the past. You do your job well, but this one habit that I've seen is self-defeating. Can we talk?"

_____ 3. "You sounded like a racist trying to keep the blacks in their *place* in a white man's world."

_____ 4. "You realize you could have handled the meeting better."

_____ 5. "Jack, you handled the meeting well until you made that statement about their loudness, emotionality, and losing control. I've heard you say things like this before, and I know you don't mean anything bad by it. However, I think your attitude in this area is going to keep you from doing your best as an administrator. To me, I think it's just a matter of learning about cultural differences."

Check the Answer Key at the end of the chapter for the correct rating and calculate your average discrepancy score by dividing the sum of the

Continued

EXERCISE 19-1   *Continued*

individual discrepancy scores by five. Review the ones you missed to learn why they are rated as they are, then proceed to Helpee Situation 2.

Helpee Situation 2

Student to teacher: "I've lived here all my life, but I don't know anybody. Even here at school I just can't seem to make friends. I try to be nice to other kids, but I feel uncomfortable inside and things just don't go right. Then I tell myself, 'I don't care, people aren't any good, everyone's out for himself, I don't want any friends.' Sometimes I think I really mean it."

Helper Responses

_____ 6. "You're in a real bind. You want to make friends but you make excuses for yourself when you don't succeed."

_____ 7. "There's nothing wrong with that. Many people learn to live secluded lives."

_____ 8. "You're concerned because you haven't been able to make friends."

_____ 9. "At times, you almost talk yourself into giving up on people, but something holds you back from doing it. This kind of problem is not a stranger to our school counseling center. Loneliness can be a painful motivator."

_____ 10. "You know there's something wrong with you, so do something about it."

_____ 11. "It's easy to get bitter if you keep reaching out to people but don't get anywhere. I guess it gets you to thinking, 'Is the problem mainly with me or with them?' Either way, you seem to realize that giving up is not the answer."

Check the Answer Key at the end of the chapter for the correct ratings and calculate your average discrepancy score by dividing the sum of the individual discrepancy scores by six. Review the ones you missed to learn why they are rated as they are, then proceed to Helpee Situation 3.

Helpee Situation 3

Student to teacher: "I can't see why you gave me a C on my paper. I worked on it three weeks. It was twice as long as Joe's and you gave him an A. That doesn't seem fair to me."

Helper Responses

_____ 12. "You don't think a C is a fair grade for your paper."

_____ 13. "You're angry I gave you a C when your paper was much

EXERCISE 19-1 *Continued*

longer than Joe's. Do you have any idea why I gave you a lower grade?"

___ **14.** "You're protesting because you think I've been unjust. The length of a paper is not necessarily a good judge of its quality, but I'd be happy to review your paper with you."

___ **15.** "There's no reason for you to be angry. A C is a good grade for you."

___ **16.** "Joe's paper met the objectives that I announced two months ago. You're convinced your paper meets those objectives, too."

___ **17.** "I'm sure your final grade will be quite good. You're doing well in my class except for this one paper."

Check the Answer Key at the end of the chapter for the correct ratings and calculate your average discrepancy score by dividing the sum of the individual discrepancy scores by six. Review the ones you missed to learn why they are rated as they are, then proceed to Helpee Situation 4.

Helpee Situation 4

For the first six weeks of school, your 10-year-old son has been assuring you that his teacher does not believe in giving homework assignments. Late one afternoon the teacher calls to express her concern. She points out that your son has failed to turn in all four of the homework projects that she has given. Later, you ask your son how he's doing in school. He replies, "I'm doing real well, Mom. It sure is nice to have a teacher that doesn't give homework."

Helper Responses

___ **18.** "That gives you a lot more free time and that must feel great."

___ **19.** "Your teacher called to tell me you've failed to turn in each of your first four homework assignments. I am surprised, disappointed, and angry that you would lie to me repeatedly."

___ **20.** "What are you working on in class now, honey?"

___ **21.** "You're a little liar! I should have known that I couldn't trust you!"

___ **22.** "Your teacher spoke to me today. She is concerned about your not having turned in any of your required homework."

Check the Answer Key at the end of the chapter for the correct ratings and calculate your average discrepancy score by dividing the sum of the individual discrepancy scores by five. Review the ones you missed to learn why they are rated as they are.

EXERCISE 19-2   Responding with Confrontation

Behavioral objective: The trainee will be able to write helper responses in a natural style that are rated as Helpful or Very Helpful on the Confrontation Scale.

Read the helpee situations and formulate your responses as though you were speaking to the helpee. Write them down as quickly as possible to retain the conversational style. If you find it difficult to discriminate the helpee's feelings, or if wording your response is troubling you, consult Appendix B, Vocabulary of Affective Adjectives, and Appendix C, Speaking the Helpee's Language with Empathic Leads. Check your responses against the criteria of a helpful response on the Confrontation Scale. If it would not be rated Helpful or better, rework it to make it Helpful or Very Helpful.

Helpee Situation 1

Johnny often makes comments to needle his teachers and fellow students. He does not let up in his attack once he gets a rise out of his victim. You have noticed that he has a tendency to back off quickly when he is firmly confronted. He says to you, "I guess you could have made something of yourself if you wouldn't have become a teacher."

HELPER RESPONSE _____

_____

_____

Helpee Situation 2

In your many years of high school teaching you have seen numerous unwanted pregnancies. Therefore, you have adopted a positive attitude towards the idea of the school's health clinic dispensing birth control measures. Another teacher comes up to you and accuses you of trying to encourage premarital sexual relations by supporting birth control counseling.

HELPER RESPONSE _____

_____

_____

Helpee Situation 3

The assistant principal asks you to give the opening meditation at an important assembly. You are an atheist and do not believe this is some-

EXERCISE 19-2 *Continued*

thing that you can honestly do. You wish to maintain your good working relationship with the assistant, yet you would prefer to keep personal beliefs to yourself. He says to you, "Can I count on you to be ready next week?"

HELPER RESPONSE _____

_____

_____

Helpee Situation 4

You are a Special Ed teacher. You have given one of your learning disabled students a classroom grade of C. As you are walking into the teachers' lounge, you overhear his regular classroom teacher say to another, "How can she justify giving McCurdy a C when the most he ever gets in my class is a D? I don't give away grades—they have to earn them."

HELPER RESPONSE _____

_____

_____

Helpee Situation 5

A particular teacher who you don't know well spoke with you briefly about some of the things she wished to bring up at the faculty meeting. You listened to her without committing yourself as for or against her views. Immediately, after the faculty meeting she says to you, "You really let me down this time. I thought you would back me up, and you just sat there like a bump on a log. Couldn't you catch my hints to jump in and support me?"

HELPER RESPONSE _____

_____

_____

Helpee Situation 6

Robert is a 13-year-old sixth grader. Teachers describe him as bright, quick-tempered, insensitive, disrespectful, and highly disruptive. The school counselor and you, the principal, have had regular contact with him, but all that you have tried has failed. You have found Robert's parents to be severe and critical. Several conferences with them have changed nothing. You decide that it would be best to send Robert to an alternate school designed to handle maladaptive junior high school

Continued

EXERCISE 19-2 *Continued*

kids. You inform his parents of your decision and they respond, "We don't want our kid moved. He's got a right to be in your school!"

HELPER RESPONSE _____

_____

_____

Helpee Situation 7

You are a junior high school teacher. You explain to your class that you will be out the next day for a religious holiday. When you return to school, the substitute teacher has left you a note describing how your students had thrown chalk and erasers, shoved their desks around the classroom, refused to take their seats, and signed the attendance roster with such names as, "Debbie Does Dallas," "Peter Pothead," "Sam Suks," and "Henrietta Hooker." You walk into the classroom and all of the students are studying your face.

HELPER RESPONSE _____

_____

_____

Helpee Situation 8

Hepworth and Larsen (1993) point out that the rate of suicide for adolescents has tripled over the past thirty years and that, "half a million young people between ages 15 and 24 attempt suicide each year and 5,000 of them succeed" (p. 255). The situation below describes an adolescent whose symptoms should serve as a "red flag" for a possible suicide.

Henry is a 17-year-old high school junior. Over the past several months he has withdrawn from his friends while his school achievement and personal hygiene have deteriorated. He appears to be quite depressed. Henry rarely smiles any more and he seems to have lost his capacity for deriving pleasure from being in varsity sports. His concentration has decreased and he appears to be chronically fatigued. You tell him that you are concerned about him and he replies, "You won't have to worry about me much longer. Everything is arranged." You note that he says this with some relief in his voice and no expression on his face.

HELPER RESPONSE _____

_____

_____

Answer Key for Exercise 19-1

Helpee Situation 1

1. 1 (reflects helpee's feelings about discrepancies)
2. 2 (tentatively points out discrepancies in helpee's behavior using an experiential confrontation)
3. 1 (gives direction very bluntly, coldly, and prematurely)
4. 1 (contradicts the expressed point of view of the helpee)
5. 3 (clearly points out discrepancies and the specific directions in which these lead; provides relevant information [didactic confrontation] necessary for the reduction or resolution of the helpee's problem)

Helpee Situation 2

6. 2 (points out discrepancy in a tentative way)
7. 1 (contradicts the expressed conflict of the helpee)
8. 1 (does not refer to discrepancy; reflects helpee's feelings)
9. 3 (firm directional statement of discrepancy)
10. 1 (premature advice tactlessly delivered)
11. 3 (firm directional statement of discrepancy)

Helpee Situation 3

12. 1 (reflects helpee's feelings about discrepancies)
13. 2 (tentative exploration of discrepancy using a questioning format)
14. 3 (firm directional statement of discrepancy)
15. 1 (premature advice; contradicts expressed conflict)
16. 2 (tentative exploration of discrepancy)
17. 1 (ignores discrepancy entirely)

Helpee Situation 4

18. 1 (ignores discrepancies)
19. 3 (clearly points out discrepancies and the specific consequences they had on her emotionally)
20. 1 (ignores discrepancies)
21. 1 (name calling; gives negative direction prematurely)
22. 2 (tentative expression of discrepancies)

REFERENCE

Hepworth, D. H. and J. A. Larsen. 1993. *Direct Social Work Practice*. Pacific Grove, CA: Brooks/Cole Publishing Company.

▶ 20

Perceiving and Responding with Immediacy of Relationship

The dimension of immediacy of relationship can be defined as communication between the helper and the helpee about their relationship as it exists at that moment in time. Thus, as Carkhuff (1971) notes, immediacy is the ability to understand the different feelings and experiences that are going on between you and another person, it is the adroitness to "tune in" to the helpee and know where the helpee is "coming from." Because this dimension involves the feelings of the helpee toward the helper, it can be one of the most difficult to deal with. It may put the helper's commitment to the helpee to a rigorous test by confronting the helper with overt or implied criticism of his or her role and competence.

Immediacy of relationship is also a difficult dimension to master because it generally involves the use of a number of other dimensions. It usually requires some high level empathy getting at underlying feelings, self-disclosure on the part of the helper, and some element of confrontation. Once again, we are dealing with a strong medicine (like confrontation) that warrants careful dispensing.

Immediacy is expressed in statements such as, "I really have a lot of respect for you," or "You're so incompetent—talking to you hasn't done me any good at all!" Obviously, the dimension of immediacy may involve varying degrees of threat depending upon the nature of the material shared. As a general rule, negative feedback is more difficult to handle than positive feedback. In addition, the perspective of time must be considered in evaluating the risk of threat to the relationship. Simply put, the more remote the timeframe, the less threat, and the more immediate the timeframe, the greater the threat. For example, "Last year I was very angry with you when you gave me an F on your final exam," versus, "You just gave me an F on your final exam—I'm very angry with you!"

If the helper responds in a defensive or evasive way, he or she may be seen as incompetent or weak, and the relationship may be threatened. If the helper is open, reasonable, and concerned, he or she may be seen as strong and capable. Even when the helpee is correct in negatively criticizing the relationship, the helper who faces the criticisms squarely and tries to do something about them will usually "pass" the helpee's test of commitment. As with the action dimension of confrontation, it is highly desirable that a strong base relationship exist before using the dimension of immediacy of relationship. Until a strong base is established, it is most often best to keep the focus on the helpee and his situation, rather than on the relationship between helper and helpee. If attention is shifted to the relationship too early, the formation of an adequate base may be impaired.

In order to be comfortable dealing with the immediacy aspect of a helping relationship, helpers should be aware of, and at ease with, their own self-image. The reason for this seems clear. Once the issue of the quality of the relationship is raised, helpers with an inadequate self-image may feel threatened by a negative evaluation and respond defensively. At this point it might prove fruitful for such helpers to do a little "soul searching" and see if they have perhaps been misusing their role for their own selfish or maladaptive purposes.

The wise helper will also evaluate the strength and nature of the helping relationship on a regular basis. The scales for rating the helpee that appear in Appendix D may prove useful in this regard. The helper should evaluate the relationship in both its positive and negative aspects, since virtually all relationships will have both strengths and weaknesses.

Oftentimes the helpee will be telling the helper how he feels about him or her without even knowing it. Many times, clues to the helpee's attitude toward the helper are hidden within other messages. The helper may recognize that there are barriers that are making it difficult for help to take place. The helper should then seek to deal with and resolve these rather than try to push ahead in a task-oriented way toward some predefined goal, since the helpee may not be working toward that goal because of obstacles in the relationship. If the relationship between the helper and helpee is strained or is not meaningful to the helpee, help is unlikely to take place.

DIFFERENT LEVELS OF IMMEDIACY

As with other dimensions, there is a scale for rating the levels of the dimension of Immediacy of Relationship (see Table 20-1).

Some low-level and very high-level immediacy of relationship responses

TABLE 20-1   Immediacy of Relationship Scale

Harmful/Not Helpful	Minimally Helpful	Very Helpful
Ignores all cues from helpee referring to their relationship. Uses own feelings about the relationship in a destructive way. Gives token or superficial recognition to helpee expressions about their relationship; postpones discussing it or dismisses it after commenting superficially.	Discusses the relationship with the helpee in a general or tentative manner. Reflects the helpee's communications about the relationship. Open to sharing responsibility for defects in the relationship.	Discusses helpee's expressions about the relationship in a direct, positive and explicit manner. Makes precise interpretations of the relationship.

can be rated using the usual helpee-helper interaction. However, longer helper-helpee interactions are often necessary to rate this complex dimension accurately. Because immediacy may involve powerful feelings, it is sometimes necessary to wait for the helper's response "to be digested" or "to sink in."

ILLUSTRATION OF THE IMMEDIACY OF RELATIONSHIP SCALE

The helpee situation below illustrates the three levels of the Immediacy of Relationship Scale. The situation assumes that the helper and the helpee have a strong base relationship. Ratings are based on the criteria of the Immediacy of Relationship Scale alone.

Helpee Situation

You are teaching an advanced French class in a Catholic high school. The topic of the day is Sartre and his existential philosophy. When you indicate that Sartre was an atheist, a lively discussion ensues. You expound upon Sartre's point of view in a nonjudgmental way. At the end of the class you are quite pleased. Many of the students who seemed to lack depth of independent thought appear to have come alive over this controversial subject. The next day you are summoned to the principal's office. Mr. Ted Birch and you have known each other for nine years. In your private conversations, he has labeled himself as a right-wing conservative and has often shown impatience with what he regards as your radical liberalism. Despite your political differences, you basically like and respect Ted. He says to you, "I just got a call from Mrs. Wright, and was she steaming! She threatened to pull all three of her children out of this school if something like this ever happens again. How can you set me up like this—trying to sell atheism to your students?"

Helper Responses

HARMFUL: "You're obviously threatened by me because I stand up for what I believe in while *you* cave in to political pressures.

> The helper attacks Mr. Birch using her own feelings about the relationship in a destructive way. She may be accurate, but she is not helpful.

NOT HELPFUL: "I was simply teaching the class about Sartre and his existential views."

> Although the helper is being confrontive and assertive, the helper is ignoring obvious cues from the helpee which apply to their interpersonal relationship.

NOT HELPFUL: "I realize that you're angry with me, but you've got to understand that I have a job to do. My job is to teach French to those kids. Sartre was a famous French philosopher and a discussion of his major beliefs fits into the curriculum."

> After superficially acknowledging the principal's anger toward the helper, the helper sidetracks away from a discussion of the immediate interpersonal relationship.

HELPFUL: "Okay, Ted, you're ticked off at me because you think I'm trying to persuade the students to become atheists. Let's face it, we've had our political differences in the past, but I think we ought to talk this situation out so our relationship isn't harmed."

> The helper accurately empathizes with the helpee in terms of the literal situation. The helper then generalizes about differences they've had in the past. Finally, the helper offers to share responsibility for preserving the relationship. The helper, however, is getting caught up in the helpee's dilemma, rather than interpreting it.

VERY HELPFUL: "Ted, you know that's not my style. It looks like her threat really got to you. The tuition payments keep us both employed, so I can live with what you're doing. A little displaced aggression never hurt a good relationship. If you'd like, I'd be happy to give her a call and do my best to take the heat off of you."

> In formulating this response, the helper observes the way the helpee is interacting and asks herself, "What is the helpee really trying to tell me that he can't say directly?" In our example the helper then begins with a simple confrontation, proceeds to offer high levels of respect and empathy and then gives a precise interpretation of what is truly going on in the helper-helpee relationship. Finally, she finishes with a suggested action plan for problem solving.

VERY HELPFUL: "Ted, my first instinct was to resent your accusation that I was being disloyal to you and disrespectful to the students. Then I realized that we both know that I am a professional educator and not a saleswoman. I guess you really felt up against the wall when she leveled those threats at you. You felt that you needed to lash out at someone. Our relationship is strong enough to take this kind of pressure."

> When the helper is rational, the helper does not need to feel threatened when the helpee expresses something negative about their relationship. By taking one step back from the interaction and observing it objectively and dynamically, the helper is in a better position to offer a helpful interpretation of immediacy. A good interpretation answers the question, "What is really going on in the helper-helpee relationship right now?" In this illustration, the helper makes a precise interpretation as to what is going on between helper and helpee, after having offered high levels of genuineness and confrontation. She then closes with a confrontation of strength about their relationship.

**EXERCISE 20-1   Perceiving Immediacy of
                   Relationship**

Behavioral objective: The trainee will be able to rate helper responses on the Immediacy of Relationship Scale with an average discrepancy score of 0.5 or less.

In the exercises below, assume that a strong base relationship exists. Rate each of the helper responses on the Immediacy of Relationship Scale using the key below. Place the number (1, 2 or 3) in the blank to the left of the helper response.

EXERCISE 20-1 *Continued*

Harmful/Not Helpful	Helpful	Very Helpful
1	2	3

Helpee Situation 1

You are a male high school teacher. You have been teaching math for eight years but have been at this particular school for two years. The department head retires. Mrs. McKenzie, your colleague, has been teaching in this high school for over twenty years. She was expecting the appointment to department head, but the administration did not believe her to be qualified because of her poor communication skills. You were chosen as the new head of the math department. Mrs. McKenzie feels deeply hurt and very hostile toward you, but she expresses it indirectly. She avoids eye contact, refuses to speak to you, and declines to attend department meetings. Several reliable sources have heard her say to other teachers, "What does he know about being a leader—he's really just a beginning teacher!" As you walk into the teacher's lounge you see Mrs. McKenzie seated by herself. You say "hello" to her. She glares at you and says, "I was just leaving!" You say:

Helper Response

_____ 1. "Oh, well, I guess I'll see you later."

_____ 2. "Mrs. McKenzie, I know that you have some very strong feelings about my appointment. I'd like to sit down with you and try to resolve some of the problems between us."

_____ 3. "I realize you're not comfortable staying in the same room with me, but I just had to get a break from those kids and put my feet up in the air—my bunions are killing me."

_____ 4. "Here we are, in the middle of February, and those kids are acting like it's the last day of school. They're inattentive, restless, giggly. I can't figure out what's going on with them."

_____ 5. "Mrs. McKenzie, you were sure you deserved the appointment and I guess you figure that I somehow have not been fair to you in accepting it. I wanted to give you time to work through your bad feelings, but I somehow think that we might both be better off if we analyze our relationship now."

_____ 6. (Sarcastically) "That's the best news I've had all day."

_____ 7. "I know you don't like me, yet I want to make this a good department."

Check the Answer Key at the end of the chapter for the correct ratings and calculate your average discrepancy score by dividing the sum

Continued

EXERCISE 20-1 *Continued*

of the individual discrepancy scores by seven. Review the ones you missed to learn why they are rated as they are, then proceed to Helpee Situation 2.

Helpee Situation 2

John is a high school student. His records indicate that he comes from an abusive and neglectful family. You have had him in your class for seven months. You like him and treat him well. He says to you, "Sure, you're always nice to me, but you have to be; you're paid for it. It's part of your job!"

Helper Responses

_____ 8. "You know what today's assignment is. I think the thing for you to do is continue working on it."

_____ 9. "You think I'm just playing a role with you."

_____ 10. "If I wasn't paid to be with you, believe me, there wouldn't be any relationship between us."

_____ 11. "I'm sorry to see that you don't trust my positive feelings toward you. I get paid to teach; I'm nice to you because I want to be. I get the feeling that you're afraid to get close because you're convinced that you'll get hurt. I'm taking that chance and I'd like you to also."

_____ 12. "You may not feel comfortable with me yet, but this is not the time to discuss such a personal matter. We have a lot of work to get done today if we expect to be ready for final exams."

_____ 13. "Maybe you're convinced that you're somehow unlikable, but I'm not. I know it's been hard for you to trust me, but it's not hard for me to like you."

_____ 14. (Sarcastically) "Wonderful. Now if you're through psychoanalyzing me, perhaps you can get back to doing your assigned work."

_____ 15. "You're pretty sure that I fake my feelings so I can pick up my paycheck. What can I do to improve things between us and earn your trust?"

Check the Answer Key at the end of the chapter for the correct ratings and calculate your average discrepancy score by dividing the sum of the individual discrepancy scores by eight. Review the ones you missed to learn why they are rated as they are.

EXERCISE 20-2 Responding with Immediacy of Relationship

Behavioral objective: The trainee will be able to write helper responses in a natural style that are rated as Helpful or Very Helpful (if a base is assumed), or Not Helpful (if a base is not assumed to exist) on the Immediacy of Relationship Scale.

Read the helpee situations, carefully determining whether a base is to be assumed. Decide what you would say if you were speaking with the helpee and write it down as quickly as possible to retain the conversational style. If you find it difficult to discriminate the helpee's feelings or if wording your response is troubling you, consult Appendix B, Vocabulary of Affective Adjectives, and Appendix C, Speaking the Helpee's Language with Empathic Leads.

If a base with the helpee is assumed, your response should meet the criteria for either Helpful or Very Helpful on the Immediacy of Relationship Scale and Helpful or Very Helpful on the scales of facilitation, facilitation/action, or action dimensions.

If no base is assumed, your response should be rated Not Helpful on the Immediacy of Relationship Scale and Helpful or Very Helpful on the facilitation dimensions. Since feelings of immediacy can be highly threatening without proper rapport, it is suggested that you avoid being too direct too quickly. By concentrating your efforts on the facilitative dimensions, you will be preparing yourself and the helpee for an honest and open encounter.

Evaluate your responses and rework them as necessary to meet the appropriate criteria.

Helpee Situation 1

Bonnie has been in your high school English class for six months. She obviously is quite fond of you. She regularly defends you to her classmates and quite often hangs around to speak with you after class. Since she is in your last period class, you find it difficult to avoid talking with her. Bonnie says to you, "Gee, Mr. Clark, I can't tell you how much I've been enjoying your class this year. You've really helped me a lot with my writing skills. (As she thrusts her chest out and smooths out her skirt, she looks you up and down with a seductive smile on her face.) I'd do anything to show you my appreciation."

HELPER RESPONSE ⎯⎯⎯⎯⎯⎯⎯⎯⎯⎯⎯⎯⎯⎯⎯⎯⎯⎯

Continued

EXERCISE 20-2 *Continued*

_____

_____

Helpee Situation 2

You are a high school teacher. Another teacher with whom you have had a good relationship for many years recently confided in you that he was gay. You were in no way bothered by this revelation and it did not affect the nature of your professional relationship. This same teacher comes up to you and quietly states, "I don't know who I can talk to . . . I'm just really scared . . . my test results and the physical exams all indicate that I've got full blown AIDS. I hope you'll continue to be my friend. I plan on teaching just as long as I'm physically able to."

HELPER RESPONSE _____

_____

_____

_____

Helpee Situation 3

You are a high school principal. Several students have been arrested at your school for possession of cocaine. Each of these students has told the investigating officers that they obtained their coke from Mr. Shaw, a new faculty member whom you know little about. Mr. Shaw has heard these allegations. He stops by your office and says, "I hope you realize that I'm completely innocent of the charges that those hoodlums are making. You do believe me don't you?"

HELPER RESPONSE _____

_____

_____

_____

Helpee Situation 4

Tony, a new student in your class, has recently transferred from an out-of-state school. He says to you, "Man, teachers are the same everywhere. They won't give you break one. Just take one step out of line and they're on your back. I don't expect you'll be any different from any of the teachers I've had."

HELPER RESPONSE _____

_____

_____

EXERCISE 20-1 *Continued*

Helpee Situation 5

Two teachers who have been teaching together on the same team for two weeks are discussing their impressions of the new team-teaching program. One says to the other, "I entered this program thinking the intellectual stimulation I'd receive from working with another teacher would be worth the change from a traditional classroom setting. So far, I'm not satisfied."

HELPER RESPONSE _____

_____

_____

_____

Helpee Situation 6

You are a young Hispanic policewoman assigned to work in an urban middle school. One of the students comes up to you in the hall and says, "You damn cops are all the same. My brother got pulled over for speeding last night. By the time your macho buddies got through with him, he was all bruised up!"

HELPER RESPONSE _____

_____

_____

_____

Answer Key for Exercise 20-1

Helpee Situation 1

1. 1 (passively ignores all expressions of immediacy)
2. 2 (discusses the relationship in a general way, willing to share responsibility for improving relationship)
3. 1 (gives token recognition to expressions of immediacy then changes the subject)
4. 1 (ignores all expressions of immediacy)
5. 3 (direct and explicit, precise interpretation of the relationship)
6. 1 (destructive)
7. 2 (reflects the helpee's feelings about the relationship in a general way)

Helpee Situation 2

8. 1 (ignores all expressions of immediacy)
9. 2 (reflects the helpee's feelings about the relationship in a general way)

Continued

Answer Key   *Continued*

10. 1 (destructive)
11. 3 (direct positive and explicit, precise interpretation of the relationship)
12. 1 (gives token recognition to expression of immediacy then postpones discussing it)
13. 3 (explicit and precise interpretation of immediacy coupled with a confrontation of strength)
14. 1 (sarcastic, destructive)
15. 2 (reflects feelings of immediacy then shows openness to sharing responsibility for improving the relationship)

REFERENCE

Carkhuff, R.R. 1976. "Helping and human relations: A brief guide for training lay helpers." In *Journal of Research and Development in Education. Human Relations: Helping (4) 2*, Winter. Athens, GA: College of Education.

▶ 21

Strategies for Change

Problem Solving/Decision Making

In Chapter 1, problem solving/decision making was identified as one of the four generic life skills isolated by the senior author and colleagues (cf Chapter 10, Gazda, Childers, and Brooks 1987). Both problem solving and decision making are dealt with in the research and applied literature without distinguishing between the two. The process of decision making in the research literature is treated as synonymous with problem solving. Fischoff's distinction (personal communication, May 17, 1984), however, is used here to provide some clarity. *Problem solving* is used to apply to a task that has a definite solution and is known to be right or wrong. *Decision making*, on the other hand, is defined as dealing with issues in which the solution cannot be specified as right or wrong. The consequences of the solution may be viewed as desirable or undesirable, but there exists no objectively correct or incorrect solution. From this perspective, then, the issues that people face and define as problems are more appropriately defined as decisions.

The model for problem solving/decision making outlined in this chapter enables helpees to reframe "problems" as decisions to which they may apply coping skills. Decision making involves making a judgment of choice between/among alternatives (Hogarth 1980), and therefore represents a commitment to a plan of action (Janis 1968). Decision making can also be viewed as a stage in the process of problem solving.

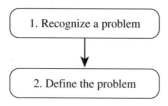

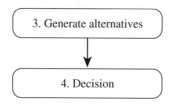

1) What are the situational elements?

2) What are the personal elements?

4. Decision

1) Most desirable action?

2) Action with most probability of success?

3) Implementation/action

5. Assess feedback

FIGURE 21-1   Model of problem solving/decision making.

MODEL FOR PROBLEM SOLVING/ DECISION MAKING

In general, the problem-solving/decision-making process occurs in five stages: recognizing a problem, defining the problem, producing alternatives as solutions, weighing and selecting from the alternatives a course of action, and assessing feedback from the implementation of a given course of action. This five-stage process is outlined in Figure 21-1.

RECOGNIZING A PROBLEM

Before a problem-solving/decision-making process can take place, a person must first recognize that an existing situation does in fact constitute a problem. Not all situations that require a solution are problem situations and therefore they do not necessitate the application of the five-stage problem-solving/decision-making model. A problem situation exists when the person recognizes that he or she is in a situation requiring the generation of an action because progress toward a goal is blocked or because progress involves choosing between two or more alternative actions (Miller, 1981). In particular, problem situations differ from *recall* situations in that "problem situations introduce a selectivity in stored information that is unique and different from recall situations" (Maier, Thurber, and Julius 1970, p. 49).

DEFINING THE PROBLEM

In Chapter 1, the phases of the helping process were described. The first phase of self-exploration is implemented to assist the helpee to define his or her problem—explore the problem (Carkhuff 1973). The purpose of this phase is to define the problem in terms of the relevant elements, both in terms of the person and the context of the environment (Carkhuff 1973; Maier 1970; Miller 1978).

Defining the problem means specifying its essential and relevant feature and the concomitant goal (Carkhuff 1973). This means to state the problem in a way that generates a search that will determine the goal and explore obstacles to the goal (Maier 1970). It is essential in understanding the problem to consider personal and social factors as well as task features (Miller 1978). In particular, personal values, assets, and limitations are essential determinants of desirable outcomes. In addition, societal attitudes and pressures impact the acceptability of particular solutions. As importantly, effective problem solving/decision making involves the ability to collect and select the information that is really necessary to solve the dilemma (Maier and Burke 1970). Therefore, definition and goal setting may involve gaining supplementary information or experience (Miller 1978). The end result is *not* an absolute "right" solution, but an individualistically based *desirable* solution. Problem solving/decision making can be conceived of as an information processing task (Gagne 1966) with task features, past experience, personal values, and societal issues constituting the relevant information.

GENERATING ALTERNATIVES

Once the problem has been defined and the goal specified, the problem-solving process interfaces with the decision-making process. The activity shifts from identifying the problem parameters to solving the problem (Simon and Newell 1971) through generating alternatives and moving into action. The first steps include searching for and formulating hypotheses or alternatives (Carkhuff 1973; Gagne 1966; Janis 1968). Brainstorming alternatives without evaluation helps to produce the elements to facilitate combining past experience into a new creative solution.

Intense emotion can interrupt the information-processing/decision-making system (Fiske and Taylor 1984). Research (Bower 1983) suggests that the experiencing of particular emotions primes associated "concepts, words, themes, and rules of inference" (p. 395). In other words, the person's emotional state may systematically bias the alternative solutions produced.

DECISION MAKING/EVALUATING AND SELECTING A COURSE OF ACTION

Once the search has delineated the possible solutions, it is necessary for the person to choose a specific course of action (Carkhuff 1973; Gagne 1966; Janis 1968). The choosing involves searching through the alternatives and weighing them or judging them according to their probability of success as well as their desirability as courses of action (Carkhuff 1973; Miller 1978). One strategy for weighing the alternatives is to manipulate mentally each proposed solution to its predicted conclusion (Maier 1970; Simon and Newell 1971). This evaluative procedure serves to eliminate some alternatives and give priority to others as possibilities based on the perceived positive versus negative outcome (Janis 1968).

It is important that preferences reflect the values of the present and immediate future (Bell and Coplans 1976). Also the value system being considered needs to be person-specific, that is, represent and reflect the preferences of the decisionmaker—whatever his or her preferences are. Awareness of the value system is particularly important to decision making (Miller 1978, 1981). Regardless of the person's level of awareness, values affect one's goals, the information one attends to and selects as relevant or critical to the decision situation, the risks one is willing to take, and the assessment of the decision outcome. Therefore, effective decision making entails establishing priorities and maintaining awareness of personal values.

As a result of the uncertainty regarding the hoped-for outcome, persons often experience difficulty in choosing between alternatives and may respond with "defensive avoidance." Accordingly, persons may procrastinate or avoid choosing, or they may try to resolve the doubts attendant to the choices through rationalization. It also is important to remember that difficulty with decision making may reflect fear—fear of making a mistake (Miller, 1981). This latter source of difficulty may be a result of the person's not being aware of having developed skills for competent decision making as well as a result of deficient skills. More importantly, the difficulty with problem solving may result in frustration if the problem is too difficult for the person's skill level, if there is pressure to solve the problem, if the person is unable to escape the problem, or if there is no substitute goal (Maier 1970). Such frustration could result in behavior that is characterized by fixation, aggression, and regression. More specifically, problem solving/decision making is impeded. Therefore, to lessen future difficulties and frustration, a final component of the problem-solving/decision-making process is to obtain feedback and access outcomes resulting from decisions.

ASSESSING FEEDBACK FROM THE OUTCOME

Once the decision is implemented as action, it is important to process the outcome so as to further develop decision skills (Miller 1981). Such assessment may be difficult. In particular, the outcome or consequence of the decision may be the only source of feedback (Einhorn and Hogarth 1978). Further, the issue may be complicated because "evidence about outcomes contingent on the action not taken is missing, or if outcomes are available, attention is not paid to them" (Einhorn and Hogarth 1978, p. 401). In this respect, it may be difficult for us to learn from our errors, as errors or more effective decision outcomes may not be obvious. It is in this area that specific training and education in problem solving/decision making may be most useful, as it seems experience may not be an effective teacher.

IMPLEMENTATION OF PROBLEM SOLVING/ DECISION MAKING IN THE HELPING PROCESS

Table 21-1 illustrates how the problem-solving/decision-making process is implemented through the application of the Human Relations Development Model presented in this text.

TABLE 21-1   Steps in Problem Solving

Facilitation phase:	Explore problem. Focus on helpee's feelings.
Transition phase:	Explore specific values in conflict. Help helpee determine if he or she chooses to take action to move toward resolution. State problem in terms of goal to be obtained.
Action phase:	Help helpee consider all possible strategies useful in reaching goal. Help helpee weigh advantages, disadvantages, and consequences of each strategy. Help helpee develop plan for reaching goal, and a time table if suitable. Help helpee evaluate effectiveness of plan.

REFERENCES

Bell, R., and J. Coplans. 1976. *Decisions, Decisions.* New York: Norton.

Bower, G.H. 1983. "Affect and cognition." *Philosophical Transactions Royal Society of London B 302,* 387–402.

Carkhuff, R.R. 1973. *The Art of Problem-Solving.* Amherst, MA: Human Resource Development Press.

Einhorn, H.J., and R.M. Hogarth. 1978. "Confidence in judgment: Persistence of the illusion of validity." *Psychological Review 85*(5), 395–416.

Fiske, S.T., and S.E. Taylor. 1984. *Social Cognition.* Reading, MA: Addison-Wesley.

Gagne, R.M. 1966. "Human problem solving: Internal and external events." In B. Kleinmuntz (Ed.), *Problem Solving: Research, Method, and Theory* (pp. 128–148). New York: Wiley.

Gazda, G.M., W.C. Childers, and D.K. Brooks. 1987. *Foundations of Counseling and Human Development Services.* New York: McGraw-Hill.

Hogarth, R.M. 1980. *Judgment and Choice.* New York: Wiley.

Janis, I.L. 1968. "Stages in the decision-making process." In R.P. Abelson, E. Aronson, W.J. McGuire, T.M. Newcomb, M.J. Rosenberg, and P.H. Tannenbaum (Eds.), *Theories of Cognitive Consistency: A Source Book* (pp. 577–588). Chicago: Rand McNally.

Maier, N.R.F. 1970. *Problem Solving and Creativity: In Individuals and Groups.* Belmont, CA: Brooks/Cole.

Maier, N.R.F., and R.J. Burke. 1970. "Test of the concept of 'availability of functions' in problem solving." In N.R.F. Maier (Ed.), *Problem Solving and Creativity: In Individuals and Groups* (pp. 155–161). Belmont, CA: Brooks/Cole.

Maier, N.R.F., J.A. Thurber, and M. Julius. 1970. "Studies in creativity: III. Effects of overlearning on recall and usage of information." In N.R.F. Maier (Ed.), *Problem Solving and Creativity: In Individuals and Groups* (pp. 44–49). Belmont, CA: Brooks/Cole.

Miller, G.P. 1978. *Life Choices.* New York: Crowell.

Miller, G.P. 1981. *It's Your Business to Decide.* Boston: CBI.

Simon, H.A., and A. Newell. 1971. "Human problem solving: The state of the theory in 1970." *American Psychologist 26*(2), 145–159.

▶ 22

Responding to Inappropriate Communication

Now we arrive at what is probably the most difficult communication situation of all—responding to communication that is inappropriate. It is difficult because it deals with values that lie in the "gray area" where it is common to find differences of opinion about what is inappropriate and what is not.

We can all probably agree on some basic categories of situations that are inappropriate. We shall look at five major categories: rumor/gossip, degrading talk, inordinate/chronic griping, inappropriate dependency, and requests to take part in inappropriate activities.

Our purposes is to learn the principles of how to respond. Then we can each decide for ourselves how we will respond to situations in real life; when that happens we will have the full context and will be able to make the choice that is best for the persons involved.

When we are faced with a situation we consider inappropriate, we have three options: (1) We might tell the person off. This would probably hurt our relationship and prevent us from helping that person in the future. (2) We might say nothing. This implies that we approve of their inappropriate request or behavior and encourages the person to continue. (3) We could give a clear refusal to be part of the inappropriateness, but at the same time show that we care about the individual as a person. This is the style of response we recommend.

This response may not appear attractive at first glance. It is difficult to deliver and it carries with it the risk of being rejected by the helpee. In this situation we want to affirm the person even as we are trying to discourage that person from the inappropriate behavior, and as we let him or her know that we are not willing to be inappropriate. It is, however, the response style that will give the most favorable results over a period of time. Other response styles only prolong the inappropriate behavior.

There is no answer you can give that will suddenly change the helpee's style. There is no simple, foolproof formula response that is easy to use and always works. But we'll suggest a guideline: POLITELY DECLINE TO TAKE PART.

The guideline is easy to state but not as easy to use. It is easy to decline, and it is usually fairly easy to be polite, but to put those two together is another thing! The key seems to be in *how* you respond as much as in *what* you say. Try these suggestions:

1. Put the "decline" into words. Make your preferences clear. Say those words with a rather matter-of-fact tone of voice—neutral and nonjudgmental.
2. Then, put "politely" into a second message. Change the subject, suggest that the other person talk about something else, or ask a question about something appropriate. At this point use a warm, enthusiastic tone of voice and effective attending skills. Naturally, your warmth *must* be genuine.
3. Determine to respond effectively, no matter how difficult it may be. If you can deal with an inappropriate communicator effectively one time, you may never again need to deal with that person's inappropriateness. It's worth a try!

With this approach we seek to deal firmly with the inappropriateness and gently with the person. Even so, it may result in a bit of embarrassment for the person with the inappropriate behavior. The embarrassment is just the natural consequence of doing something inappropriate. Let him or her live with that and hope that he or she learns from it. There is some risk with this approach, but the potential for harm is greater if we don't use it.

TYPES OF INAPPROPRIATE COMMUNICATION

Behavioral objective: The trainee will recognize and be able effectively to respond to five types of inappropriate communication.

Five types of inappropriate communication are listed below with examples. While these situations may not occur in what we usually think of as helpee/ helper relationships, we will use that terminology, referring to the person whose communication is inappropriate as the helpee. The person who habitually communicates inappropriately may not be asking for help—but probably is in need of it—and the potential may exist for you to become a helper.

Rumor/Gossip

A rumor is an opinion or statement without known authority for its truth. Its emphasis centers on an *organization or group*, not on a person. Rumors are not necessarily spread with the knowledge of their inappropriateness or inaccuracy, but it seems inevitable that even "neutral" rumors quickly become distorted as they move from person to person. For example, the innocuous report, "There was a lot of talk in the staff meeting about vacation days, but I don't know if there is anything in it for us," can quickly become, "All the departments but ours are getting an extra week of vacation next year." Sound ridiculous? Perhaps, but if you think about it, you will probably recall actual situations that you know of in which an innocent remark quickly became absurdly different or, worse, yet, vicious and harmful.

Rumors often begin without having any names linked with them. This soon changes, probably as a result of carriers trying to make the story more believable as they pass it along. This considerably increases the damage that can be done to specific persons, groups, or organizations. What is said in the section below about responding to gossip also applies to responding to rumor.

Gossip is a rumor of an intimate nature; the focus is on the character or behavior of a *person*. Gossip may open with lines as blatant as, "Did you hear the latest about . . . ?" or with a feeble attempt to be subtle, "You know, I'd be the last person to say anything against anyone, but . . . ." For most persons, the problem is not in knowing how to recognize gossip, but in knowing how to avoid becoming a part of it.

Nobody wants to become the victim of gossip, so we may be afraid of cutting off a gossiper because we do not want to make that person angry and thus become the subject of his or her gossip. We may unwittingly reinforce the person by our silence, and we may even accidentally become a "carrier."

The helpee situation below has five responses that illustrate ineffective ways of responding to rumor or gossip plus an effective response.

Helpee Situation

Teacher to teacher: "Did you know that Mr. McCoy and that new counselor Ms. Spring are dating? She is probably getting her promotion because of her relationship with him. You know what they say; it's not *what* you know but *who* you know."

INAPPROPRIATE HELPER RESPONSES: Responses in which the helper is polite but does not decline to take part in it.

1. The helper wants to hear more: "You're kidding. Mr. McCoy and that young counselor!"
2. The helper pretends not to be interested but encourages more: "Now, we can't jump to conclusions. I do see them together at lunch, but how do we know for sure? It can be very dangerous making assumptions."

3. The helper responds with passive acceptance as though nothing can be done to influence the nature of the conversation: "Well, I guess these things happen, and there's not much we can do about it. We see what we see and hear what we hear, don't we?"

Responses where the helper declines to take part in it, but is not polite.

4. The helper is disrespectful to the helpee by giving her advice on something she already knows: "Kelley, did you know that people can get hurt by gossip, regardless if it's true or not? It's always important to think before you talk, and check out the facts. I prefer not to be involved in this. Maybe you should go talk with them and not me."
5. The helper is curt with the helpee. This response may damage the relationship and not improve the situation. "Don't waste my time with it! I am busy right now, and have more important things to do than listen to stories about the love life of two faculty members."

APPROPRIATE HELPER RESPONSE: In the appropriate response, the helper attempts to be warm and respectful of the helpee, and tries to avoid sounding superior, but clearly declines to interact further on the subject, for example, "I guess you want to help me keep informed about what's going on around here, and I appreciate that, but this seems like something I really don't need to know about. There *is* something else I'd like to hear you talk about, and *that* is . . . ." The helper seeks to communicate acceptance of the helpee as a person without condoning the helpee's inappropriate behavior. This is probably as demanding a communication situation as any, especially when it involves responding to a friend or coworker.

Degrading Talk

Here we have a variety of ways to insult individuals or groups of people. Many slang "labels" that are put on people are deeply hostile in nature, and are often damaging even when used with what a person may think is playful intention. Labeling divides people from one another.

A classroom in which a teacher uses sarcasm will not be a healthy classroom. Sarcasm, heard so much in popular television sitcoms is hostile. The TV laugh track leads some people to think sarcasm is witty, but it is not; it is mean.

To generate an atmosphere in which education and personal growth flourish, do all that you can to diminish the amount of degrading talk. Do this in two ways:

1. Be an encourager. Fill your classroom, and your other relationships, with empathy, respect, and warmth. A *lift-up* brings students to life; a *put-down* destroys spirit.

2. Resist being part of a degrading conversation. Learn how to *politely decline to take part in it*. The situation below shows how this might sound in a conversation.

Helpee Situation

Helpee: "They are the poorest excuses for human beings I ever saw! Not worth a plug nickel. Let me tell you how stupid and ignorant those people are!"

   INAPPROPRIATE HELPER RESPONSE: "I guess you know what you're talking about." (This response fails to reject the helper's inappropriate behavior, and therefore invites the helper to say more degrading things.)

   APPROPRIATE HELPER RESPONSE:

1. "You seem to have pretty strong feelings about some things, and I'm willing to try to understand your feelings and ideas if that can be done without running people down. Otherwise I'd rather talk about something else."
2. "Your experience and attitude seem quite different than mine. If you wish to talk objectively about your attitudes, we can do that, but I have no interest in just listening to a disrespectful emotional attack on a group of people. Would you like for us to have a rational, fair-minded discussion?"

Inordinate/Chronic Griping

Inordinate griping is exaggerating a small complaint; chronic griping is continued complaining about something that cannot or need not be changed. Griping or complaining in any form is unpleasant to hear. When it is inappropriate, it should not be supported.

On the other hand, excessive griping sometimes signals a significant and legitimate complaint. If so, it should be attended to with your best and most facilitative efforts, although it may result from deficient personality adjustment and, if so, be outside the scope of your help. Then, your best option is to accept the person as a person, support his or her behaviors that are appropriate, and ignore as best you can the inappropriate and unpleasant parts of the behavior. If you need to respond, you may express your own opinion or findings on the same subject (situation 1) or gently challenge the helpee's assertion (situation 2), if this can be done without antagonizing the person.

Helpee Situation 1

Helpee: "That guy is really a rotten teacher. I bet he's like that because he doesn't understand America. He just came here while he was in high school, you know."

   Helper: "I find I can learn from my teachers regardless of their cultural background. Having different types of teachers gives me different views and makes learning interesting." If the helper thinks the helpee would be receptive, the helper could add, "It sounds like you have trouble with people who behave differently than you."

Helpee Situation 2

Helpee: "The only reason he gets to teach here is because of equal opportunity. Otherwise he would never have gotten the job."

Helper: "You seem to think a person's ethnic uniqueness determines his or her ability to teach. I'm interested in knowing where you got that information."

You are not likely to be able to stop the inappropriateness, but you do not want to reinforce useless behavior. With some individuals, overreacting with strong emotion will reinforce their useless actions. Your goal is to relate in a friendly way, and to state your attitude toward the inappropriate behavior in a clear and respectful manner, without conveying annoyance, anger, or hurt toward the other person.

Inappropriate Dependency

It is easy, especially in lower grades, for teachers to allow students to become inappropriately dependent upon them. You may have students who have been in classrooms with teachers who encouraged and fostered weakness and dependency on the part of the students. The purpose of education is to teach competence and independence. It is the teacher's role to know how to assist the students in moving from dependence to mature independence and interrelatedness.

Inappropriate dependency usually arises from fear. Some students believe they will not be able to deal with an impending situation; therefore they seek to be sheltered by the teacher or to remain helpless so that facing the object of the fear can be postponed. Some of these fears are real and some of them are irrational.

Dependency also arises from a natural need for attention and for interaction with other persons, but it can grow into a neurotic dependence if persons do not have adequate options for expressing themselves. If students find that their ego needs can be met by being sheltered and cared for by the teacher, they will resist giving up their dependency, and their behaviors may regress to those of an earlier developmental stage.

Inappropriate dependency often results in the student's feeling hostile toward the teacher. The countermeasures for dependency are: (1) recognizing situations that are likely to develop into overdependence and exercise prevention; and (2) knowing how to deal constructively with a dependent person.

The process for helping the dependent person uses the communication skills learned in earlier chapters. Particular aspects are summarized as follows:

1. Find out, through facilitative communication, what the situation is. Assist the helpee in exploring and understanding that situation, its roots, and its implications.

2. If the helpee reveals exaggerated or unfounded fear, probably more fear will be revealed after further facilitative communication.
3. If the helpee discloses "real" fear, an intervention program must be devised. Give the helpee support, information, and as many success experiences as possible to restore the helpee's confidence in his or her ability to cope with the feared situation. Start with what the helpee can do and progress gradually toward the goal behavior. The helpee should be assisted in working toward changing the situation or in securing help to change the situation, as indicated.

Inappropriate Activities

Here we suggest how you may respond when people want you to take part in activities that are potentially harmful to other persons. This would include acts that are illegal, unethical, of questionable judgment, risky to the safety of others, or that encourage an inferior level of performance. These situations may carry a high potential for serious problems.

You must decide if the talk is idle chatter or something concrete, and estimate the effect it may have on others. This will guide the style of your response. If the inappropriateness does not significantly threaten anyone's welfare, you may deal with it by seeking to understand the helpee and trying to facilitate his or her self-understanding. If risk to persons or property is involved, protective action must take precedence over facilitation. Still, this can usually be done without alienating the helpee. You should deal with the helpee as warmly and respectfully as possible but express your views clearly and firmly. Your response may: (1) point out undesirable consequences that might occur and/or (2) offer alternative actions that are appropriate, and (3) it must clearly state or imply what behavior would be appropriate.

If you are aware of inappropriate behavior of a serious or potentially serious nature, you owe it to your organization, your coworkers, and your students to take steps to prevent possible damage. This may mean talking with your superior about it, a step that may take courage and may carry with it the possibility of making you unpopular with the other individual or your coworkers, but for the long-term success of the organization there is no alternative.

Helpee Situation

A group of teachers is assigned to a task force. They are to develop a proposal for some immediate changes to relieve a problem of sexism in the curriculum. They have been allowed to meet on a school day, away from school, at a local conference center. Early in the afternoon, one of the teachers says, "We worked hard all morning. Let's cut out early."

INAPPROPRIATE HELPER RESPONSES:

1. "Sounds good to me. We've earned the time off by working so hard. Besides, how is anyone going to know we left early?"

2. "I agree. I've been on these pseudo task forces before, and nobody ever takes our suggestions seriously anyway. It's just a waste of time."

APPROPRIATE HELPER RESPONSES:

3. "You're probably right, that it will take a struggle for us to get our suggestions put into place, but a lot of other teachers are counting on us, and I think we can make a difference if we give it our best."
4. "I'd be uncomfortable with doing less than the best we can. The task we've been given is a worthy task. We have the ability to do what we have been asked to do, so I suggest we work hard today and push our ideas into policy in the weeks ahead."

EXERCISE 22-1   Practice Responding

Write responses to the situations below in which the helpee's communication is inappropriate. If possible, role play the situations with another person.

Helpee Situations

1. Teacher to teacher (gossip): "When you were in the principal's office did she say anything about Mr. Bell? I heard he is going to be sued by a parent for some sort of unethical behavior. What do you think he did?"
2. Student to teacher (excessive dependence): "You are so much nicer that any teacher I ever had. You treat me better than my parents do. I would like to come over to your house and help you with your chores on Saturday. Not for pay; just because I like you so much."
3. Student to principal (degrading talk): "We should have a chance to be in a school where everybody is the same. Then we could concentrate on learning, instead of having to put up with insults from those (uses hostile racial terms to describe people who are different than he)."
4. Parent to teacher (gossip): "You are so much better than Ms. Harris, whom my kids had last year. She always came to class late and she didn't make the kids work. I think she was more concerned with her social life than the class. I should write a book about all the run-ins I had with her. Can you believe that one day she . . . ?"
5. School secretary to teacher (interrupting a busy teacher for the fourth time in an hour, with the same griping): "Rain, rain, rain. All it does is this stupid, stupid rain. I'm sick of it."
6. School secretary to new teacher (inappropriate activity): "Welcome to the real world! You can forget all you learned at the university. It

EXERCISE 22-1 *Continued*

doesn't work here. These kids are impossible to teach. If you have to beat on them a little, physically, do what you have to do; just don't tell me about it."

7. Student to teacher (excessive dependence): "I know I've done it before, but I forget how. Won't you go with me to the library and check out the book for me?"

8. Teacher to parent (degrading): "Your son is smart enough to do well in school but he would rather try to get through by cheating and conning people. The other teachers and I think he must have learned such attitudes at home, so therefore I don't think you and I have anything to talk about."

9. Custodian to teacher (inappropriate activity): "Take home whatever supplies you need. The school will never miss them. We are all underpaid anyway."

10. Secretary to teacher (rumor): "I overheard the principal on the phone to the superintendent's office, talking about redistricting. Do you suppose that they may close this school next year?"

11. Teacher to teacher (with the same complaint he has whined every day for seven months): "There is no reason why this floor couldn't be clean and shiny, if the night custodian would simply do his job."

▶ 23

Anger—Friend and Foe!

Anger is an unpleasant emotion that is here to stay. It is a *result* of problems, and it can *cause* problems. It is common—if you aren't angry, someone near you is. It is strong, with the capacity to lead to destructive behavior if we let it, yet it can be useful. It is often misunderstood.

Anger is a secondary emotion. It follows other emotions that may result from external forces each of us face:

1. *Losses* such as the death of a loved one, physical impairment, or unemployment lead to feelings of pain, sorrow, grief.
2. *Threats* such as crime, war, and high unemployment lead to feelings of fear, anxiety, insecurity.
3. *Frustrations* that result when we are blocked from getting our needs met lead to feeling helpless, weak, inadequate.
4. *Rejection*, being pushed away by others, is the most agonizing human experience and leads to feeling vulnerable, mortal, worthless.

These primary feelings easily turn to anger. When facing these common conditions, some persons get angry easily and cannot control their anger, while other persons may not get angry, or, if they do, they can control it.

The difference lies with the internal condition of the individual. The following internal conditions are related to feeling angry in response to the external conditions above and to having difficulty in controlling the anger:

1. *Guilt*, real or imagined.
2. A sense of *helplessness*. This may be from low self-esteem or from a lack of emotional or physical help from others.

This chapter is adapted from Richard P. Walters. 1981. *Anger: Yours, Mine and What to Do about It.* Grand Rapids, MI: Zondervan.

3. *Unrealistic expectations.* This may be from excessive self-esteem or from having become accustomed to abusing power.
4. *Aimlessness;* lack of purpose in life.

The emotion of anger has a strong physiological component, triggered by the autonomic nervous system. When faced with one of the external forces listed above, we respond as if under physical attack and the body prepares itself for fight or flight. You know the physical effects: increases in the heart rate, respiration, perspiration, and secretion of adrenaline, and so on. These physical reactions often occur even though we don't need them, and the "gut" reaction interferes with the processes of thinking and, of course, communicating.

We do have a choice about what we do. Although the body may be signaling "fight" or "flight" and the mind is bewildered, we are capable of choosing from among four alternatives:

1. Expression of the anger feeling in *rage*—volatile, explosive, destructive behavior toward objects or other people.
2. Expression in *resentment*—holding the feeling within, stifling it, denying the direct outward expression of it, which is self-destructive.
3. *Indignation*—keeping the feeling but using the energy to take long-term constructive actions against the conditions causing anger in oneself or others.
4. *Resolving the feeling* by reducing or removing the causes of a particular incident of anger.

Rage and resentment are destructive and usually harmful options. Indignation, used thoughtfully and cautiously, can be very beneficial in correcting injustices or advancing worthwhile causes. Resolution is probably the course we will follow most frequently.

Resolution begins with first aid techniques used to "buy time" while the physical activation subsides. In this emergency phase, many familiar tactics can be useful.

FIRST AID FOR ANGER

1. Remind yourself that even though you feel angry you are still in control of your behavior.
2. Turn your attention to something else. The tried and true method of counting to ten is one way, but you may need a more demanding task. Recite the alphabet backward, count backward from 200 by 7's, concentrate on using your sense of touch to investigate a nearby object that you long have taken for granted. The principle is to divert your attention, temporarily, from the anger provoking stimulus to anything neutral.

3. Relax your breathing. Take a deep breath, hold it a second, release it slowly through your mouth.
4. Separate yourself from the scene of conflict, even for a couple of minutes, if possible.
5. Maintain positive thoughts. Visualize yourself in the most pleasant, relaxed conditions you know.
6. Use music. Listen, play, or sing.
7. Channel the energy into something constructive. Rake the yard or write a report—jump vigorously into a project, physical if possible.
8. Do something you enjoy.
9. Talk with a friend.
10. Talk with yourself. Out loud, even. Yes, that's helpful and it's safe if no one's around. Look yourself eye to eye in a mirror as you talk about your anger. Silly? Maybe, but it's useful because it helps you bring the circumstances into perspective. Writing down your thoughts will do the same thing.
11. Relax. Give yourself a neck rub, put your feet up, take a short walk, use systematic muscle relaxation—whatever you can do in the circumstances and that has worked for you in the past.
12. Laugh. True laughter, incompatible with anger, will drive anger out.
13. Cry if you need to. When we repress feelings that need release we are putting those very feelings into control of us.
14. Measure the issue. Is it worth being angry about?

Obviously, circumstances dictate what you can or cannot do. Usually you will be able to do a couple of these—enough to give you the breather you need.

First aid helps, but it is not enough. Many of us become complacent after using such first aid and do not go on to the "cure." That's a bad mistake. If the roots of anger remain they will sprout again, and probably soon. Strategies for cure may include intensive counseling, possibly psychotherapy, but there are many things that people can do to help themselves.

A CURE FOR ANGER

1. Learn to be aware of your anger and to accept it as a legitimate emotional experience, even though you wish to be rid of it.
2. Undo, to the extent possible, any damage done to others.
3. Decide if your goal is to be free of angry feelings, or if it might be more constructive to keep the feeling and use the energizing effect to enhance your indignant protest against the forces that cause the feeling.
4. Find and analyze the sources of anger. This is where talking with others is particularly important. An anger "diary" is useful; carry a 3 x 5 card for a couple of weeks, making a note of what is happening each time you feel angry. Or write "anger" at the top of a pad and start writing words that

come to mind with free association. Either of these exercises will generate material that you (and your friend or counselor) can explore for clues about the sources of anger.

5. Look beyond the precipitating event that triggered the feeling. The probability is high that emotional pressure has been building for a long time.
6. Make a firm commitment to yourself, and perhaps to others, to not be controlled by anger; that you will not express it in rage or resentment.
7. Plan constructive actions: (a) to talk with persons you are angry with; (b) to confront when necessary; (c) to have a group meeting of persons involved, if appropriate; (d) to forgive those who have hurt you; (e) to get whatever outside help might be useful.
8. Rehearse your plan and carry it out.

INITIAL RESPONSES TO AN ANGRY PERSON

Each of us has had an experience of receiving an attack of anger from another person without warning and for no apparent reason. Two elements are present in most instances when an outburst of anger occurs: (a) a precipitating situation or incident, and (b) a readiness on the part of an individual to become angry. The external and internal conditions that lead to the readiness may be multiple and obscure to you. Being aware that many external and internal conditions affect each of us at all times and must certainly underlie expression of anger should help you respond to that *person* rather than to that person's anger *behavior*.

Every classroom has in it students who are bombarded with the external conditions that lead to anger and whose internal conditions allow anger to flourish. Some of the students are self-controlled all the time, and all of the students are self-controlled some of the time, but there will be occasional outbursts of anger by students, and teachers need to know how to respond to angry persons.

The information below outlines the aspects of communication that are unique to responding to an outburst of anger. These considerations and helpee behaviors precede using the model in its "regular" manner. When those conditions are met, helping can begin. Here are guidelines for first aid responses to an angry person.

1. Know and understand your own response to anger. Anticipate the ineffective responses you might be inclined to give. Use the model, as applied in the exercises dealing with an angry person, to respond effectively.
2. Remember the dynamics of anger. Frequently an attack comes from a person who is unhappy because of events or needs not related to the precipitating incident. As soon as you show the angry person that you are trying to understand those needs, you have a friend.

3. Allow the angry person to talk and to let angry feelings spill out. When the anger is allowed to flow from the helpee, it will usually dissipate quickly. The angry person is not going to feel good or be receptive to your help until the bad feelings are communicated and understood. It is futile to try to force logic or information on a person who is filled with strong emotion—at that moment it is simply not possible to use it.

4. Accept the person's right to be angry and accept him or her as a person of worth, even though you may not agree with the stated reasons for being angry. You must always allow the other person the freedom to be wrong.

5. The angry person is not functioning with optimal accuracy. Anything you say or do is likely to be misinterpreted. This means that your communication must be particularly effective. You'll have the best chance of success by following these suggestions: Show nonverbally that you are listening. Nod affirmatively, pay close attention, do not crowd the person or give any motion that might be interpreted as anger on your part.

   React calmly, but with clear meaning. If it seems appropriate to speak, you might say something like, "I'd like to listen to what you want to say," or, "This must be very important; please let me know more about it." *Say only enough to show your acceptance of and your attention to the angry person.*

6. If there is a quick solution to the precipitating incident, give it. If, for example, the person is angry because a coworker did not assist with something, help out if your duties permit you to do so. This is first aid for anger, not a cure.

7. If you have been part of the problem, admit it, fully and willingly. If you do not, no restoration is possible and the problem can only become more serious. Do not deal with the helpee's feelings when you should be taking action. If, for example, the person is angry because you are not doing something that you are responsible for doing, do not sit around and listen to the anger, get up and do your job!

8. Seek something about which you can compliment the other person, or something about which you can agree, but do not use this as a "technique." It can bring you and the other person close together only if you are genuinely seeking to develop your areas of common interest.

9. Always communicate helpfully. Your good communication adds pleasure to the lives of others who, in turn, will communicate more helpfully with other persons.

CRISIS MANAGEMENT

On occasion—although we wish it were not so—you will find yourself in a situation in which a person is experiencing a major trauma and is unable to cope with it. You may be the person on the scene who is best able to decide what to do first, how to do it, and do those things that keep a bad situation from becoming worse.

The guidelines listed below suggest the most important principles and tasks that are usually part of managing a crisis of the most urgent sort, in which life or health is threatened. While the components may often be implemented in the order listed, you will use your own judgment about priorities in the situation at hand.

1. Protect life and human welfare. After that, and perhaps with much less priority, protect physical property.
2. Manage debilitating emotions. For anger, use the more detailed information in this chapter. For fear, offer realistic reassurance. Do what can safely and reasonably be done to reduce actual dangers. For suicidal impulses, remove the individual from the possibility of self-harm, get him or her into a setting in which self-destructive behavior is not possible, offer hope that *makes sense and is meaningful to him or her.*
3. Establish who is in charge. By its nature, there is no time for a committee meeting in a crisis. Firm leadership—a benevolent dictator—is suitable.
4. Notify professionals. Arrange for immediate support and, if possible, long-term response that will relieve the causes of the trauma, heal its effects, and prevent recurrence.

Some crises are emotionally intense, but allow more time for resolution. In these situations the helper expects the helpee to be as involved in discussion, thinking through and choosing a plan of action, and implementing the plan as possible. The helper is directive only to the extent absolutely necessary.

1. Define the problem. Some have said that a problem defined is half-solved. Certainly we are unlikely to solve a problem without defining it. Doing so makes a transition from emotional chaos to rational problem-solving. The helpee may find it very helpful if you create a facilitative atmosphere, so that it is easy for him or her to talk about the situation they are in. Doing so, they often find many answers.
2. List alternatives. Persons who are caught up emotionally in a problem are not very creative. You may find that a solution that seems quite obvious to you has not occurred to the helpee. Brainstorm with him or her about approaches to relieving the perceived problem.
3. Identify people involved, and how they are influenced by each of the alternatives.
4. Make a plan. The strategies for change in Chapter 21 may be very helpful to you at this point.

In all situations, recognize the limits upon what you can do. Bad things happen to good people; you can't stop that. Your best efforts to relieve or prevent human suffering will sometimes not be enough; you can't help that. You and I are responsible to do what we can do, nothing more. When we have done that, we do well to take satisfaction in having given our best efforts. If we dwell on what might have been, criticize ourselves for other response scenarios we can imagine in our minds, we only weaken our confidence and endurance to do those things that remain around us that are worth doing. Do your best, let go of the rest, and stay strong to help the next.

STRATEGIES FOR RESOLVING THE ROOTS OF ANGER

Schools have an obligation to help angry students understand the origins of their distress and to offer appropriate help. It is part of the school's mandate to help students develop emotional health; it is part of maintaining an atmosphere that aids learning and protects students from one another; and it is practical because it reduces burnout among teachers.

Any one person may give only a portion of the help a student needs, but collectively the school often can do enough. Table 23-1 lists some of the strategies that may be used in a school to resolve or alleviate root causes of anger.

HELPING RESOLVE CONFLICT BETWEEN TWO OTHER PARTIES

Have you ever been the referee in a fight or been put into the awkward position of being there when two of your friends were verbally scrapping with each other? Has it happened in the classroom?

Conflict is a normal part of vigorous, healthy relationships. It can be a very constructive force: It is energizing, brings out creativity, can force people to evaluate their point of view, and can lead to greater harmony and cooperation. Or it can be destructive.

We don't pretend that you will be an expert conflict negotiator in one quick lesson, but if you skillfully use the suggestions below, you are very likely to be effective in helping two parties in conflict resolve their differences. These simple, common-sense procedures are the ones used in high-level labor management and political conflicts. They are likely to work in any situation—in the classroom, in supervision, in marriage or family counseling—at the very worst these procedures are going to be better than the alternatives.

If it is possible to have some structure for the discussion, that can help a lot. You might suggest these ground rules for the discussion:

1. Everyone listens.
2. Everyone gets a chance to talk.

TABLE 23-1   Strategies for Coping with Anger

External conditions	Strategies that reduce the stress and promote better mental health in angry persons

from THREAT
    to SENSE
    OF SAFETY
	Help them see circumstances more accurately: desensitization to irrational threat; growth in skills for coping with actual threats.

from REJECTION to ACCEPTANCE	Help them have realistic expectations: aid friendship building; help them learn if rejection is real or imagined; if real, learn why; improve social skills.

from LOSS
    to GETTING
    NEEDS MET
	Teach about grief: to reduce fear about their emotional response to the loss; to help them acquire substitutes for loss. Guide them toward finding new ways to get needs met.

from FRUSTRATION to SUCCESS	Help them test the validity of their skills; aid growth in coping skills and other life skills

Internal conditions	Strategies to strengthen internal resources, thereby diminishing vulnerability to anger

from GUILT
    to FREEDOM (which
    may call for apology
    and/or restitution)
	Is the guilt real or imagined? Identify any conflicts between belief and behavior remedy offenses committed against others.

from HELPLESSNESS to CONFIDENCE	Human development programs that enhance self-image: support groups; counseling

from UNREALISTIC
    EXPECTATIONS
    to PERSPECTIVE
	Discussion or counseling groups that bring the student more accurate understanding of "the real world" and of his/her self

from AIMLESSNESS to DIRECTION	Vocational/educational guidance: learning decision-making techniques; defining and working on attainable goals; voluntarily being accountable for behavior to a group or person

3. The goal for the discussion is for everyone to be fully satisfied at the end.
4. That goal is not attainable, but it's worth working toward. And, it's possible for everyone to be reasonably satisfied.
5. If you are in a position of responsibility (as a supervisor, teacher, parent) you will exercise your authority so that you can protect all parties in the dispute, and you will make the final decision if you have to.

Your role is to be the guide; to lead the others into effective processes. The steps listed below may not be followed in exact sequence, but each element is

EXERCISE 23-1   Responding to Anger

Part of the skill in responding to anger is being able to take it—to perceive accurately and respond calmly under complex and emotionally charged circumstances. These conditions cannot be simulated very well by printed helpee situations. If possible, ask someone to take the helpee role and together verbally act out the situations below. If that is not possible, write the initial response that you would give in a helper role. In responding to each of the situations, you are the teacher.

Helpee Situations

1. Parent to teacher: "The school is supposed to offer band instrument lessons, but when I talked to the music teacher she said that only certain kids were eligible. She said a child has to make a certain score on some test. I don't know how any test can prove whether or not a child should have lessons! I'll tell you one thing, my child is as talented as any kid in school. I think it's because we weren't born in the U.S."

2. High school student to teacher: "This whole society is a ripoff society! Everybody feeds off somebody else! *You're* part of it! You may *say* you're here to help us, but you're just in it for the money. You have a union just like all the other ripoffs. You couldn't care less about the students."

3. The principal, Ms. Jones, calls to you as you are walking to your car after school. She catches up with you and angrily begins confronting you about an incident that occurred that day. She said you sent a student, Ray Smith, to the office instead of bringing him to the office yourself. Instead of going to the office, the student wandered around the halls for half an hour. The principal ends by saying, "You know the rules. I don't want this to happen again."

4. Custodian to teacher: "I wish you'd do something about these kids and their gum. It is everywhere—the school is covered with it. We've got more than we can do with our sweeping and waxing and emptying the trash and everything else without cleaning up all the filthy gum! But you high and mighty teachers don't care what we have to do!"

5. Elementary student to teacher: "I don't like you! You never choose me to do anything special!"

6. High school student to teacher: "You have it in for me. You always make a fool of me in front of the whole class. You ask me the hardest questions every time just to pick on me. I don't think I've done anything to deserve this, unless it's to have a skin color that's different than yours."

EXERCISE 23-1   *Continued*

7. High school student to teacher: "This class is a waste of time! There's no reason in the world why I should have to study this stupid stuff! How is this going to help me get a job? I can work in fast food and no where else, and you know it, 'cause it's people like you that keep it that way for people like me."

8. High school student to teacher: "My friends say that I get P.O.'d real quick, and that it happens a lot. I guess they're right. But my life hasn't been the same since my best friend killed himself."

9. Student to parent: "You've made me look the fool to the whole school. I don't have a friend left! You should be proud of me, but you're not. You should be thankful I've got my act together, but all you have done is show me that the smartest thing I could do is move out of this place where nobody cares about anybody else."

10. Parent to student: "You don't know anything about gratitude, so go ahead and move out, and we'll both see how quick you find out how much hard work it takes to make it in this world. Then maybe you'll be thankful for all I've done for you, and can show at least a little respect to the people you live with."

usually necessary in order to create the level of trust and understanding that is necessary for agreement on solutions to the conflict. Here are the steps you help involve every person in:

1. Listen very carefully with ears and eyes, using good attending skills.
2. Understand feelings, but do not follow them. For example, we may feel like hitting each other, or walking out, but we don't.
3. Separate facts from fiction; double-check the facts. Eliminate slanted communication such as half-truths, exaggerations, irrelevant remarks.
4. Clearly state the problem and the solution as each person views it.
5. Ask for all solutions to the problems. None is too silly to consider.
6. In the process of steps 3, 4, and 5 it is helpful to ask one party to restate the problem (or suggested solution) to the other party, to see if perception is accurate. This is similar to the empathy process of reflecting the content and feelings. The greatest source of conflict between persons (or groups) is misunderstanding, and the process of reflection is probably the most useful single method of reducing misunderstanding. You can use this frequently in your own statements as mediator and can also ask them to do it.
7. Find areas of agreement. Write these down clearly, but don't keep going over and over them; move on to the troublesome items and find ways to agree on those (step 5).

8. Make a decision.
9. Summarize, clarify again (step 6), and present expectations for the future.

The procedures—simply acquiring clear understanding of one another—aren't magic, but sometimes the results would make you think so. Conflict resolution requires a willingness to live within the limits of situations that don't allow every person to have everything he or she wants. Adjustment is part of life. As helpers, we can always treat each person with respect and work toward solutions that are equitable. These may be a lot better than what that person has been used to.

▶ 24

Applying the Communication Model to Other Situations

Up to this point the interpersonal skills model outlined in Chapter 1 has been directed toward the primary communication skills of a helper in a helping situation—understanding communication types, responding effectively to requests, listening when appropriate, using the transition and action dimensions effectively, and dealing with anger and inappropriate communication. This chapter expands on the model and discusses other important communication situations, such as giving and accepting compliments, communication in employment relationships, responding to dissatisfaction, responding with constructive criticism, and responding to an administrative dilemma. How an individual handles difficult interpersonal situations in many cases determines his or her value as an employee to the organization. Remember that in each of these special communication situations the key to increasing your probability of success (i.e., getting your point across effectively while at the same time maintaining the relationship with the individual) depends on the base relationship that is established according to the model developed throughout this manual.

GIVING COMPLIMENTS

Compliments are a legitimate and important part of the expression of warmth. They are only helpful when used honestly; unfortunately, this isn't always the case. Walters (1980) describes the following types:

1. *Bait.* Given by persons fishing for a compliment in return.
2. *Motivator.* Given to urge the person to work harder.
3. *Foot in the door.* Used as an introduction to criticism—first the good news, then the bad news.
4. *Bandaid.* To cover up the hurt that has been inflicted upon the other.
5. *Set up.* Cheap flattery used to weaken your resistance to an attack.

A few persons are leery about receiving compliments. There are several possible reasons:

1. They think the compliment might be phony.
2. Receiving a compliment gives them a standard of performance to live up to in the future.
3. They have a habit of denying compliments, perhaps having been taught this style of self-negation as a reaction to being proud.
4. They can't believe it and feel they don't deserve it, which is often a sign of low self-esteem.

If people tend to be leery about trusting compliments, is it safe to give them? Or will people think *you* are phony simply because five out of the last six compliments they got seemed phony to them? They might. There is some risk, but it's a risk worth taking because people need to receive all the affirmation and encouragement they have earned. Risk is minimal when the following conditions are met:

1. The compliment is deserved.
2. The person knows you have been in a position to know whether or not it is deserved.
3. You want to give the compliment. It doesn't mean you have to like the person. You may even be struggling with envy. These circumstances may even enhance the value of the compliment to the receiver. But, most of all: If you want to give it, give it; if not, don't.
4. You say it in your own style. Keep it short and simple.
5. To the best of your ability you are giving the compliment for the other person's benefit, not yours.

ACCEPTING COMPLIMENTS

While we're at it, let's consider the reverse side of the compliment—our behavior in accepting them. This is also an issue of helper warmth because if a compliment is not accepted effectively it conveys anything but warmth. The sad fact is many persons are clumsy when they are given a compliment. They may respond by denying or minimizing the achievement or characteristic that is being complimented. For example, the following compliment is given by one teacher to another teacher, "You did an excellent job in your presentation to the faculty this morning. I especially admired how you handled the question-and-answer period." The teacher who has been complimented responds, "Oh, I thought it was probably pretty boring. In fact, I felt pretty awkward trying to answer a couple of those questions. They should have had someone else up there." This kind of response to a compliment is rather typical, yet it actually punishes the person who has given the compliment. This kind of response challenges the validity of the perception and integrity of the statement of the person giving the compliment. It will probably leave that person feeling rebuffed and unlikely to offer a compliment to the other person again.

Many persons are suspicious of the genuineness of compliments. They may believe that the person who is complimenting them is fishing for a compliment in return, using flattery for some hidden purpose, trying to manipulate them, or is praising them as an introduction to giving criticism. However, compliments are usually genuine, and when they are not, it is obvious.

Accept a compliment as you would accept any other gift from a friend; If it makes you feel good, say so. For example, a person says to a coworker, "Delores, it's hard to put this into words, but I want you to know I'm glad that we get to work together. You care a lot about the kids but also a lot about the rest of us. What you said to me this morning especially meant a lot to me." An appropriate response would be, "Thank you! It makes me very happy to hear you say that."

The most meaningful compliments often come as a surprise, which makes them difficult to respond to easily. But, since the person giving the compliment has revealed genuine feelings, you can reveal yours in your response. Don't be reluctant to accept the compliment. Simply say something along the lines of, "That's really kind of you to say that," or "Wow, thanks! I appreciate that!"

If you use the principles and skills taught in this book you will earn and deserve lots of compliments. When they come, accept them graciously, enjoy them, draw energy from the affirmation; and you'll become even more enthusiastic about living and more effective in everything you do!

COMMUNICATION IN EMPLOYMENT RELATIONSHIPS

In the ideal employment situation the needs of all members of the organization are met in ways that are satisfying to each person involved and that contribute to the fulfillment of the goals of the organization. Good communication among the members of the organization is the first step toward creating ideal conditions. A desirable goal is for there to be a relationship each to each among members of the organization, such as we have earlier defined as a base relationship between a helper and a helpee. In this relationship administrators understand the goals and needs of their subordinates (empathy), value their options, believe in their potential, consider their needs as important (respect), and create a pleasant working environment (warmth).

When these conditions exist in an organization, each person wants to do his or her best. They are more productive and happier, and organizational goals get met. Supervisors who relate to their people with the styles taught in this manual will more than likely enjoy great success, and the job will be easier because of the cooperation they receive. The same relationship styles that produce better learning and fewer discipline problems in the classroom will produce better teaching and fewer conflicts among the faculty.

The relationship between supervisor and employee should be congenial and show mutual caring without undue familiarity; be personal but do not show favoritism; be relaxed but purposeful. From this relationship supervisors can be as direct as the situation requires but allow employees all the freedom and flexibility in the performance of their duties as their competence allows. Good communication builds relationships that strengthen supervisors' ability to achieve the best efforts of their team, because the team members are satisfied with the relationship.

RESPONDING TO DISSATISFACTION

One type of interaction that frequently occurs between an administrator and teacher or between a department head and department member results from dissatisfaction with some aspect of the working conditions. The interaction below illustrates several ways of responding to a situation of this type.

Helpee Situation

Teacher to principal: "This semester I seem to have practically every problem child in the seventh grade. Sometimes my classroom seems like a madhouse. If Billy Watson and his buddy, Ralph, weren't *both* in the class together, maybe things would be okay. I specifically asked that they be assigned to different rooms but, as usual, nobody listened to my recommendation."

Helper Responses

HURTFUL: "I'm afraid you're imagining things. You know that we listen to what you say."

HURTFUL: "My job is to decide who does what. Your job is to do it."

HURTFUL: "You're probably just having a bad day. We all have our bad days. The reason you have those students is because we thought you were the best person for the job."

INEFFECTIVE: "You say some of your students are giving you a hard time today?"

INEFFECTIVE: "Maybe you're not getting enough rest at night."

MINIMALLY HELPFUL: "Right now you sound mistreated by the way things have been handled and discouraged about how things are going in the classroom. This must be pretty important to you. I'd be glad to talk with you about it and see if there are some other options for us at this time." The principal—in the helper role—must decide whether or not the complaint is legitimate. This judgment determines, in part, the nature of the response. Both of the level 4.0 responses illustrated below assume a base relationship between the teacher and the principal.

ADDITIVE (principal believes complaint is unfounded): "The situation in your classroom has made you pretty uncomfortable. You say it seems to you that we did not honor your request to separate the problem boys this year. Yet, it sounds to me that there may be more to it than that."

HELPEE (reply to previous response): "Well, I don't know, I'm just so confused. I've always thought of you as being fair—a good person to work for—but when I look at what I'm doing, and see what others are doing, it does seem like I get the worst end of things quite often."

ADDITIVE (helper recognizes complaint as legitimate): "It's been rough for you—it's been getting you down. Now that you point it out to me, I see you're right—I *have* tended to give you more of the difficult students. But it's been because you're skilled in dealing with them, and not for any other reason. Your classroom performance has been excellent. I didn't realize that working with some of these students was such an unpleasant task for you. Maybe there are some other arrangements that will be more satisfactory."

HELPEE (reply to previous response): "Well, it wasn't the work so much but I just couldn't understand why I got all the problem students. It's a compliment in a way, I guess, but it would be nice if you could spread the load around a little more."

RESPONDING WITH CONSTRUCTIVE CRITICISM

Probably the most difficult situation in supervision occurs when it is necessary to talk with employees about such things as their deficiencies in performance of duties, infractions of rules, or undesirable interpersonal relationships. In terms of this communication model, such interactions often involve conditions and techniques of the action phase of the model. Whether or not this communication is accepted depends on (1) the quality of the base relationship, and (2) the skill with which the helper utilizes the action-phase condition of confrontation and other action-phase strategies such as problem solving.

The occasion of confrontation does not need to be extremely uncomfortable for either supervisor or subordinate. It can, in fact, be a time of constructive advance in skills and understanding for both parties. Follow the suggestions below to maximize the benefits of these occasions.

1. Don't get overly caught up in the crisis of the moment. Keep the long-range relationship in mind.
2. Take care not to accuse prematurely. Listen to the employee's story. Be alert for new data that are relevant to the situation.
3. Give the employee an opportunity to take the initiative in explaining and correcting the situation. Follow the principle of allowing the employees/ helpees to do as much for themselves as they are capable.
4. Put the criticism and the problem area in perspective by discussing employees' areas of strength. To let employees mistakenly feel that they are doing nothing right is tragic, but it happens frequently. Again, stay alert for the effect of the interaction on the employees.
5. The best protection against remedial supervisory work is prevention of problems through clear task assignment and other preparation of the employees to carry out their duties.
6. Avoid "hit and run" confrontation. Things are rarely as simple as they appear on the surface, so allow for explanation of the problem and ample time for interaction.

The following dialogue illustrates an effective administrator implementing the communication model and the resolution of a problem. In this example, a principal is talking to two of her teachers (helpees) about their inappropriate behavior that had been reported to her and that she had subsequently verified. Assume a base relationship between the principal and two teachers in her school.

HELPER (principal): "The reason I wanted to see you two together is to discuss a complaint I had a few minutes ago from one of the other teachers."

HELPEE (teacher): "Okay, what is it?"

HELPER: "It was about the excessively loud talking and laughing in the teachers' lounge this morning. You both know that I rarely get a report like that about either of you from one of the other teachers, but with several classrooms in the area of the teachers' lounge the noise was apparently very disruptive to the surrounding classrooms."

The principal began the conversation by explaining the purpose and tempered the criticism by pointing out, indirectly and briefly, that the behavior of the teachers is generally at a very high professional level.

The teacher may respond to what the principal says in any of the ways a helpee might respond to a confrontation. Several of these are illustrated and discussed below as alternative endings to the dialogues. In each of the alternative endings to the dialogue above, the helper responses are effective and consistent with the high levels of the communication model.

HELPEE: "Who said that?"

HELPER: "You seem surprised to think that one of your colleagues would come to me with this kind of complaint. It sounds like your perception of the situation is different from the one that I heard."

> This response emphasizes the helpee's probable feelings and reactions. It seeks to get the focus of the interaction back on the helpee's behavior. Answering the question that the teacher asked would not facilitate the helpee's exploration of the problem.

HELPEE (angrily): "That's a lie! How could we be making noise when we were grading papers in the lounge all morning? You don't know what you're talking about. You *never* do!"

HELPER: "You have strong feelings about this, so it's something we need to talk about right now. Let's all go in my office so we'll have more privacy."

> The helpee belligerently tries to bluff her way out of this situation. The principal must firmly retain control so she can deal with the original incident in a constructive way, as well as with the helpee's display of animosity for her.

HELPEE: "You talk a lot about teamwork. How can we work as a team if we are not allowed to speak with each other?"

HELPER: "You're saying that we need to strike a happy medium between no interaction at all, on the one hand, and disruptive behavior on the other."

> The helpee has overreacted to the helper's response and in effect distorted her message. The helper's response in this situation afford an opportunity for the helpee to disclose more.

HELPEE (Both look at floor and say nothing.)

HELPER (After about thirty seconds of silence): "There are several things that you might mean by your silence, but I would prefer not to guess about what you're thinking. I would rather hear directly from you, and I hope that you will give me your ideas about this matter."

> When the principal offers to listen to the teachers' perceptions and feelings related to the situation, the response communicates high-level respect.

EXERCISE 24-1   Responding to an Administrative Dilemma

Each of the situations below describes a dilemma for a person who has administrative responsibility for another person. Consider the implications of each alternative action in terms of the communication model.

Helpee Situation 1

A principal overhears two teachers talking about a new teacher who has been hired on a temporary basis to replace another teacher who is on medical leave of absence: "Did you hear that the new teacher just graduated two weeks ago; she's been in college for four years. Let's introduce her to the real world. We'll show her she's not so cool!"

What should the supervisor do? (1) Ignore it. (2) Warn the new teacher so she will be prepared for what may happen. (3) Talk to the two teachers immediately. (4) Talk to the two teachers individually when convenient.

If you choose (1), explain why. If you choose (2), (3), or (4), write a statement consistent with the communication model for the supervisor to use in opening the conversation with the person involved.

Helpee Situation 2

You are a principal. Ms. Bryan, the person speaking to you in this situation, is a teacher's aide in the classroom of Mr. Smith. Ms. Bryan says to you, "I really don't know what to do about this, but I think I need to talk to you about it. I think some things need to be done. Mr. Smith has been treating some of the students terribly. Yesterday I saw him shove Bill Richards when he wouldn't cooperate. He thinks no one saw him but I did, and it's not the first time it's happened either. But I'm afraid to talk to him about it."

What should you, as principal, do? (1) Acknowledge hearing the complaint but take no other action. (2) Talk with Mr. Smith and warn him that this kind of behavior is unacceptable. (3) Talk with Mr. Smith about whether or not he is getting along well with Ms. Bryan. (4) Talk with Bill Richards. (5) Other (describe). Explain your choice and write a statement that would be appropriate to use in introducing whatever course of action you would take.

Helpee Situation 3

Six weeks ago Mr. Bridges, the principal, hired Ms. Johnson as the new school secretary. Ms. Johnson replaced a secretary who had been at the school for many years. She was hired with a clear understanding that it was for a trial period of two months and subject to review at the end of

EXERCISE 24-1   *Continued*

that time. Although Ms. Johnson's work seemed to be satisfactory in most ways, Mr. Bridges thought he had sensed annoyance from several of his teachers, and he had a general uneasiness about her dependability. He had about decided that he had hired the wrong person.

What should Mr. Bridges do? (1) Wait until the end of the trial period and see if the situation changes. (2) Warn her that her performance to date is not satisfactory. (3) Talk with some of the senior teachers to get their impressions of Ms. Johnson's work. (4) Encourage her to begin looking around. Explain your choice and write a statement for Mr. Bridges to use as an initial statement in the conversation.

Helpee Situation 4

You are a principal and Ms. Sanders is a teacher on your faculty. During the last month she has been late to work several times. She has given you a variety of reasons: "My car wouldn't start. The clock didn't go off. I had to call a cab and they didn't come. I thought I was going to be sick so I waited." Today she was an hour late. When she reported in she explained, "The place where I leave my baby wasn't open on time. There just wasn't anyone there, so I had to wait for them to come. I couldn't bring Mikey here! I tried to call you but you were busy. Didn't you get my message?"

You check with the secretary and she states that she had not received a call from Ms. Sanders that morning. Later in the day another teacher mentions that she had left her child at the same daycare center at 8 o'clock, the time that Ms. Sanders indicated the center was closed. Describe what you would do and say.

Helpee Situation 5

One of the teachers in your school, Ms. Jenkins, has created problems for you on several occasions as a result of spreading inaccurate accusations about other staff members in the school. Today, she comes to you to talk about one of your most trusted and valuable teachers. She says, "I hate to be nosy, but it seems like Mr. Jackson is coming to school in the morning with liquor on his breath. Maybe that explains why he has so many discipline problems in his class lately." Describe what you would do and say.

Helpee Situation 6

You are in the teachers' lounge this morning when one of the janitors, Mr. Jones, walks in and begins pouring himself a cup of coffee. A first-year teacher in your school is sitting in a chair next to the coffee pot and

Continued

EXERCISE 24-1   *Continued*

you overhear her say, "You can't use this lounge. It's only for the *teach-ers*. You have an area down in the basement." Describe what you would do and say.

Helpee Situation 7

Ms. Arlan was transferred to the school where you are principal. You weren't eager about her transfer to your school because of things you had heard about her. Her former principal told you, "If it weren't for things she says, she would be the best member of our team. It's just that she keeps things in a constant uproar because she is so opinionated. Actually she's *great* with the students."

You have wondered if Ms. Arlan's problem in the other school might have been due to overreaction on the part of the principal, so you approved the transfer. Everything has gone very smoothly during the first few weeks of the school year and, from your frequent observation, Ms. Arlan appeared to be an asset to the faculty.

Just now, two of your other teachers enter your office. One of them is crying and the other appears angry and says, "We just knew it wouldn't work out and it *hasn't*. That big mouth you brought in here just shot off her mouth to Rose. I told her to apologize to Rose but she just stomped off. There is *no way* we are going to put up with that stuff all year long. Something has to be done about it, and done about it now!"

Describe what you would do and/or say.

REFERENCE

Walters, R.P. 1980. *Amity: Friendship in Action*. Boulder, CO: Christian Helpers, Inc.

▶ 25

The Encouraging Teacher

Encouragement is a fundamental concept instrumental in helping teachers to improve relationships with their students and in creating an atmosphere of cooperation and democracy in the schools. In general, encouragement conveys to students that they are understood and accepted—that they are "fine as they are." Encouragement is not a new psychological idea. The concept was introduced with the Individual Psychology of Alfred Adler (1939) and was clarified and refined by Rudolph Dreikurs (1971). This chapter will briefly describe the concept of encouragement as a necessary component of the human relations life skill.

ENCOURAGEMENT AND THE FACILITATIVE RELATIONSHIP

A facilitative relationship requires more than establishing contact and rapport with students. A facilitative relationship requires mutual trust and respect. Trusting human nature, oneself, and others is truly encouraging. Respecting both oneself and others allows for cooperation and equality to exist between teachers and students.

In order to establish and maintain a cooperative relationship, teachers must know how to align the interests and goals of the students with their own. A cooperative relationship is one in which the student and teacher accept one another's goals. Winning the student's cooperation is a prerequisite for learning, and maintaining it requires constant vigilance. Often, this facilitative relationship is the first constructive relationship in which the student learns by experiencing the give-and-take of life. It is a relationship in which

This chapter was contributed by Timothy D. Evans, Ph.D., Associate Professor, College of Education, University of South Florida.

the student feels not only understood and accepted, but also experiences the anticipation of success (Dreikurs 1967a).

However, conveying mutual respect, trust, cooperation, and understanding are not the only therapeutic agents in establishing a facilitative relationship. Encouragement is also an essential skill for relating to students. Rudolph Dreikurs (1964) taught that a child needs encouragement like a plant needs water. Alfred Adler (Griffith 1991) emphasized that an educator's most important task, perhaps his "holy duty," is to see to it that no child is discouraged at school and that a child who enters school already discouraged has his or her self-confidence restored. Education is possible only for confident children who look hopefully and joyfully upon the future.

Educators have an obligation to encourage students and to prevent them from failing. In addition to ensuring friendly teacher-student relations, encouragement provides the guidance which enables students to develop into responsible individuals.

Effective teaching depends on an educator's ability to encourage parents, children, and other teachers. Teachers and parents sometimes inadvertently discourage students by having too high expectations and being overly ambitious for them. When we tell students they could do better, we are really implying that they are not good enough as they are. Students misbehave only when they are discouraged and convinced they cannot succeed on the "useful" side of life. Thus, student success depends on the school's ability to provide encouragement. Conversely, student failure reveals an inability of the school to encourage. Reversing discouragement requires a counteraction found in the psychology of encouragement. No student is able to initiate or sustain corrective efforts without encouragement. Encouragement stimulates hope, belief in oneself, and a sense of belonging (Dreikurs 1964).

More than others, discouraged students need opportunities to feel important, appreciated, and respected. Yet, it seems that the students who need encouragement the most generally receive it the least. Instead of minimizing their weaknesses in order to build on their strengths, we chastise them for their innumerable indiscretions. Instead of recognizing their efforts or improvements, we focus on their mistakes. Instead of allowing them to feel a sense of belonging through meaningful contribution, we isolate them even further through various means of punishment and/or control. Conventional methods for correcting students' faulty behaviors do nothing more than ridicule, humiliate, and punish—responses which only incite increased misbehavior. Students regard such punitive methods as confirmation of their lack of self-worth and convince themselves that they do not belong in school. Rather than cooperate, these students look for ways to undermine school authorities.

Because most educators confuse *encouragement* with *praise*, traditional usage of the term encouragement prevents a full appreciation of both its significance and its complexity in application. To encourage a discouraged student requires the restoration of a student's faith in himself or herself, the recognition of a student's strength and ability, and the belief in a student's dignity and worth. Without encouragement, cooperative learning and human development are not possible. Encouraging and accepting students as they are helps them to become who they are and to go as far as they can go in doing what they do.

CHARACTERISTICS OF ENCOURAGERS

Meredith and Evans (1990, Evans 1989) constructed a theoretical framework founded upon Adlerian principles and Third Force Psychology (Combs 1962) to describe the characteristics of an encouraging person. According to their model, an encouraging person possesses three of the characteristics of a fully functioning person: (1) an adequate and realistic view of self, (2) an adequate and realistic view of others, and (3) an openness to experience.

Adequate and Realistic View of Self

Encouraged people like themselves. They can be kind to themselves even when things go poorly, and they are satisfied with who they are. These individuals tend to see themselves as liked, valued, worthy, and capable. This adequate and realistic view of self allows them to meet life anticipating success. With this strong sense of significance, they are free to contribute and help others.

To have a realistic and adequate view of self requires us to do away with interfering ideas that lower our self-confidence, placing us in competition with others. Discouragement must be replaced with enough hope and confidence that no matter how poorly things go, we are capable of improving the situation.

Adequate and Realistic View of Others

Encouraged people accept themselves and are able to extend the same privilege to others. Those who practice encouragement believe and trust in other people. They are comfortable with human nature and can allow others to be themselves. These individuals identify with others and this is expressed through a high degree of accepting and trustworthy behavior. This identification with others prevents them from moving in ways that are harmful or injurious to others, for to do so would be to injure themselves. They believe all people are worthwhile simply because they exist. The encouragement process has to begin with acceptance of students as they are, not as they could be. This requires trust and faith in human nature.

The encouraging teacher knows that students, if shown respect, will learn merely for the enjoyment of learning. The motivation to learn does not come from doubting oneself; rather, it results from self-acceptance (Dreikurs 1964). Thus, the encouraging teacher frees students to be themselves and to develop their unique resources.

Discouraging educators, on the other hand, lack faith in human nature. The discouraging teacher feels too responsible for a student's learning and believes that students will not learn unless they are monitored and controlled with external reinforcers. These teachers do a lot of grousing. They are constantly reminding, nagging, advising, judging, or scolding. Grousing not only does nothing to improve the situation, it conveys a lack of trust and confidence in the student's ability to be a responsible learner. Teachers who talk too much end up in conflict with their students and train their students to be teacher-deaf.

Lacking faith in human nature, we unknowingly discourage our students by rejecting them as being weak or inferior. This attitude demonstrates a lack of faith in their ability to function in the present. We imply that when young children are bigger or older they will be more capable, but because they are so small they are not ready for the task. Anything we do that supports a student's lack of faith in himself or herself is discouraging (Dreikurs 1964).

Encouraging teachers display faith in their students by involving them in the learning process. For example, students are allowed to evaluate their own coursework through the use of portfolios instead of grades. They are trained to conduct parent-student conferences instead of teacher-parent conferences. Finally, students are permitted to manage their own discipline problems through the use of classroom meetings (Meder and Platt 1986).

The statements below contrast encouraging statements that imply faith and respect with discouraging statements that convey doubt and disrespect.

Encouragement	*Discouragement*
(Conveys faith and respect)	(Conveys doubt and disrespect)
"I think you can do it"	"Let me do it for you"
"You have what it takes"	"Be careful; it's dangerous"
"You're a hard worker"	"Don't forget your assignment"
"What do you think?"	"Let me give you some advice"
"I could use your help"	"When you're older you can help"

Openness to Experience

Teachers who are encouraged are not fearful of mistakes, but are open to their experiences. These teachers believe a day without mistakes is a day misused. They realize that all learning involves mistakes, and they view mistakes as challenges—opportunities for growth and discovery which contribute to our development as human beings. By allowing us to experience the consequences of our behavior, mistakes teach us the natural order of life.

Encouraged individuals have the courage to be imperfect. When they err, they mobilize their energy to improve the situation rather than waste energy blaming others or berating themselves as inferior.

If we are programmed to view mistakes as a loss of status, we arrange our lives to avoid making mistakes even if it means doing absolutely nothing or only attempting those things we do well. Although this behavior is often criticized as laziness, procrastination, or a lack of motivation; in actuality, it reveals an overly ambitious person who is fearful of losing status by making a mistake.

Traditional educational practices, by being mistake-centered, deprive our children of the experiences which promote growth and development. Education impresses upon children their deficiencies, their smallness, and their limitations while at the same time expecting them to be much more than they can be.

In education, mistakes determine the value of the work. A final mark is not determined by a student's effort, cooperation, or brilliant ideas, but by how many mistakes were made. All of this contributes to the already tremendous discouragement of our students.

By emphasizing mistakes, teachers curtail students' willingness to work and inhibit their development as human beings. Think of the times you worked hard to learn something, but performed poorly. Did negative feedback stimulate you to want to continue your efforts? Or, would you have been more likely to continue had the teacher focused on your strengths and recognized your efforts?

By not tolerating imperfection and acknowledging it as inherent in the learning process, educators destroy students' self-confidence and undermine their courage to meet the challenges of life. If we want our students to accomplish something in school, we must convey a faith and trust in their strength to rise to the occasion. We must minimize the mistakes they are making by emphasizing all the good things they have done, not all of the things they could have done.

Discouraged individuals are overly impressed by everything that's wrong in the world. They lack an adequate and realistic view of themselves and because they are critical of themselves, they are critical of the people around them. They believe that the only way to "count" is to be perfect. Consequently, their lives are limited to performing only those few things they do well. Instead of striving to contribute, they strive for the impossible—perfection.

Ironically, mistakes themselves seldom do much damage. The real danger is in how we interpret our mistakes. We can either correct mistakes and move on, or we can waste energy worrying about our status. Feelings of inferiority generally do more damage to our self-confidence and self-esteem than the consequences that the mistake itself produces.

PRAISE

Encouragement is not praise. Encouragement is based on a fundamental faith and trust in human nature. Praise is based on the belief that students will not learn or behave appropriately unless they are controlled through external rewards or punishment.

Teachers commonly use statements of praise such as, "You did better than anyone else," "If you do the work, you'll receive a gold star," and "I want you to do your best." Although these may appear to be innocuous statements that mean well, they are statements which, over time, will generate discouragement. All praise is at odds with creating a learning atmosphere characterized by cooperation, mutual respect, and friendly interactions.

Teachers having human relations skills are better equipped to create an encouraging environment conducive to learning. Instead of giving advice, rewarding, and "doing things" for students, the facilitative teacher knows how to give statements of encouragement, "I can tell you put a lot of effort into completing your assignment," "I will leave it up to you to decide, but I could use your cooperation," or, "I think you will do what is right." These statements are more likely to create the friendly relationships that lead to a cooperative atmosphere.

Praise always contains elements of judgment, evaluation, and doubt in one's ability to function appropriately. By its very nature, praise communicates disrespect and is therefore designated as a low level (one-level) response on the Global Scale of Responding (see Chapter 14).

There are three levels of praise, each of which inhibits good relationships from developing. These three levels are categorized as flattery, rewards, and superlatives (Dreikurs 1967b).

Flattery is used by teachers in an attempt to help students feel good about themselves. For example, "John, that's a handsome shirt." This type of flattery does little harm other than to make a judgment about John and is a form of politeness that is considered innocuous and is rarely taken seriously. Flattery is problematic in that it often sounds insincere or even controlling.

The second form of praise is more discouraging than simple flattery. This form of praise involves a system of *rewards* designed for classroom management and motivation. Because rewards bribe students into behaving as requested, rewarding these behaviors conveys a lack of faith in their ability to make sound choices on their own. Rewards also deny them the opportunity to learn from the consequences of their behaviors, and thus, to develop their inner strength. Although rewarding desired behaviors may coerce short-term compliance, it does not foster long-term change. Rewards do not teach cooperation.

For example, teachers will sometimes reward "good" behavior in hopes of setting an example for others. A teacher may tell a student, "Mary, you've completed your homework assignment without any mistakes. Since you followed my directions and had a perfect paper you may be first in line for lunch." Rewarding good behavior in front of the class can easily promote discouragement. Those who attempted the lesson, put forth a great deal of effort, but had poor results may feel punished and give up.

This type of praise may even backfire with the student it intends to reinforce. If Mary has learned that when she does what she is told she is to be rewarded, a lack of praise could be interpreted as scorn. Or possibly, Mary might decide that she will only contribute if she receives a reward. Today's students often consider rewards to be their right and insist upon being rewarded for everything. Even more seriously, students sometimes consider that being punished gives them the right to retaliate against those who inflicted the punishment. Students often retaliate by fighting, neglecting schoolwork, not eating, or misbehaving in ways that are extremely disturbing to teachers and parents.

Finally, the use of *superlatives* represents the most discouraging level of praise. Telling someone, "You did a great job," "You're the best student," or "You did a terrific presentation," can set students up for failure by virtue of the fact that the praise sets standards that are impossible to match. No one can perform perfectly all of the time. Students logically question whether falling short of being "the best" in their next endeavor will render themselves as less valued than previously. In this case, they may conclude that it's safest to do *nothing* in order to avoid completing an assignment. Clever students learn how to appear busy while moving from project to project—never completing anything. By not finishing a project they can avoid being evaluated, and with it the possibility of failing while maintaining an image of greatness. Using superlatives as a form of praise—especially with overly ambitious and/or perfectionistic students—can result in students completing few, if any, assignments.

ENCOURAGEMENT

Encouragement is a means of relating respectfully. It conveys faith in a student's ability to handle a task. Encouragement neither evaluates nor judges. Instead of threatening students to obey authority, encouragement challenges students to develop their own strengths and resources.

Encouragement focuses on effort or improvement. Praise is always outcome-oriented. "You put a lot of effort into completing your assignment" is encouraging while "Great job! You got all the problems correct" praises. Praise always evaluates the outcome of the work whereas encouragement acknowledges effort and improvement, allowing the student to evaluate the quality of his or her own work.

Encouragement can be given anytime. Praise can only be given for correct or impressive results. Process-oriented encouragement, by being unconcerned about perfect outcomes, can be given in any situation. The encouraging teacher can find something hopeful to say to or about even the most disruptive students. This could be as simple as noticing how a student sat still for five minutes and how this behavior contributed to the welfare of the class.

Encouragement separates the deed from the doer. Although an encourager recognizes an individual's misbehavior as disturbing, this does not label the individual as "bad." Discouraged individuals are entitled to respect and dignity despite their behavior. Praise does not separate the deed from the doer; they are seen as one and the same.

Encouragement teaches self-control. Every time we encourage a student, we discipline that student. Self-discipline occurs when a teacher says, "John, I trust that you will choose to concentrate on your work and do your problems." This teacher conveys to John that he has control over his thoughts, feelings, and behavior. There is no reference to rewards or punishment, but only the faith that John will make the choice to be in charge of himself.

Praise conveys that the control lies outside of oneself—that students must rely on external authority to sanction their behavior. For example, "John, since you did not do your homework, you'll need to move your desk next to mine. If you complete the assignment, then you can leave for lunch on time." Here, there is no recognition of John's ability to make decisions or exert control over himself.

Encouragement points out specific behaviors. For example, "Tommy, you made progress in learning how to dress yourself without anyone's help." Encouraging statements provide specific information about the effort or improvement; yet, the overall quality of the work is left for the student to evaluate.

Encouragement is acting instead of talking. In times of conflict, talking is the worst thing one can do. Talking will provide an opportunity for arguments in which the student will defeat the teacher. Never explain to students what they already know or have heard. Students will become teacher-deaf when lectured repeatedly and are threatened with punishment. Talking is to be used for friendly conversations and problem solving and not for disciplinary means. Instead of talking, teachers can learn how to behave and move more effectively, especially in moving away from the conflict.

Implementing Encouragement

In order to implement encouragement in the classroom, teachers need training in (1) establishing and maintaining an encouraging attitude, (2) recognizing the various levels of encouragement and discouragement (e.g., Feeling like a failure as a person is more discouraging than feeling like a failure at a specific task), (3) setting goals with the student based on his or her level of discouragement, (4) increasing student commitment to the goals, (5) understanding a student's private logic and redirecting his or her interfering ideas toward cooperation and contribution, and (6) developing a student's social interest.

In addition to developing the above skills, teachers can learn to use the language of encouragement. The following examples compare statements which either encourage or discourage students (Dreikurs, Grunwald, and Pepper 1982):

Encouragement	*Praise*
"You put a lot of effort into your work"	"I'm proud of you when you do well"
"You're a fine person"	"You did better than anyone else in the class"
"I know you did your best"	"Next time, if you work harder, you can get an A instead of a B+"

SUMMARY

Today, in an era when so many teachers, parents, and students feel discouraged, encouragement is desperately needed. While encouragement is not a new psychological idea, relatively few educators utilize this valuable concept. Based on mutual respect and dignity and focusing on a person's strengths rather than weaknesses, the principles and practices of encouragement are essential for creating a stimulating learning environment. As more and more educators are discovering, encouragement is a key element in restructuring and improving our schools.

REFERENCES

Adler, A. 1939. *Social Interest.* New York: Putman.
Combs, A., Chairman. 1962. *Perceiving, Behaving, Becoming.* Washington, DC: Association for Supervision and Curriculum Development.
Dreikurs, R. 1964. *Children: The Challenge.* New York: Hawthorne/Datton.
Dreikurs, R. 1967a. *Adult-Child Relations.* Chicago: Alfred Adler Institute.
Dreikurs, R. 1967b. *Psychodynamics, Psychotherapy, and Counseling.* Chicago: Alfred Adler Institute.
Dreikurs, R. 1971. *Social Equality.* Chicago: Alfred Adler Institute.
Dreikurs, R., B. Grunwald, and F. Pepper. 1982. *Maintaining Sanity in the Classroom.* New York: Harper and Row.
Evans, T. 1989. *The Art of Encouragement.* Athens, GA: University of Georgia, Center for Continuing Education.

Griffith, J. 1991. "Back to school." *Individual Psychology Reporter 8*, 1–4.

Meder, F., and J. Platt. 1986. *Class Meetings* [video]. Sacramento, CA: California State University, University Media Services.

Meredith, C. 1986. "Democracy in the family." *Individual Psychology 42*, 602–610.

Meredith, C., and T. Evans. 1990. "Encouragement in the family." *Individual Psychology 46*, 187–192.

APPENDIX A

Research Scales

Research Empathy Scale

1.0	1.5	2.0	2.5	3.0	3.5	4.0
An irrelevant or hurtful response that does not appropriately attend to the surface feelings of the helpee. However, in instances where content is communicated accurately, it may raise the level of the response.		A response that only partially communicates an awareness of the surface feelings of the helpee. When content is communicated accurately it may raise the level of the response; conversely, it may lower the level of the response when communicated inaccurately.		A response conveying that the helpee is understood at the level he or she is expressing; surface feelings are accurately reflected. Content is not essential, but, when included, it must be accurate. If it is inaccurate, level of the response may be lowered.		A response conveying that the helpee is understood beyond his or her level of immediate awareness; underlying feelings are identified. Content is used to complement affect in adding deeper meaning. If content is inaccurate, the level of the response may be lowered.

KEY WORDS—Empathy Scale
Level 4.0—underlying feelings, additive
Level 3.0—surface feelings reflected
Level 2.0—subtractive
Level 1.0—irrelevant; hurtful

Research Respect Scale

1.0	1.5	2.0	2.5	3.0	3.5	4.0
A response that overtly communicates disrespect. The helper may attempt to impose his or her own beliefs and values onto the helpee, seek to focus attention on himself or herself by dominating the conversation, instantly challenge the accuracy of the helpee's perception, or devaluate the worth of the helpee as an individual by communicating that the helpee is not able to function appropriately on his or her own. These responses leave the helpee wishing that he or she had not talked to the helper, and probably preclude future interactions.		A response in which the helper withholds himself or herself from involvement with the helpee. This may be communicated by declining to enter a helping relationship, by ignoring what the helpee is saying, or by responding in a casual or mechanical way. Such responses tend to terminate the interaction.		A response that communicates that the helper is open to or will consider entering a helping relationship. It communicates recognition of the helpee as a person of worth, capable of thinking and expressing himself or herself and able to act constructively. The helper suspends acting on his or her situation.		A response that demonstrates the helper's willingness to make sacrifices and bear the risk of being hurt in order to further the helping relationship. This results in the helpee experiencing himself or herself as a valued individual and stimulates deeper interaction by allowing the helpee to feel free to be himself or herself.

KEY WORDS—Respect Scale
Level 4.0—involved; committed
Level 3.0—open
Level 2.0—withholds
Level 1.0—imposes; dominates; devaluates

Research Warmth Scale

1.0	1.5	2.0	2.5	3.0	3.5	4.0
The helper has disapproving facial expression or appears disinterested. Helper turns away or does other tasks while the helpee is talking. Affect is not congruent with the helpee's affect.		Expressions and gestures are absent or neutral; responses sound mechanical or rehearsed.		Clearly shows attention and interest; nonverbal behaviors vary appropriately as helpee's emotions vary.		The helper is wholly and intensely attentive to the interaction, resulting in the helpee's feeling complete acceptance and significance. The helper is physically closer to the helpee than at level 3.0, and may make physical contact.

KEY WORDS—Warmth Scale
Level 4.0—intense nonverbal communication
Level 3.0—clear nonverbal response
Level 2.0—gestures absent or neutral; voice sounds mechanical
Level 1.0—visibly disapproving or disinterested

Research Concreteness Scale

1.0	1.5	2.0	2.5	3.0	3.5	4.0
The helper responds to the helpee's personally relevant feelings and experiences in abstract or vague terms, in a specific but inaccurate manner, or in a premature and hurtful fashion.		The helper responds to the helpee's personally relevant emotions and situations and intellectual terms that do not incorporate the helpee's frame of reference. The helper does not focus on specific manifestations of helpee concerns. The helper may ask the helpee to be more specific yet fails to model that specificity.		The helper responds to the helpee's personally relevant material in clear, specific, and concrete terms. The helper mostly centers his or her attention around most things that are personally important to the helpee. The helper accepts abstractions on the part of the helpee but models specificity.		The helper responds fluently, directly, and quite thoroughly to specific concerns of the helpee and actively solicits specificity from the helpee. During the earlier stages that may involve asking for clarification of vague or abstract helpee statements. During later stages it may entail assisting the helpee to enumerate clear and definite alternatives that derive from the interaction, summarizing the helpee's newly acquired self-understanding, or outlining plans for future action.

KEY WORDS—Concreteness Scale
Level 4.0—models and actively solicits specificity
Level 3.0—specific
Level 2.0—general; solicits specificity
Level 1.0—vague; inaccurate; premature; hurtful

276

Research Genuineness Scale

1.0	1.5	2.0	2.5	3.0	3.5	4.0
A response in which the helper uses his or her feelings to punish the helpee, or a response in which the helper's communications are clearly unrelated to what other cues indicate the helper is feeling. There is considerable incongruence between the helper's feelings and his or her verbal and/or nonverbal expressions. The helper may be defensive (unaware of his or her feelings), or quite false and deceitful (communicating feelings that the helper is plainly not experiencing).		A response in which the helper's communications are slightly unrelated to what other cues indicate he or she is feeling. There is incongruence between the helper's feelings and his or her verbal and/or nonverbal expressions. The helper responds according to some preconceived role.		The helper demonstrates no incongruence between expressions and feelings. The helper gives a controlled expression of feelings which facilitate the relationship, refraining from expressing feelings which could impede the relationship.		The helper is spontaneous and dependably real. The helper's verbal and nonverbal messages, whether they be positive or negative, are congruent with how he or she feels. In the event of negative responses, the helper communicates these constructively, in an effort to open up new areas of inquiry.

KEY WORDS—Genuineness Scale
Level 4.0—spontaneous; fully congruent
Level 3.0—controlled expression
Level 2.0—role played
Level 1.0—punitive; defensive; deceitful

Research Self-Disclosure Scale

1.0	1.5	2.0	2.5	3.0	3.5	4.0
The helper actively remains detached from the helpee and reveals nothing about himself or herself, or discloses something personal in order to meet his or her own needs exclusively. The helper changes the focus of the interaction to himself or herself, resulting in the helpee feeling overwhelmed and thinking that the helper is not interested in the helpee, or becoming disillusioned with the helper's ability to help.		The helper does not volunteer any personal information. The helper may answer direct questions, but only hesitantly and briefly. The helpee, then, gets to know only what he or she asks about the helper.		The helper reveals personal ideas, attitudes, and experiences relevant to the helpee's concerns, in a general fashion, revealing his or her feelings at a surface level. Therefore the helper's uniqueness as a person is not communicated. The helpee, then, knows only a little about the helper's ideas or experiences that may be useful in dealing with his or her own problems.		The helper freely and spontaneously volunteers specific information about his or her own personal ideas, experiences, and feelings when they are relevant to the helpee's interests and concerns. These may involve a degree of risk-taking on the part of the helper. The helper reveals his or her uniqueness as a person.

KEY WORDS—Self-Disclosure Scale
Level 4.0—volunteers specific material; risk taking
Level 3.0—volunteers general material
Level 2.0—does not volunteer
Level 1.0—withholds; overwhelming role reversal

Research Confrontation Scale

1.0	1.5	2.0	2.5	3.0	3.5	4.0
A response which does not allow any consideration of discrepancies existing for the helpee. The helper may accept the discrepancies expressed by the helpee, may contradict the expressed or felt conflict of the helpee, ignore the discrepancies, or give direction prematurely. In any of these instances the helper is closing off possible fruitful avenues of investigation.		The helper does not explicitly draw attention to discrepancies in the helpee's behavior. The helper does not overtly accept or deny these discrepancies but does not point them out to the helpee, either. The helper may simply remain silent about the discrepancies or reflect the helpee's feelings about them. The helpee, therefore, is not explicitly aware of possibly useful areas of inquiry.		The helper indicates discrepancies without pointing out the specific directions in which these lead. The helper is tentative in comparing diverging communications expressed by the helpee. This allows the helpee to explore different areas in which he or she may become aware of diverging trends in his or her behavior.		A response which clearly points out discrepancies which the helper has noticed and the specific directions in which the discrepancies lead. This focuses the helpee's attention on specific discontinuities in his or her behavior. It facilitates the helpee's dealing with areas of which he or she had been unaware or brings out more clearly a discrepancy of which the helper had been only vaguely aware.

KEY WORDS—Confrontation Scale
Level 4.0—firm directional statement of discrepancy
Level 3.0—tentative expression or exploration of discrepancy
Level 2.0—does not refer to discrepancy
Level 1.0—accepting; contradicting; ignoring; premature advice

Research Immediacy of Relationship Scale

1.0	1.5	2.0	2.5	3.0	3.5	4.0
Helper ignores all cues from helpee that deal with their interpersonal relationship, or uses his or her feelings about the relationship in a destructive manner.		Helper consciously gives token recognition to helpee expressions about their interpersonal relationship but postpones discussing it or dismisses it after having commented on it superficially.		Helper discusses the interpersonal relationship between himself or herself and the helpee, but in a general rather than a personal way, which obscures the uniqueness of their relationship. The helpee may make literal responses or reflections to the helpee's expressions. Helper is open to sharing responsibility for any defects that may exist in the relationship.		Helper relates the helpee's expressions to himself or herself in a direct and explicit manner. The helper makes precise interpretations of the helper-helpee relationship.

KEY WORDS—Immediacy of Relationship Scale
Level 4.0—explicit; current
Level 3.0—open; general
Level 2.0—postpones; dismisses
Level 1.0—ignores; destructive

APPENDIX B

Vocabulary of Affective Adjectives

VOCABULARY OF AFFECTIVE ADJECTIVES

Kind-Helpful-Loving-Friendly-Thankful

admired
adored
affectionate
agreeable
altruistic
amiable
amorous
appreciative
aroused
benevolent
bighearted
brotherly
caring
charitable
cherished
comforting
compassionate
compatible
congenial
conscientious
considerate
cooperative
cordial
dedicated
dependable
devoted
diligent
empathic
fair
faithful
fatherly
fond
forgiving
friendly
generous

genuine
gentle
gallant
giving
good
gracious
grateful
helpful
honest
honorable
humane
idolizing
indebted to
involved
just
kind
longing for
long-suffering
loving
mellow
merciful
mindful
nice
obliging
open
optimistic
passionate
patient
neighborly
respectful
rewarded
sensitive
sharing
sincere
sociable
soft-hearted
straightforward
sympathetic
tender

thoughtful
tolerant
treasured
trustful
unassuming
understanding
unselfish
warm-hearted

_____
_____
_____
_____
_____
_____
_____

Curious-Absorbed

analyzing
attentive
concentrating
considering
contemplating
curious
diligent
engrossed
imaginative
inquiring
inquisitive
investigating
occupied
pondering
puzzled
questioning
reasoning
reflecting
searching
thoughtful

From *Amity: Friendship in Action, Part II: The Skill of Active Listening*, pp. 41–47. Copyright 1980 by Richard P. Walters. Reproduced by permission.

weighing
wrapped up

_____

_____

_____

_____

_____

_____

Happy-Peaceful

accepted
amused
at ease
blissful
brilliant
calm
carefree
charmed
cheerful
clear
comfortable
complete
contented
delighted
ecstatic
elated
enjoying
excellent
fantastic
fine
fit
full
giddy
glad
glorious
good
gratified
great
happy
in high spirits
inspired

joyous
jubilant
laughing
lighthearted
magnificent
marvelous
optimistic
overjoyed
peaceful
pleasant
pleased
poised
proud
refreshed
rejoicing
relaxed
relieved
renewed
revived
safe
satiated
satisfied
serene
settled
smiling
soothed
splendid
sunny
superb
sweet
terrific
thrilled
tickled
tremendous
wholesome
wonderful

_____

_____

_____

_____

_____

_____

Miserable-Troubled-Hurt-Frustrated

abused
aching
afflicted
awful
battered
bothered
bruised
burdened
clumsy
crabby
cramped
cut to the heart
deprived
desolate
desperate
despairing
destitute
dismal
displeased
dissatisfied
distressed
disturbed
divided
dreadful
futile
harassed
hassled
hemmed in
hindered
horrible
imprisoned
jammed up
loaded down
lost
lousy
mistreated
oppressed
pathetic

VOCABULARY OF AFFECTIVE ADJECTIVES

peeved
perturbed
pitiful
poor
pressured
pulled apart
restless
ridiculous
rotten
ruined
sore
stabbed
strained
strangled
suffering
swamped
temperamental
terrible
threatened
thwarted
tormented
trapped
tortured
uneasy
unfortunate
unhappy
unlucky
unsatisfied
unsure
upset
wiped out
wounded
wretched
_____
_____
_____
_____
_____
_____
_____

Ashamed-Guilty-Embarrassed

apologetic
awkward
blamed
branded
chagrined
cheapened
condemned
conscience-stricken
contrite
degraded
denounced
disapproved of
disgraced
dishonored
disreputable
doomed
embarrassed
evasive
exposed
foolish
humbled
humiliated
in a bind
in trouble
judged
punished
put down
rebuked
red-faced
regretful
remorseful
ridiculous
roasted
shamed
sheepish
silly
slammed
sorry

wicked
wrong
_____
_____
_____
_____
_____
_____
_____
_____

Disgusted-Suspicious

arrogant
callous
cynical
derisive
despising
detesting
disgusted
displeased
distrustful
dogmatic
doubting
envious
grudging
hesitant
jealous
loathing
mistrustful
nauseated
nonchalant
offended
pompous
queasy
repulsed
revolted
sickened
skeptical

sneering
wary

_____
_____
_____
_____
_____
_____
_____

Playful-Joking-Witty

agreeable
amusing
breezy
clever
easygoing
free and easy
frisky
fun-loving
funny
genial
good-humored
happy-go-lucky
hearty
hospitable
humorous
joking
jovial
jolly
lighthearted
mischievous
original
lively
quick-witted
smart
sociable
sparkling
spontaneous
sportive
sprightly

spry
turned on
uninhibited
vivacious

_____
_____
_____
_____
_____
_____

Weak-Defeated-Shy-Belittled

all in
at the mercy of
bashful
bent
broken-down
chicken-hearted
cowardly
crippled
crushed
deflated
demeaned
dependent
dominated
done-for
drained
drowsy
exhausted
failing
fatigued
feeble
fragile
frail
hungry
helpless
imperfect
impotent
inadequate

incapable
incompetent
ineffective
inefficient
inept
inferior
insecure
insulted
intimidated
laughed at
needy
neglected
no good
paralyzed
powerless
puny
put down
run down
scoffed at
self-conscious
shattered
small
smothered
spineless
squelched
stifled
strained
tearful
timid
tired
troubled
unable
unambitious
unfit
unsure of self
unqualified
unstable
unworthy
useless
vulnerable
walked on
washed up
weak

VOCABULARY OF AFFECTIVE ADJECTIVES

whipped
wimpy
worthless
yellow
_____
_____
_____
_____
_____
_____
_____

Lonely-Forgotten-Left Out

abandoned
alienated
alone
betrayed
bored
cast aside
cheated
deserted
discarded
disliked
disowned
empty
excluded
forsaken
friendless
hated
hollow
homeless
homesick
ignored
isolated
jilted
left out
lonely
lonesome

lost
neglected
ostracized
outcast
overlooked
rebuffed
rejected
scorned
secluded
shunned
slighted
snubbed
stranded
taken lightly
ugly
uninvited
unimportant
unwanted
unwelcome
_____
_____
_____
_____
_____
_____
_____

Angry-Hostile-Enraged-Irritated

aggravated
aggressive
agitated
angry
annoyed
aroused
belligerent
bitter
boiling
bristling

brutal
bullying
burned
contrary
cool
cranky
critical
cross
cruel
disagreeable
displeased
enraged
ferocious
fierce
fighting
fired up
frenzied
exasperated
fuming
furious
harsh
hateful
heartless
hostile
incensed
indignant
inflamed
infuriated
irked
irritated
mad
mean
out of sorts
outraged
perturbed
provoked
pushy
quarrelsome
raving
ready to explode
rebellious

resentful
revengeful
ruffled
sarcastic
spiteful
steamed
stern
strung out
stormy
unkind
vindictive
violent
vicious

_____
_____
_____
_____
_____
_____
_____

Interested-Excited

active
alert
aroused
attracted to
bubbly
bustling
busy
challenged
delighted
eager
enthusiastic
excited
exuberant
fascinated
flustered
impatient
impressed with
inspired
involved

keyed up
quickened
resourceful
responsive
spurred on
stimulated
tantalized
thrilled

_____
_____
_____
_____
_____
_____
_____

Confused-Surprised-Astonished

aghast
air-headed
amazed
appalled
astonished
astounded
awed
awestruck
baffled
bewildered
bowled over
breathless
changeable
dazed
dismayed
disorganized
distracted
doubtful
dumbfounded
emotional
forgetful

gripped
horrified
in doubt
jarred
jolted
mixed up
muddled
mystified
overpowered
overwhelmed
perplexed
puzzled
rattled
ruffled
shocked
speechless
staggered
startled
stunned
stumped
swamped
taken aback
torn
trapped
tricked
uncertain

_____
_____
_____
_____
_____
_____
_____
_____
_____

Sad-Depressed-Discouraged

below par
bereaved
blue

VOCABULARY OF AFFECTIVE ADJECTIVES

brooding
broken-hearted
burned out
bummed out
dejected
demolished
depressed
despondent
destroyed
disappointed
discouraged
down-and-out
downhearted
dreary
drooping
dull
falling apart
forlorn
gloomy
glum
grief-stricken
grieved
heavy-hearted
hopeless
in the dumps
let down
lifeless
low
melancholy
moody
moping
mournful
oppressed
pained
pessimistic
sad
serious
shredded
solemn
sorrowful
tearful

troubled
unhappy
weary
woeful
wrecked

_____
_____
_____
_____
_____
_____
_____

Vigorous-Strong-Confident

able-bodied
accomplished
adaptable
adequate
adventurous
alive
ambitious
assertive
assured
blessed
boastful
bold
brave
capable
certain
clever
cocky
competent
competitive
confident
courageous
daring
determined
dignified

dynamic
effective
efficient
encouraged
energetic
equal to the task
favored
fearless
firm
fit
forceful
fortunate
gifted
hardy
healthy
in control
important
independent
intelligent
keen
lion-hearted
lucky
macho
mighty
peppy
potent
pumped
prosperous
qualified
powerful
reliable
responsible
secure
self-confident
self-controlled
self-reliant
sharp
shrewd
skillful
smart
solid

spirited
stable
strong
sturdy
suited
sure
successful
together
tough
triumphant
victorious
vigorous
well off
well suited
wired
wise

_____
_____
_____
_____
_____
_____
_____
_____

Afraid-Tense-Worried

agonizing
alarmed
anxious
apprehensive
boxed in
cautious
concerned
cornered
disturbed
dreading
edgy
fearful
frantic
frightened
hesitant
horrified
in a cold sweat
jittery
jumpy
on edge
panicky

petrified
nervous
numb
quaking
quivering
restless
scared
shaken
suffocated
terrified
trembling
troubled
up tight
uncomfortable
uneasy

_____
_____
_____
_____
_____
_____
_____

Speaking the Helpee's Language with Empathic Leads

Speaking the Helpee's Language with Empathic Leads

Of all the dimensions that have been identified and researched, empathy continues to emerge as the key ingredient of the helping relationship. In order to empathize, or deeply understand the feelings of the helpee, the helper must first attempt to enter the helpee's phenomenological field. That is, the helper must try to enter into the helpee's personal and subjective frame of reference, focusing on how the helpee perceives, integrates, interprets, and experiences his or her world. It should be noted, however, that this is a highly imperfect process. It is, of course, impossible for us to be the helpee, so the best we can strive to do is arrive at a reasonably correct but limited understanding of the unique person with whom we are interacting.

When trying to communicate empathically, we will generally prove most effective if we (1) remain open-minded, (2) consider most of our judgments as working hypotheses subject to revision, and (3) use empathic leads that match the language style of the helpee.

Human beings receive information about their environment through their sense organs and store such information in their brains. The perceptual modalities that we use to gather this information may be grouped into five major categories: (1) vision, (2) audition, (3) kinesthetic (body sensations), (4) gustation (taste), and (5) olfaction (smell). Smell and taste seem to play a minor role in helping us gain information about our world. Sight, sound, and body sensations are our primary representational systems.

As we mature, we tend to favor or rely on the information provided by a particular representational system or combination of systems. In order to identify which of the representational systems is most highly valued by the helpee, the helper need only pay careful attention to the predicates (words that make a statement about the subject of a clause or sentence) that helpees use to describe their experience. When helpers systematically match the predicates of their communications, they send clearer messages that are more easily decoded or understood by the helpee. That is, when you "tune in" to the helpee by assessing his or her "wavelength" and then adjust your verbal communications to that wavelength, you maximize accurate communications and minimize distorted communications.

The following phrases, grouped under modality strengths, may prove useful when you trust that your perceptions are accurate and the helpee will be receptive to your communications:

Visual

From your point of view . . .
You were green with envy when . . .
As you see it . . .
I see what you mean, you . . .
It was an eye-opener when . . .
Looks like you . . .
You're beginning to see that . . .
From your perspective . . .
That was a shining example of . . .
You're trying to show me . . .
Your goal is in sight; you . . .
I get an image of you . . .
I visualize you . . .
You want to shut your eyes to . . .
You went blank when . . .
It's hard for you to focus on . . .
Clearly, you want . . .
You want to keep an eye on . . .
. . . really caught your eye
You see yourself . . .
Can you picture him . . .

Auditory

Sounds like . . .
Your internal dialogue tells you . . .
As I hear it, you . . .
It didn't sound right when . . .
What you're saying is . . .
You'd swear that . . .

What I hear you saying is . . .
You went silent when . . .
He really bent your ear when . . .
You were speechless when . . .
It all suddenly clicked when . . .
I can tune into your wanting . . .
When I listen between the lines I hear . . .
You had a blast when . . .
I'm listening to you express . . .
She rings your bell when she . . .
You can almost hear yourself saying . . .

Kinesthetic

You get shivers down your spine whenever . . .
You feel . . .
It touched you when . . .
You had your hands full when . . .
You feel sick to your stomach if . . .
You'd like to hold off until . . .
You felt pinned against the wall when . . .
You're trying to grasp the meaning of . . .
Your whole body senses . . .
From your standpoint . . .
You felt it was abrasive of him to . . .
You find her very cold because . . .
You'd like to get your hands on . . .
You're not going to crawl back to . . .
You feel like you're being pulled apart when . . .
He really tripped up when . . .
Your hands get clammy when . . .
You felt as though . . .
It's rough for you when . . .
You felt overloaded when . . .
You got burned up over . . .
You felt crushed because . . .
You're trying to get a handle on . . .
Your guts tell you that . . .
You have a gut feeling about . . .
It felt right when you . . .
You wanted to tear him up when . . .
You get up tight over . . .
You resent being held back by . . .

It pains you when . . .
It is a pain in the neck when . . .
You wanted to kick him in the butt because . . .
Your knees start to knock if . . .

Olfactory

Something about . . . really stinks
You smelled trouble when . . .
You think it stinks when . . .
You got a whiff of . . .
You seem to have a real scent for . . .
To you, it smelled of . . .
It had the aroma of . . .

Gustatory

You want to savor the memory of . . .
You thought it was in poor taste to . . .
You thought it was sweet of him to . . .
It takes a sour individual to . . .

Nonspecific or Mixed Modalities

You think . . .
You believe . . .
You mean . . .
It seems to you . . .
You're . . . (identify the feeling, e.g., mad, elated, depressed)
You're aware of . . .
You know . . .
You sense that . . .
In your experience . . .
I understand you to mean . . .
You're convinced that . . .
You're sure . . .
There's no doubt in your mind that . . .
It really knocked your socks off when you heard she . . .

The next group of phrases, also grouped under modality strengths, may be of help when you wish to be most tactful, when you are having trouble perceiving the helpee clearly, or it seems that the helpee might not be receptive to (or may react defensively to) your communications.

Visual

...: does that accurately summarize your view?
... is that a colorful example of what you mean?
... is that a clear picture I'm getting?
... are we seeing eye to eye?
... do I have it in proper focus?
Let me see if I understand you, you ...
... does that cast some light on the subject?
... is my fantasy accurate?
... am I getting the picture?
... is that on target?
... am I sharing your view?
... is that your perspective?
... is that a distorted view?
... is that what you have in sight?
... is that the way it looks to you?
... am I gaining any insight?
... is that what you envision?

Auditory

What I guess I'm hearing is ...
Does it sound reasonable that you ...
This is what I think I hear you saying ...
Something tells me that maybe you ...
... does that sound accurate?
Could you be trying to tell me that ...
It seems to me that you're saying ...
As I hear it, you ...
... do I hear you correctly?
... am I in tune with you?
... does that click?
... am I tuning in to you?
... does that ring a bell?
... is that good listening?
... did I hear you right?

Kinesthetic

... is that the way you feel?
I get the feeling that maybe ...
Perhaps you're feeling ...

Is there a chance you're feeling . . .
I'm not sure I understand; you're feeling . . .
Maybe it's a little tough for you to . . .
Do you perhaps feel held back by . . .
. . . how does that grab you?
I somehow sense that maybe you feel . . .
. . . am I getting in touch with you?
You appear to be feeling . . .
Maybe you're feeling . . .
Do you feel a little . . .
I guess you feel somewhat . . .
. . . do I have a good handle on it?
. . . how does that sit with you?
. . . did it rub you the wrong way?

Olfactory

Perhaps you smelled something fishy when . . .
Maybe you sniffed trouble when . . .

Gustatory

. . . do I get the flavor of what you mean?
. . . did that perhaps leave a bitter aftertaste?
Perhaps you felt that . . . was a tasteless remark?
Is it conceivable that you're a little bitter about . . .
Maybe I'm out to lunch, but . . .
It was like rubbing salt in your wounds when she . . .

Nonspecific or Mixed Modalities

Could it be that . . .
I'm not sure if I understand you . . .
. . . is that the way it is?
Correct me if I'm wrong, but . . .
Is there any chance that . . .
I somehow sense that maybe you feel . . .
I wonder if . . .
I guess that you're a little . . .
. . . is that what you mean?
It appears you . . .
Is it conceivable that . . .
Could you try saying . . . and see if it fits?
Is it absurd of me to think that . . .

An additional method of sensitively communicating with helpees involves your carefully assessing their talents, abilities, interests, occupational preferences, or actual occupation. You then consciously train yourself to use words and expressions that the helpee will likely identify with. This style of verbal communication will usually further solidify your rapport with the helpee. It is perhaps interesting to note that some experienced high-level helpers actually appear to communicate in this style unconsciously. That is, they do not have to focus on their choice of words, these kinds of phrases just flow from the helper-helpee interaction.

Helpee	*Helper*
Football player	"Let's see if we can tackle that problem first."
Mechanic	"No, you don't sound crazy but I think you can use a tune-up."
Plumber	"I think you'd feel better if you flushed some of that junk out of your system."
School band member	"You'd like to get more in step with the other kids."
Truck driver	"That's a heavy load to haul."
Carpenter	"That goes against your grain, doesn't it? "Did I hit the nail on the head?"
Student teacher	"I think if you can spell out your stated objectives, you'll be able to plan your future more carefully."
Baseball player	"You'd like to at least get up to bat, even if you do strike out."
Computer programmer	"Your system is overloaded."
Engineer	"Let's see if we can draw up some plans."
Business student	"You'd do well to look at your assets and liabilities."
Accountant	"What's the bottom line for you?"
Police officer	"I'd like to help you find some goals to shoot for."
Librarian	"Perhaps we need to research some of those personal problems."
Dry cleaner	"You'd like to smooth out some of the wrinkles in your marriage."
Writer	"How about us examining your childhood chapter by chapter?"
Lawyer	"Have I presented my case to you clearly?"
Doctor	"Now that we've diagnosed the problem, let's see if we can write a treatment plan to correct it."
Realtor	"Do you think its worth your investment?"
Forester	"If you took that step, would it leave you out on a limb?"

Dancer	"You're doing pretty well. You just need to polish up some of your moves."
Ship captain	"You're heading into uncharted waters."
Secretary	"I guess you might want to file that guy under 'L' for loser, huh?"
Soldier	"We just need to run you through some basic training in communications."
Sailor	"Do you think it's time to pull up anchor?"
Fisherman	"Are you gonna fish or cut bait?"
Electrician	"Do you feel like you're overloading your circuits?"
Pilot	"It looks as though there are clear skies ahead."
Paramedic	"Can your wife count on you to come to her rescue?"
Journalist	"I can see the headline now—'Mr. Jones Is a Model Citizen!'"

Scales for Rating the Helpee

APPENDIX D

Scales for Rating the Helpee

All scales presented up to this point have dealt with rating the helpers in their interaction with helpees. The three scales presented here are used to rate helpees. These scales look at the extent of the helpee's desire for problem solving. They are analogous to the commitment of the helper to the helpee, which is measured on the Respect Scale, except in this case it reflects the commitment of the helpee to the task of problem solving.

The three scales are Helpee Help-Seeking Scale, Helpee Self-Exploration Scale, and Helpee Action-Implementing Scale. These three scales are designed so that helpees must be at high levels on the Help-Seeking Scale before they can be at high levels on the Self-Exploration Scale and, likewise, they must be high on the Self-Exploration Scale before they can be high on the Action-Implementing Scale. Thus, the three scales roughly form a continuum of helpees' commitment to the process of their own problem resolution or personal growth.

The action dimensions should be used only after high levels of self-exploration have been achieved. Therefore, you will find the scale of helpee self-exploration to be an excellent indicator for timing the introduction of action responses.

The three helpee rating scales are outlined in the following sections and the levels are defined.

HELPEE HELP-SEEKING SCALE

The Help-Seeking Scale is a measure of whether or not the helpee wants to be involved in a helper-helpee relationship. Helpees are rated on this scale according to the strength of their desire for help.

Level 5—Helpee actively seeks help.

Level 4—Helpee accepts help when provided.

Level 3—Helpee is open to being helped; will consider entering a helping relationship.

Level 2—Helpee admits need for help but avoids entering a helping relationship.

Level 1—Helpee overtly refuses available help, or the helpee participates in helper-helpee relationships in order to qualify for benefits extrinsic to the aims of the helping relationship.

HELPEE SELF-EXPLORATION SCALE

The Helpee Self-Exploration Scale is a measure of the extent to which the helpee is actively searching for new feelings and experiences. Helpees are rated on this scale according to the strength of their desire to self-explore.

Level 5—Helpee actively searches for new feelings and experiences (even if fearful).

Level 4—Helpee volunteers personally relevant material with spontaneity and emotional proximity.

Level 3—Helpee volunteers personally relevant material but mechanically and with no feeling.

Level 2—Helpee responds mechanically and with no feeling to personally relevant material introduced by the helper.

Level 1—Helpee avoids all self-expression, is defensive, and provides no opportunity to discuss personally relevant material.

HELPEE ACTION-IMPLEMENTING SCALE

The Action-Implementing Scale is a measure of the degree to which the helpee participates in the determination and practice of problem-solving or growth-directed behaviors. The course of action is defined as the steps helpees take toward solving their problems and includes training or psychotherapy, socialization, education, restitution, physical exercise, relaxation, or other efforts.

Level 5—Helpee follows the course of action to the extent that it exists; doing everything known to be done for that situation at that time.

Level 4—Helpee accepts part of the course of action.

Level 3—Helpee considers following the course of action as it is evolving.

Level 2—Helpee accepts helper communication that is high on action dimensions.

Level 1—Helpee rejects or avoids helper communication.

APPENDIX E

Sensory Modality Checklist

▶

APPENDIX E

Sensory Modality Checklist

The Sensory Modality Checklist assesses the strengths of each of your major sensory modalities—auditory, visual, and kinesthetic. Use it to discover your preferred cognitive style for learning and self-expression.

There are ten incomplete sentences and three choices for completing each. Some of the choices contain more than one option. If any one of those options seems typical of you, score that answer. All of the options do not have to apply to you. Score the three choices by rating (3) to the answer most typical of you, (2) to your second choice, and (1) to the last answer.

SENSORY MODALITY CHECKLIST

Score (3) to the answer most typical of you. Score (2) to your second choice, and (1) to the last answer.

1. When I want to learn something new, I usually
   A (3) want someone to explain it to me.
   B (2) want to read about it in a book or magazine.
   C (1) want to try it out, take notes, or make a model of it.

2. At a party, most of the time I like to
   A (3) listen and talk to two or three people at once.
   B (1) see how everyone looks and watch the people.
   C (2) dance, play games, or take part in some activities.

3. If I were helping with a musical show, I would most likely
   A (1) write the music, sing the songs, or play the accompaniment.

B (3) design the costumes, paint the scenery, or work the lighting effects.

C (2) make the costumes, build the sets, or take an acting role.

4. When I am angry, my first reaction is to

A (3) tell people off, laugh, joke, or talk it over with someone.

B (1) blame myself or someone else, daydream about taking revenge, or keep it inside.

C (2) make a fist or tense my muscles, take it out on something else, hit or throw things.

5. A happy event I would like to have is

A (1) hearing the thunderous applause for my speech or music.

B (2) photographing the prized picture of a sensational newspaper story.

C (3) achieving the fame of being first in a physical activity such as dancing, acting, surfing, or a sports event.

6. I prefer a teacher to

A (2) use the lecture method with informative explanations and discussions.

B (3) write on the chalkboard, use visual aids, and assign readings.

C (1) require posters, models, or inservice practice, and some activities in class.

7. I know that I talk with

A (2) different tones of voice.

B (1) my eyes and facial expressions.

C (3) my hands and gestures.

8. If I had to remember an event so that I could record it later, I would choose to

A (2) tell it aloud to someone, or hear an audio tape recording or a song about it.

B (3) see pictures of it or read a description.

C (1) replay it in some practice rehearsal using movements such as dance, playacting, or drill.

9. When I cook something new, I like to

A (2) have someone tell me the directions, a friend or TV show.

B (3) read the recipe and judge by how it looks.

C (1) use many pots and dishes, stir often, and taste-test.

10. In my free time, I like to

A (1) listen to the radio, talk on the telephone, or attend a musical event.

B (2) go to the movies, watch TV, or read a magazine or book.

C (3) get some exercise, go for a walk, play games, or make things.

Total all "A" choices—Auditory. *20*
Total all "B" choices—Visual.   *21*
Total all "C" choices—Kinesthetic. *19*

Look at the three scores you added for Auditory, Visual, and Kinesthetic. They will range from 10 to 30; together they will total 60.

The Auditory score means that you learn and express yourself through sounds and hearing. The Visual score means that you enjoy learning and expressing yourself with your eyes, seeing things written, colors, and imageries. The Kinesthetic score means that you learn and express yourself through physical, muscular activity, and practice.

If the scores are within four points of each other, you have a mixed modality which means that you process information in any sensory modality with balanced ease.

If there are five points or more between any of the scores, you have a relative strength in that modality as compared to the others. You may have two modalities that seem stronger than the other one. This means that you learn more easily and express yourself more naturally in the modality with the larger score(s).

There are, of course, no right or wrong choices of sensory modalities. This checklist is a criterion-referenced achievement scale, revealing the sensory modalities that you have learned to depend on and enjoy the most. You can practice to improve your skill in any modality with the goal of achieving a mixed and balanced modality of sensory strengths.

INDEX

INDEX